TO VENTURE
FURTHER

ALSO BY TRISTAN JONES

SHERIDAN HOUSE MARITIME CLASSICS

TO VENTURE FURTHER

AN INCREDIBLE BOAT JOURNEY ACROSS THE WATERWAYS OF THAILAND

TRISTAN JONES

ESSEX, CONNECTICUT

An imprint of Globe Pequot, the trade division of
The Rowman & Littlefield Publishing Group, Inc.
4501 Forbes Blvd., Ste. 200
Lanham, MD 20706
www.rowman.com

Distributed by NATIONAL BOOK NETWORK

First published 1991 by Grafton Books,
A division of HarperCollins Publishers.

First Sheridan House paperback edition 1999.

British Library Cataloguing in Publication Information available

Library of Congress Cataloging-in-Publication Data

Names: Jones, Tristan, 1924-1995, author.
Title: To venture further : an incredible boat journey across the waterways of Thailand /
    Tristan Jones.
Description: Essex, Connecticut : Sheridan House, [2023] | Series: Sheridan House
    maritime classics | First published: New York, N.Y. : Grafton Books, 1991. | Summary:
    "In this memorable exploit from a master storyteller, legendary sailor Tristan Jones
    makes an exceedingly difficult passage through the infamous Kra Penninsula in a small
    fishing boat"— Provided by publisher.
Identifiers: LCCN 2022054242 (print) | LCCN 2022054243 (ebook) | ISBN 9781493073283
    (paperback) | ISBN 9781493076055 (ebook)
Subjects: LCSH: Henry Wagner (Boat) | Kra, Isthmus of (Thailand)—Description and
    travel.
Classification: LCC DS589.K73 J66 2023 (print) | LCC DS589.K73 (ebook) | DDC
    915.93—dc23/eng/20221109
LC record available at https://lccn.loc.gov/2022054242
LC ebook record available at https://lccn.loc.gov/2022054243

And I set forth upon that stormy sea,
In that small ship, with that small company
Which until then had not forsaken me. . . .

We kept our eyes straight-turned toward the mornings
And with our oars gave wings to our mad flight,
Till we were come unto that narrow strait
Where Hercules once raised his landmarks
To warn men not to venture further. . . .

NOTE: I have had this in my head for years. It may be left over from a previous existence. If it is not, my apologies to its author, living or dead.

Tristan Jones

For Som, Anant, Nok, and Thailand;
and for
Thomas Ettenhuber (1964–1988)
"the great Achilles,
whom we knew . . ."

Contents

Part Three ... And the Other

Maps

From originals prepared by Thomas Ettenhuber, Fellow of the Royal Institute of Navigation

11

TO
VENTURE
FURTHER

Foreword

by Thomas Ettenhuber, mate in *Henry Wagner:*

The events described here, and that I witnessed, all happened. After I read the typescript of this book, I told Tristan that I thought things had been a mite different in perhaps one or two cases, but he said, "Thank God you do see them differently, I wish it were more!"

Tristan Jones is not an easy man to venture with into anything. He drives himself too much to be very tolerant of others' failings. He can explode, yet he is never unkind. He is, for others, a meticulously careful captain; no one on our venture, except himself, was ever injured. He is much more affable than his account, perhaps, shows. I know of few people who didn't feel better for meeting him.

At the start of our Kra venture it had seemed to me that only Tristan's Atlantis cause was right: Now I see that everything had been exactly right and that Tristan had known that, all along. We four crew had started out all as strangers, boys and youths, with little in common, hardly understanding, in fact not liking, each other much, except for Nok and Anant. We now feel a thousand times better about ourselves and each other. At the start it had seemed as though we were headed for chaos; and we were, but by sheer will and knowledge, Tristan brought us through, and made for us sense of it all.

Now, over a year after our great Kra venture ended, we are all still friends, still working together for our Atlantis cause. How

15

many small, tight expeditions, no matter how well financed, well publicized and well organized, have been able to state that?

Five years ago I was a student in Bavaria, West Germany. Everyone said there was no more adventure in the world. Surely this was one of the most astonishing adventures ever?

PART ONE

THIS . . .

"Gorau dial, dangos cwm a'i ffadau."
"The noblest vengeance is to show a wrong, and forgive it."

Yr Hen Gyrys o Ial,
The White Book of Rhyddich,
Wales, fourteenth century

1

Atlantis Endeavor

True adventurers are not as films usually depict them: They plot, they plan, they have their *reasons*.

Why should anyone, in his right mind, want to persuade severely disabled youngsters to tackle a challenge that would make grown, able-bodied men blanch?

Why, indeed.

And why Atlantis?

A few months before I lost my leg, I had formed a society with the aim of investigating the legend of the sunken continent of Atlantis. I was convinced that there were many grounds for believing that behind the musty legends there were elements of fact. That perhaps before a cataclysm, ten thousand years ago or more, a highly civilized race of sea wanderers had colonized many parts of the earth from their ocean continent.

In 1982, after my left leg was amputated above the knee and I found myself among disabled people, I knew where our sunken continent *really* was. It was right around us, every single one of us. Its inhabitants, derided by others who had not their disadvantages, sank lower and lower, every day of their waking lives, into depths of gloom and self-deprecating misery that few who were not in their place might even start to imagine.

The two incidents—the forming of the society and the loss of my limb—showed me that the guiding spirit of the universe had a purpose for me. I had been fated to lose my leg. In that way I was shown that the sunken continent that I had searched for was, in fact, the disabled children of our world. I left the hospital in New York, my body wrecked, penniless, in medical debt to my ears, but swearing to myself that somehow, alone if need be, I would try to raise some of our sunken continent, even if it was only by the span of a hair, or I would die in the attempt.

I set out from San Diego in 1983, in a thirty-six foot trimaran, *Outward Leg*. Even then I suspected that my ocean-voyaging, as an "example" to other amputees, would be almost a waste of time and effort. By the time I sailed into London, in 1984, fourteen thousand miles later, I knew that my original intent had been based on errors, both mine and other people's.

My first error had been to trust promises that had been made but, were not, in the event, kept. Had they been, my job of reaching and possibly inspiring disabled people would have been far easier, and showed far more results than it did, and far more quickly.

My second error—and this was a far more grievous one— was in not realizing before I started my voyage that the vast majority of disabled people in this world will never get within even hailing distance of a modern, state-of-the-art ocean-going yacht, much less sail in one. My error here might be more understandable when you consider that I had been, for forty-eight of my sixty-two years, voyaging at sea. But perhaps not. Anyway, *mea culpa*.

That there were a few disabled people who might have been able to afford a yacht was undeniable. But they were a tiny minority. The vast majority of disabled people are poor. To set them a valid example, I would have to do something using methods, materials, and resources that were readily available to them.

Without big sponsors and the media support that they can engender, it seemed futile for me to carry on the voyage from London by the "normal" route—to Gibraltar and through the Mediterranean to Suez. It would not be "newsworthy" enough.

To attract the attention of disabled people to my efforts in *Outward Leg*, I set out from London for Suez by another, far more difficult route: across the North Sea, up the Rhine, and down the Danube rivers, through the "Iron Curtain," through the Black Sea, and so into the Eastern Mediterranean. Thomas Ettenhuber, who was to play a major part in the Atlantis venture, joined me as mate in Nuremberg.

On the rivers Rhine and Danube I was in an ocean-sailing boat; one beyond the wildest dreams of most disabled people. All the way through Europe they had come on board, eight hundred and more of them. Leg amputees, arm amputees, the deaf, the dumb, and the blind. All I could do was carry them in *Outward Leg* a short distance on the rivers whenever I could, hoping to brighten, even if only for a short while, their existences, and to lighten their despair; the despair that I knew myself only too well. Yet all the time I had known that was not enough.

In some countries I had watched the disabled being gently brought on board by careful attendants; in others they had crawled aboard of their own volition. In some countries they had, more often than not, been politely ignored by the general populace; in others (as we passed further east) they were frequently derided.

By the time I reached Istanbul, in the summer of 1985, I had made up my mind.

To try to overcome the general public's attitude to disabled people, as I had seen them, something drastic would have to be done: We disabled would have to try to meet a previously unmet challenge, to show the world that we might not only try to keep pace with the able-bodied, but that we might even *set them a challenge of our own*.

We would not, as so many other worthy disabled people had done, follow in anyone else's footsteps. We would not try to overtake anyone but ourselves and nature. We would set the challenge, the pace, and the course for everyone else, disabled or not. We would be *Number One* for at least once.

There was a big snag. Who, outside ourselves, would ever support such a seemingly forlorn enterprise? Who would insure our crew? Who would pass me or my crew as medically fit to take on such a rigorous endeavor? Who would give us license? Who would dare to take on the awesome responsibility for welfare and lives?

The answer had come eventually: no one but me.

I had looked closely, in the West, at various organizations that existed to ease or broaden the lot of the so-called "handicapped" (hateful word—visions of a cap-in-hand!). I even knew some of the organizers of some of those worthy concerns. I knew that they, no matter how good-hearted they might have been, would never even look twice at such a proposition as mine. It was far too risky. If it failed, if anyone should die or be seriously injured, I should be looked upon as a crazy pied piper who had cajoled innocent children into a deadly trap, and they would, rightly, feel responsible for having aided me.

There could be but one attempt at what we were to do. Only success would justify my intentions. There would be no room at all for failure of any kind. As in any endeavor where this was the case, the fewer people involved, the better. Only I could take the blame for any failure. But by the same token only our crew, and not I, could take any praise for success. I would not deserve to share their accolades, for I would have bargained with the devil. But to achieve my aims, to kick disdain and derision in the teeth, I would bargain with a hundred devils if need be.

I had no resources other than my small income from writing magazine stories, a not overgenerous advance on a book, and my small naval pension. No bank manager, quite rightly, would have dreamed of considering any of my income, except the latter perhaps, as any kind of security for a loan. All I had was my knowledge, my heart, my soul, and my dream. Those, laid out on the table in some posh London or New York office, would not have looked much.

The matter of money—or the lack of it—dictated that our effort would have to take place where sustenance, labor, and materials were relatively cheap. It would also have to be where interference from "authorities," ill intentioned or not, would be minimal, or even better, none. The question then was, *where?*

2

The Challenge

Our Atlantis endeavor would overcome a challenge. The challenge would have to be something that had never been done before by anyone else, disabled or not. It would have to be within limits that I could tackle. And that meant it would have to involve a boat. The boat would have to be cheap enough for other disabled people to be able to afford to follow our example. That put *Outward Leg* out of the running. Not many disabled people could afford a quarter of a million dollars.

Using cheap, simple boats meant that ocean voyages were out. Any boat meant for sensible ocean voyages with a crew of disabled people on board would be prohibitively expensive for us to build and fit out. Accidents happen—and they could happen very easily at sea to leg or arm amputees. Boats carrying such people across an ocean, or even offshore, should, I think, in most parts of the world, carry a doctor. That would mean one less berth for the disabled crew and more expense. I would have to choose an area where medical assistance, should it be needed, would be available within a day, or at the most two.

These considerations led me to one conclusion: Our challenge would have to be in coastal waters or on rivers.

Then there was politics to consider. I had three projects in mind: one to navigate in a small craft through the Black Sea to the Soviet Union, and then to negotiate the rivers Don and Volga to the Caspian Sea, to reach Iran on its north coast.

Another project had been to haul a boat from the shores of the Mediterranean, in Turkey, to the River Euphrates, and to navigate from its headwaters through Syria and Iraq down to the Gulf of Iran.

Both these projects I shelved. To make our way then through the Soviet Union would have entailed about a year's negotiation for permits, with no assurance that they would, in the end, be forthcoming. The Turkish and Syrian governments had been amenable enough when it came to permits to haul and launch in the River Euphrates, but the then-raging Iraq–Iran war ruled out reaching the Gulf.

I was left with the third project: a crossing of the Isthmus of Kra. The Kra is the thinnest part of the long peninsula that dangles down from Indochina like the tentacle of a dead octopus; Burma, Thailand, and Malaysia all have territory in the peninsula, and Singapore is at its tip. The layman knows of the Yangtze: The navigator knows the Kra.

Our aim would be to get a genuine sea boat across the isthmus by way of the riverheads, with a short portage, if need be, across the watershed divide, from the Andaman Sea (part of the Indian Ocean) to the Gulf of Thailand (a part of the South China Sea).

Although ancient Chinese legends told of heroic attempted passages across the Kra, and although several navies had sent expeditions to cross the isthmus in the last century, there was no written or certain record of any crossing ever having been successfully accomplished. Even the Japanese Army had failed.

A waterway from sea to sea across the Isthmus of Kra has been a dream of the peoples of Thailand for centuries. The distance across the narrowest part of the isthmus by land, if the maps available might be trusted, was anything from forty to eighty miles, east to west. That, I knew, might not be the way to cross. But it was in the realm of possibility, I realized, that we might find a viable route for such a waterway. It might, at least, be a gentler route than the one that had been recently mooted, which involved blasting through the mountains of the isthmus using atomic devices.

We might be the first navigators in recorded history to pass across the Isthmus of Kra from sea to sea. We might be the first of many future navigators, who will take their ships across when the trans-Kra canal is built. When the next century's navigators pass along it, they might remember that the first people ever to make the passage had been disabled. Thus, with our effort we would reach not only into the Gulf of Thailand, but also into the hearts of people yet unborn. It was a prospect worthy of any self-respecting writer of the sea, or of any navigator worth his salt: a voyage into the future!

Consider again the seven conditions I had set for a suitable project for disabled youngsters. The expedition must be:

FIRST: in a boat
SECOND: within the capabilities of disabled youngsters
THIRD: comparatively inexpensive
FOURTH: within one or two days' reach of medical help
FIFTH: something never before done by anyone
SIXTH: something that contributes some good to society as a
    whole
SEVENTH: politically possible

The projected Kra crossing seemed to meet all of these conditions.

Until we had been in Thailand for three months, I said nothing much about my Kra project to Thomas. On our voyage, whenever a possible crossing of the Kra had been discussed, we always spoke of it jocularly, as though *Outward Leg* might make the attempt, but inside I had known that would be, physically, hardly possible; the rivers would be far too shallow for her. It would not be, anyway, as surely within the aims of our Atlantis endeavor.

In late 1985, having emerged from the Soviet Empire in Eastern Europe, we had *Outward Leg* refitted in Cyprus. We then flew to the United States, where by signing my books at boat shows —hundreds a day—and by giving lectures about our trans-European leg, we earned the money to take *Outward Leg* twelve thousand miles east to Thailand, which we fetched in June 1986. My first job in Phuket was to write about the voyage of *Outward Leg* east from Istanbul in the book *Somewheres East of Suez*. By early September the book was finished.

We were anchored in Ao Chalong, a bay on the south side of Phuket Island. The shelter from the southwest monsoon was good enough; not perfect but good enough, to give us some respite from rolling seas. The scenery, of islands, sandy beaches, and green hills, was splendid.

It must have been disconcerting for Thomas when I told him,

ten thousand miles from his home, that I would no longer continue on a voyage-in-error.

Thomas said, "Isn't it a bit late to realize, after three years and twenty-six thousand miles, that you've made a mistake?"

Thomas's question was a tough one. In the two years since he had left Nuremberg to sail with me, his English had improved so much that many of my fellow Britons took him for one of their own countrymen. It was not easy for me to tell him that my decision had been made long before we arrived in Thailand; in fact, only weeks after he had joined *Outward Leg*.

"There're no mistakes in exploration, Thomas," I told him. "You can only 'mistake' what's been 'taken' before. What you mean is 'error.' That's a good navigator's word."

At first Thomas looked downcast. Then I told him what our venture would be. I dived into the cabin and showed him my map of the Kra area, and described to him in glowing terms the wonders that we might find there, in that territory almost blank on the sea chart. I showed him the more modern maps and old sea charts. Their features were almost completely different from each other.

But Thomas is a hard nut. The more I explained to him of the difficulties on the Kra crossing, the more his face brightened.

Finally I said to him, "Are you on, then?"

He grinned. "What else?"

"It's not going to be as easy as ocean sailing," I warned him.

"How do we start? What's the first job?"

The dry season would be upon us in a month's time, and would last until late May or June, when the rains would start to teem down. "Build a base, find a suitable boat, find a crew, train them, learn enough Thai, teach them enough English, reconnoiter the Kra by land and its rivers by boat as far as we can. . . ."

Thomas nodded. "Okay. We start tomorrow?"

"Today."

"Easy," he said.

"We'll see. It's all got to be prepared during the dry season. Between now and next May, when the monsoon rains start."

"What do we do then?" Thomas asked.

"Start off ourselves for the Kra, to cross it."

"In the rain?"

"We can't navigate dry rivers. . . ."

"*On one leg?*" was his in-joke question.

"*Better than none,*" was my in-joke reply.

3
Words

When I consider some of the subjects I must deal with in this story, I imagine in my mind's eye some people, somewhere in Western urbandom, breathing heavily by the time they reach the end. I can imagine one in particular, whose only arduous venture in life might have been a half-mile jog trot around Hampstead Heath, having a mild attack of apoplexy, even. At the least he will say I am antisocial, or a relic of the Raj, or racist, or biased against everyone who wasn't born with a Royal Navy rum-tot measure within handy reach. Some might even put me down as a killjoy. Don't believe them. I've enlivened the company of more people, of every different hue, probably, than they've had hot breakfasts.

Many, many of the Thais that we were to encounter during the course of our odyssey through their southland were to be good, honest, friendly people. But good, honest, friendly Thais, bless them, are so run-of-the-mill that to tell you only of them, I would be failing in my task as a storyteller. The exceptional makes the best of a story. For the rest, the hosts of good, friendly, honest people, I know my readers are worldly-wise enough to accept their existence as taken for granted.

Thailand, then Siam, was a land that during the colonial period cleverly kept its independence. She did this mainly by handing over bit by bit, as sops to greedy British and French imperialists, her own ancient colonies in what are now Laos, Cambodia, and

Malaysia. During the Second World War her government will-
ingly joined hands with Japanese aggressors intent on reshaping
the Eastern world, for good or ill. Since then, over the past four
decades, Thailand had been under threat from communism both
from within the country and without. This had kept the army,
with American backing, in control of practically everything. For
many reasons, not the least of which was that the Thai national
parliament still met for only twelve days a year, the army was in
charge of a vast network of patronage that reached into every nook
and cranny of Thai life, even to the remotest villages. But the
army, in the main, left foreign tourists alone. There was no sense
in killing or frightening off a goose that might soon be laying
golden eggs all over Thailand.

Whether this army control was a good thing or not is not for
me to say. To be able to grasp the nub of that question, I would
have to be a Thai historian a hundred years hence. Be that as it
may, on one stage of our journey the Thai Army would help us
a great deal.

Our first problem was language (unlike in the films, the natives
do not speak fluent American English). Very few Thais, then, in
Ao Chalong, on the level at which we were ourselves, spoke
anything but Thai or some form of *Chao-leh*, the language of the
Andaman sea peoples. None that we knew spoke any good, understandable English, or any other non-Thai language. Interpret-
ers, for us, were out. What few there were cost money. They
were accustomed to dealing with—they sought out—rich Western
farangs and Japanese tourists. *Farang* is the Thai word for foreigner.
It usually means anyone of European descent, no matter how
remote. Like the Arab *feringhi*, it is probably derived from
"Frank," meaning "European." We were not well off by any
means; our aim was to deal with and for poor people locally. We
set to, while we were in Phuket, to learn the Thai language at
least sufficiently well for everyday dealings.

Landing on a *really* foreign shore—except perhaps when you
have paid to be whisked expensively around about by a tour
operator—is like being mentally born again. For the young it's
easy to be born and maybe as easy to be reborn, but for us older
people, it's not as easy to put more into an already full bucket.
Much gets spilled, no matter how carefully it's poured.

I've never been to a language school, although I understand, fairly well, seven languages besides my own. Often, when people have asked me how I learned them, I have jokingly replied: "Argued my way out of jail." (About Spanish I was half-serious.)

The best way to learn a language is to immerse yourself in it. When I am working and thinking day and night in one language, in the course of writing a book, it is almost impossible for me to absorb and learn words or phrases from another language. That's why I was much slower at learning the little Thai I know than I was at any other language I understand. It wasn't that learning Thai was too difficult; it was that I was far too preoccupied with other things, like earning the money for the Atlantis endeavor.

In the three months that I had been writing *Somewheres East of Suez*, Thomas, in his dealings with local fishermen and boat people, had been picking up odd words and phrases of Thai every day; each day a little more. Thai is not an easy language for a foreigner to learn to speak understandably, much less correctly. For a start it has an alphabet all of its very own. Although its grammatical construction is closer to German than English—and so more accessible to Thomas than to me—he soon discovered that each vowel has five tones. Sung in the wrong tone, the word for "mother," for example, means "dog" or "horse." As you may imagine, the wrong tone here could lead to some embarrassment. Thomas, to a young Thai lady, accompanied by her mother: "Ah, I see you've brought your horse along."

In ordinary, everyday Thai speech, there are thirty-one ways of referring to close family relatives; three ways—or more—to say "you," according to whom you're addressing, and five ways to say "I,". Which way you use depends on who you are, your age or status, where you are, and to whom you are speaking.

Soon, over the months that followed, Thomas was speaking Thai much more colloquially than I. In the course of his dealings with fishermen and shore side folk, he, of necessity, learned "fishing" Thai. I learned most of mine from books, in odd moments between writing articles and letters in English, French, German, and Spanish. My Thai speech, to the Thais, must have been slow, strained, and stiff. My grammar must have given them headaches.

In the following year, in the course of the tale I tell here, most times I dealt with Thais I found myself thinking like a racing jockey in full tilt at the Grand National, but seeming to be heard as if I were a visitor from Mars afflicted with a sore larynx and a bad stutter. No fault of the Thais, of course. It's their country, their language.

In further chapters of this story, for the sake of our patience, yours and mine, I shall play a trick on you. Do not be fooled by it: I shall pretend that everyone involved always understood each other perfectly. I shall leave it to you to imagine all the silent pauses, the continual graspings for meaning, the sweaty, knitted brows, the heated exasperation, the dumb resignation. I will not —I could not—write of my interminable palavers with Thais as they were spoken, or of the time it took, when Thomas was not about (and often when he was), for any clarity or understanding to be reached.

It could take an hour or more, at first, for me to get my hands on a screwdriver, unless I could hobble to our toolbox myself. It wasn't that our Thais didn't know what a screwdriver was: How does anyone understand a closed fist and twisted wrist? No wonder they might think I was indicating the manipulation of the throttle of a motorcycle, and, thinking I wanted to hire a motorbike to take me somewhere, would run up the beach and away through the palm trees and call one over for me from the track a hundred yards beyond.

Our language makes us. Any society that has five ways to say, "I" must have a rigid class structure. We found that this was certainly so in Thailand. Among the Thais themselves, every small detail was an indication of their status: their work, their house, their family, the way they were dressed, their speech, their gestures, their tone of voice, their generosity or lack of it (a great mark of respect for someone was to let him pay for everything). We *farangs* tended, where our appearance, dress, or social connections were concerned, to escape from this stereotyping. In many areas we were well and truly beyond the pale. But if we needed to get anything done at all, if we expected any Thai's effort or loyalty, or even interest, there was no escaping our obligation to be generous. But we could never be excessively so; that would have been looked upon as foolish, and we would lose face.

But if we were not generous, we would soon have no face at all, and be called *kee neeao*—meaning "sticky shit," the colloquial term for a miser.

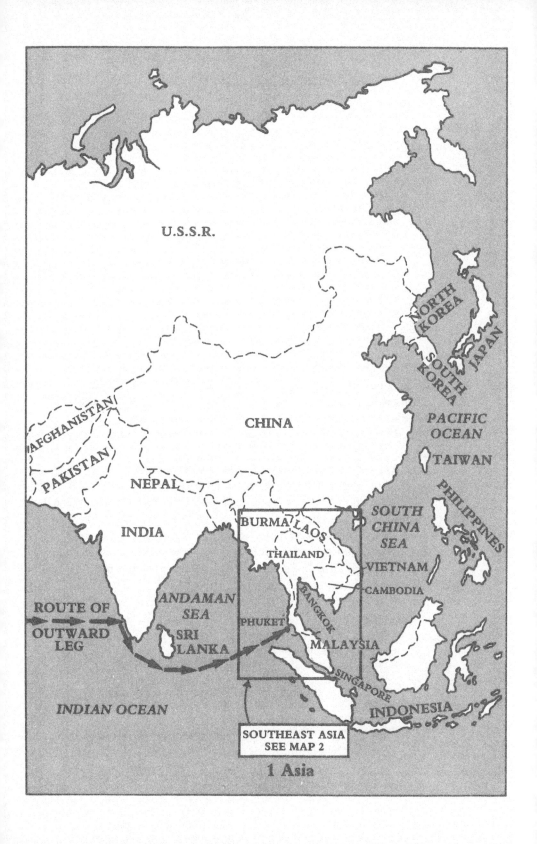

1 Asia

4
Deeds

Our Thai boys never knew, never had an inkling, until we reached the Gulf of Thailand and even the capital, of how the gospel of their actions might reach thousands—millions—of other disabled people. I tried to explain, but it seemed to make no sense to them. They thought only of the here and now. Perhaps that is the essence of all simple bravery.

There was never any question, until we reached Bangkok, of my appealing to any other motive in our boys than earning their living. To have talked to our boys about setting an example for others would have sounded, to them, gibberish. For me to have even dared to suggest that we might do good for people we had never seen would expose me, behind my back, to extreme ridicule for a week. Our Muslim boys came from a hard background. All their lives they had been made fun of for their physical flaws. They lived in a very limited world. If they couldn't see it, to them it did not exist. Anyone else's misfortune was tough luck. To help someone who was not friend or family was, to them, the act of an outright fool, who probably had too much money and deserved to be overcharged or robbed. ("*If Allah should send a fool, take his money. If he should send an infidel, kill him, praising Allah!*") But to take a boat from A to B, and be paid for it, that was a different, far more serious matter.

The matter of "generosity," as I reckoned the Thais saw it, needs to be clarified. In a feudal society (from which rural Thailand was still emerging) there was more to employment, and especially where *farangs* were employing, than mere work on the one hand and payment on the other. There was an agreement that a basic wage would be paid, but there was also an unspoken understanding that there would be extra payment ("tea money") for any extra effort; sometimes extra payment regardless. To the recipient, tea money was a favor bestowed to save face for the payer from the embarrassment of having to employ people. It was wrong, some-how, to have to depend on others, but the extra payment made it right. But besides money, food, and, in many cases, accom-modation, would be provided. This meant that my crewmen, in effect, became part of my family. This put the responsibility for my crew's well-being fair and square on my head. For people arriving from a Western urban society this kind of relationship might demand, on their part, a great deal of adjustment, but for me it was perhaps easier and simpler. It was a direct throwback to my relations with my first skipper way back during my days in a sailing barge in the English Channel and North Sea before the Second World War.

I was ready and willing to take responsibility for all my crew's actions, but woe betide them if they made fools of themselves. But there was a snag here; to keep any sense of order in our effort, and to make the preparations for it, I had to learn a new rule. I call it the *chai yen*, "cool heart," rule. Let me lead you to it, step by step.

Whenever they encountered *farangs*—the strange, big-nosed, big-boned, hairy people from out of the sky—the Thais silently, smiling, excused our lack of manners and our ignorance of Thai custom. There were a hundred examples of this Thai generosity every time I observed their interplay with *farangs*: They excused the terrible way that *farangs* pointed with a finger. The *farangs* did not know that this was considered obscene and threatening. The *farangs* did not know that almost until modern times, warlords had roamed the land, and upon entering a village would point their finger at a whim at peasants and have them killed out of mere wanton brutality.

The Thais excused—how many times?—the way a *farang* would fondle the head of a young girl in public. Or even a boy or an adult, come to that. They seemed to know that the *farang* could not realize that the head was the most sacred part of a person, the vessel of the eternal spirit of that being, so that the rest of him or her hardly mattered. The main tourist areas of Phuket Island, and so the main concentrations of *farangs*, were on the west coast. Ao Chalong Bay, where *Outward Leg* was anchored, was on the south coast. Except at the height of the tourist season (November to February), when a few visitors rented bungalows, and coaches called to drop tourists off for boat trips to head out and wreck the coral around nearby islands, the only farangs in Ao Chalong were other "yachtties" (as they called themselves) from the dozen or so foreign yachts at anchor in the bay. They were of several nationalities: British, German, American, French, with a strong Australian presence.

At the start of the tourist season the yachtties sailed their boats around to the west coast of Phuket, to work charters with tourists. The yachtties mostly lived on board their boats, some in conditions not too far removed from those of the local Thai fishermen. They had that much in common, but little else. The majority of the fishermen were Muslim, with strict rules of conduct. Generally the yachtties and the fishermen kept to their own groups. There was not much interaction between them, yet very little friction, if any.

Most of the *farang* yachtties were men. They had no need to try to get to know the local Muslim women of Ao Chalong, a futile hope. Only a few miles away by hired motorcycle was Patong, bursting with bars full of mostly non-Muslim girls and women, who were mechanically available for a few dollars.

The average Thai man's view of women seemed to be that they were either goddesses, wives, potential wives, or whores, and the whores didn't matter.

The whores came down, little sweet-faced girls as young as twelve, from the semidesert of the Esan in Northeast Thailand, and they had silk dresses wrapped around them, and they were shoved into a bar. Big-bellied, often elderly, hairy white-skinned men with loud voices and long noses would buy them out of the bar, ride around with them clinging to the back of hired motorbikes, then take them to some hotel room, and there do what they might with them. To the lasses it was reasonable enough. They'd never even heard of AIDS, and if a baby started to develop, it could soon be got rid of. "Mama-san" would see to that.

The white men, yellow men, brown men, sometimes black men (the girls tried to avoid these; black skin is disdained in Thailand among the lower orders) would talk at the girls, who would pretend to understand every word they said, and smile at them the whole while because the mama-san told them it was good for business. When they went into a hotel or a restaurant, the Thai staff, able to speak some kitchen English, would tell the *farang* how welcome he was, and how pleased they were to see him, and smile and bow and *weh* to him. This is the Thai way of greeting: to press the palms together and hold them in front, similar to the Western attitude of prayer. The height at which the palms are held indicates the degree of respect shown.

But at the same time, unnoticed by the dazed *farang*, the staff glared swiftly at the "service girl," and under their breaths they cursed her and called her a whore and told her to get as much money as she could out of the *farang*, while the going was good.

And the *farang*, seeing all the smiles and gentle talk all around him, would imagine that everyone in the place approved of him bringing his great clumsy, lustful self and his (to them) cheap little Esan whore into their restaurant or hotel, and he would fondle her head, and point to the staff with his forefinger, then lumber across the room beaming, and thank everyone in his ridiculously loud, and to many Thais frightening, voice. And leave a big tip, the clumsy, grinning oaf, at the end of the meal. Then he would leave the place along with his girl-child, imagining that everyone loved them and thought he was the best thing that had happened to Phuket since Siam changed itself to Thailand. It was promoted by tourism touts as "the Smiling Thai Welcome."

But not the girl. She knew very well what the Thais thought of them both, the vituperative cracks that would fly around after they had left, but never once would she stop smiling, not for one second.

This was nothing unusual. It was so common, this scene, that it became to me boring and embarrassing to watch, so that I soon avoided it wherever possible. It happened all day and all night, I knew, and every day and every night. It was a process, just like canning pilchards or tomatoes. An industry, with thousands of people dependent on it, was made of this process. At Patong Beach, vice, hypocrisy, and pretense made money hand over fist. To watch, silently, the antics of the fooled *farangs*, was almost to feel pity. But pity demanded generosity of the spirit, and for them I had but little. It was all so crude, dumb, and dreary, once my insight penetrated past the loud noise, the tinsel, the silk, and the colored lights. And for all this pretense these men had paid to be flown ten thousand miles or more!

Patong's reputation as a sinkhole of vice was known world-wide. Its position as a center of exploitation not only of male tourists, but of the women and girls who pandered to them, was not so notorious or obvious. There were robberies, sometimes with violence. But what did it matter, people said, when the perpetrator, caught and duly sentenced, might pay someone poorer than he to serve his prison sentence for him? Or, some claimed, to stay free, his name on the prison register?

As I mentioned before, there were few dealings between the local inhabitants of Ao Chalong and the yachtties; between them and the youngsters that we worked with there had been even less, until Thomas and I happened along.

We found that the Thai ideas of relations between captains and crewmen were very different from those in the other areas of the world that I have sailed in, and especially in the West.

In Thailand, for those in charge the rule must always be "speak softly and carry a big stick." The big stick might be simply a silent frown or, in serious cases, an implied—but never stated —threat of suspension of generosity. "Speak softly" was very real. There could be no raising of voice, no show of temper. To the Thais they would mean that I had lost my *chai yen* (cool heart), and I would immediately and irrevocably lose face, and lose the respect of the culprit. By making him lose respect for me, I had, by his lights, committed an unforgivable offense against him. If someone made an error or a blunder, even an honest one, there could be no direct confrontation with the culprit; no outright criticism. The blunderer, offended beyond reason, would simply disappear, and probably never turn up again. I could not, in that case, complain. By losing cool heart, I had committed a far greater offense than he.

We learned that the extreme complexity of relationships be-tween people of different sexes, backgrounds, areas, and ages ex-tended throughout Thai society, even down to the association between two small boys of apparently similar backgrounds, one perhaps six months older than the other. The older one was nat-urally, without any reflection, considered superior by both. The elder addressed the younger as "younger brother." The younger addressed him as "elder brother," or risked offending everyone around them.

Because of the extreme complexity of relationships between Thais, because of the risk of gravely offending them, albeit quite unawares, it seemed to me the best move for a *farang* employer of Thais would be to find a good Thai foreman, make sure he knew the job, put him in charge, then get as far away from the place of work as he could, appearing only on paydays, and if he wanted his men to work really hard the following week, with a crate or two of whiskey (unless they were Muslim).

But in a boat, and especially in a small boat on an exploratory expedition, the skipper could not escape. It was simply not possible. Lives might very well be at stake for much of the time. Neither could I hide away. Someone had to be responsible for the whole conduct of the venture. My solution was, as we shall see, to appoint a Thai as nominal captain and let him deal with minor matters on board among the crew.

The tourist industry promoted Thailand as the "Land of Smiles." At very close range, and observing the Thai smile incessantly, I found that the Thai smile, like the Chinese laugh, had about five hundred different, very precise meanings. Only a very few of these gave any true indication that the smiler liked us, or agreed with us, or approved of our actions. But most of the smiles were—although pleasant indeed to the beholder—mere matters of politeness.

Among our crew, at first, many smiles were cheerful-seeming signals of a boyish need, a continual search for approbation. We learned it was only when their continual smiling had diminished somewhat that our Thai lads had begun, very slowly, to accept us.

We learned that loyalty, true gratitude, courage, and honesty could wear a Thai smile, but so, too, could avarice, pretense, disdain, contempt, and in a few cases remarkable for their rarity, even barely disguised anti-*farang* racism.

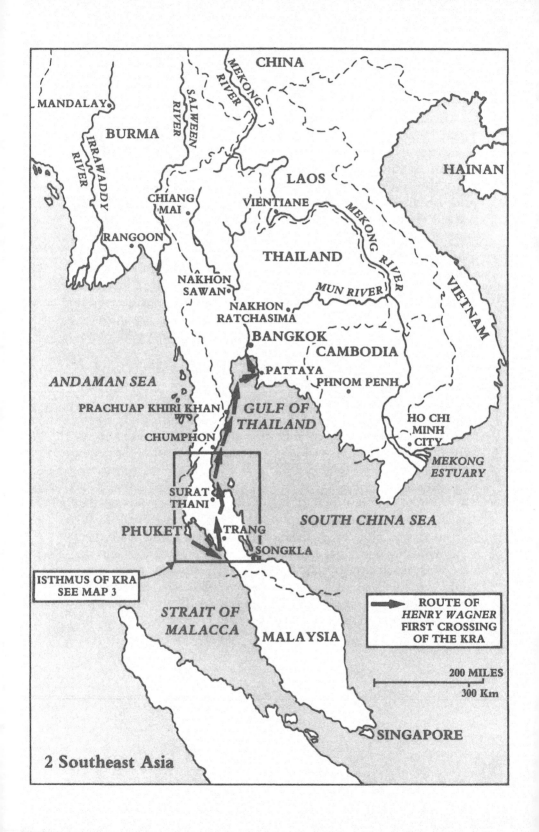

2 Southeast Asia

5

Karma . . . and a Motorbike

My first job, when I went ashore in November 1986 to start work on the Atlantis endeavor, was to get up the sandy beach. One of the worst surfaces for a one-legged person to negotiate on a prosthesis or with crutches is an inclined beach of sand. There is usually a harder stretch, fairly easy to walk on. But further up, on the tide rise, where the sand is powdery, the going can be difficult indeed. A walking stick or crutches cannot find a firm surface to push against, and a false foot sinks into the sand. In tropical heat walking on beaches can be a misery. I always tried to have someone with me when I crossed or walked along a beach, so I could grab at his shoulder whenever I was in danger of losing my balance and falling over.

As it was, alone, from Panama to Malaysia, by way of the rivers Hudson, Thames, and Danube, I had fallen over on beaches and foreshores scores of times. The way I rose was to roll over so that my weight was on the side of my good leg; then, raising and twisting my upper torso at the same time, I would stick the bottom of my cane into the ground and, using both arms, push my whole weight up, until it could be supported on my one good leg. But in sand the cane sank. It was then like trying to walk on water.

On one occasion, months before, companionless, on a deserted beach on the Zubair Islands in the Red Sea, at around noon, I had fallen over. It had taken me two hours, under a broiling sun, to drag myself first to the shade of a rock, to recover from the shock, and then to a stretch of beach where the sand was hard enough for me to push myself up to a standing position. It had very nearly killed me.

Off the beach, for a man in his sixties with one leg amputated above the knee, probably the best means of transport ashore would be a small car specially adapted to his disability. No matter how ingeniously devised his prosthesis, although he might be able to bend his false knee, he simply would not be able to press his false foot down on a brake or a clutch.

A specially adapted car might have been all very well in countries with good paved roads, but in most tropical countries, outside of the cities, the story was very different. Good roads were few and far between. Most of the roads were mere tracks. These had very rough surfaces that, in the rainy season, turned to mud. Many of the tracks were too narrow for a car to pass. Anyway, a car would be far too expensive for me. I might feed my crewmen for a year or more on what even a secondhand car might cost.

The answer, of course, was a motorcycle. They were plentiful enough in the less remote areas of Thailand. But when a motorcycle stops, it has to be supported by one of the driver's feet depending on which way it leans over. If I was on a motorcycle and it leaned over to the left, because in a sitting position I have no way of stiffening the knee, my prosthesis would simply buckle, and the bike, and me with it, would fall down onto the roadway—if there was a roadway. The solution, of course, was a sidecar on the left side of the motorcycle.

In Phuket town, there was good news. In a letter waiting for me at the post office, the British magazine *Yachting World* had accepted a story from me about our voyage east from Israel in *Outward Leg*. Then, away from the new concrete tourist shops and hotels, on a thronged side street of more interesting old wooden Chinese shops, we found a secondhand, Japanese-designed, Thai-built bike for sale. It had 56,000 miles on the clock, but it seemed to be in fair condition and, most important, by the time we finished bargaining with the Chinese-Thai shop owner, it was cheap: only $200.

On this occasion there was no doubt that Thomas's growing

command of colloquial Thai helped a great deal to get the price down. We didn't succeed in getting it down as far as a Thai might have done. But ours was not a language problem: a two-tier price system prevailed; the higher price for *farangs*, the lower for Thais.

We would find this two-tier price system throughout the country, wherever tourists went in any number. It prevailed in shops, in hotels, in theaters, in museums, in temples, in cinemas. It was based on the premise that *"as* farangs *have more money to spend, they must pay more."* But this premise was not true: Many Thais had far more money than I shall ever see (unless you buy another copy of this book for your friends).

To my Western sailor's way of thinking, the two-tier system was corrupt, it was bare-faced extortion, and it was nothing less than financial racial discrimination. The fact that this money-gouging discrimination was aimed against me made it not one gnat's gullet less odious than it would have been if it had been aimed against anyone else. Many people had tried, and would try, to change my view on this, but the two-tier price system remains to me, as I write, nothing but outright robbery. Every time I encountered it, I wondered to myself what the outcry would be if Thai visitors in Britain were charged more for goods and services than the British. How many shops and pubs would promptly lose all the regular trade they had? How many bleeding hearts would be gathered in Trafalgar Square or banging on the door of Number Ten?

But to be fair, once the average Thai seller had a glimpse of what we of the Atlantis endeavor were about, the higher *farang* price, while not being brought down to the Thai level, would at least be reduced to some extent.

Because aluminum was made in Thailand, it was cheaper than in the West. A light aluminum sidecar, a mere cage with an open top set on a wheel, put us back only another hundred. For three hundred I had my shoreside transport. I still have it, with many of its original bits replaced, 31,000 miles later.

Normally you change gear on a motorbike with your left foot. I couldn't do that. Instead, Thomas made a quick sketch for me, and we headed down the street, into an oily shambles of a corrugated-iron workshop. There, a Chinese-Thai welder fitted a piece of pipe to run up from the gear fulcrum, so that I could change gears with my left hand.

Then, to a crowd of curious shop workers' utter amazement

and evident amusement, I hobbled over the oily concrete floor, cocked my false leg over the bike, mounted it, kicked the starter with my good foot, and started off.

Later, we were to realize that it was not only the simplicity of my gear-changing lever that had amazed the Thais. Nor was it my swift transformation from a hobbling, semidependent old *farang* buffer into a cocky king of the road. Their amazement, I believe, had more to do with their Buddhist belief in karma.

I can put my own thoughts about karma only in Western terms. I do not claim to know a great deal about the Buddhist philosophy, and I am certainly no expert; I doubt if any Westerner under the age of ninety can be. I believe that the Buddhist philosophy can be a great force for peace in the world. But I also think that its widely accepted practice on one level had, to me as a disabled person, at least one drawback.

Buddhists believe in reincarnation. They believe that we all have thousands of different existences. If a person is good, in his next reincarnation he will be on a higher plane than in his present one. If a person is not good, if he does not "gain merit," then his next existence must be on a lower plane. In life there is misery: To reach nirvana (oblivion) is the aim.

In Buddhist society a widely held belief is that if someone has some flaw in him, it is a punishment; a result of bad actions in a previous existence. Not the flawed one's fault, you understand, but his previous form's fault. But whether the fault is the flawed one's or not, it is his fate. It is his karma. To be considered good, to gain merit and rise to a higher plane in his next existence, a person must accept his karma. Therefore, and here's the rub, anyone assisting a flawed one to resist his karma is jeopardizing his own rise to a higher plane in his own next existence. Helping a flawed one does not make merit. It slows down a person's escape from suffering in life, on the way to nirvana.

On the expedition ahead, among fishermen and peasants (and among many townspeople, too), we were to encounter this outlook time and time again. I must be clear: What might seem to Western eyes a seeming callousness in attitudes to the disabled was not, I believe, caused by lack of charity; it was, I am sure, rooted in a strong, ingrained unwillingness to resist the wheel of fate.

On the levels in which we moved in Thailand, it was soon obvious that a deep belief in spirits pervaded almost every facet of life. To the Thai everything has a spirit: every tree, every creature, every blade of grass, every feeling, every thought; they were even in the wind and rain.

Some spirits were good, some were not. Some spirits wished you well, some wished you harm. Thais endowed their spirits with all the human qualities: guile, or jealousy, or even stupidity. If someone knew he was being pursued or persecuted by a harmful spirit, one of the ways in which he might fool it was by disguising himself. A person might take another name (most Thais hide their real names) to fool the bad spirit. Or he might try to embarrass it into going away by making a fool of himself; perhaps going to the extent of turning his clothes inside out, or doing something else utterly ridiculous: such as, even, being a *farang* (and so, rich), yet riding an old three-wheel motorcycle, on one leg.

6

A Captain

Kee-nok was the Thai slang word for foreign tourist. It meant birdshit—because it was something that fell out of the sky. It is pronounced very much like the surname of the leader of the British Labour party.

Because it seemed to have fallen out of the sky, I named my motor cycle *Kee-nok*. Thomas grinned, fetched a laundry marker from a nearby shop, and wrote the name on the front mudguard. A laughing passerby, a dark-skinned lad, understanding our Roman script, politely took the laundry marker from Thomas and wrote it for us on the other mudguard in the Thai alphabet. Everyone around broke out into loud laughter. Our onlookers gazed upon us now with more respect; some might even have been awed. We knew more about them than they had imagined.

I glanced at the lad who had written the name in Thai script, and realized, with a shock, that he had only one good arm. Even we disabled can be shocked at the disablements of others. His right arm was cut short just below the elbow. It was bare. He had made no attempt to hide his disablement. I liked him for that.

"What happened to your arm?" I asked him in gestures.

"I was in a bus accident," he gave us to understand in a mixture of Thai and very broken English. "I have a motorcycle, too. I borrowed it from a friend, but it's broken. I've taken it in to be repaired."

Thomas broke in: "I've seen him before, driving along the road at Ao Chalong." He spoke to the youth in Thai, asking him his name and where he lived, then he told me, "His name is Som, he lives on Rawai Beach."

Rawai Beach was six miles away.

"Come on, hop in my sidecar. I'll give you a lift." I gestured. The rich cannot afford not to be generous.

At Rawai Beach we all three sat at a beachside stall next to Som's family's house and drank coffee. From the look of the house, his family was neither rich nor poor by local standards. Out in the bay long, open fishing boats, some with a few tourists on board; passed by, their longtail engines popping. Using what little Thai I knew, and what little English the youngster knew, and with Thomas's help, we talked.

Som was a tall lad, nineteen years old. Like most Thais, he was slim but strong. He was very deeply tanned, almost black. He had a handsome face with regular features, and the standard good teeth. Among his own people he did not seem to be self-conscious of his amputated arm. Naturally when young women appeared, or among strangers, he tended to try to hide it by turning his body, or lowering the end of his stump under the table. His father, he told us, was captain of a small boat. He had learned some English at his secondary school, but at the age of sixteen, after his accident, he had been unable to attend anymore. He had wanted to go on to higher education, but now that he was disabled, there seemed to his family to be no point in it, he told us. It seemed a pity. He was obviously a bright lad.

"What's to stop you earning your living?" I asked him.

"No one will employ me."

"Why not?"

"Bad luck." He was shy and perhaps embarrassed. I tapped my plastic leg with my walking stick. He laughed.

"You're lucky *today*," I observed.

"They don't think I can manage with one arm," he explained the obvious.

"You drive a motorbike."

He stared out down the beach. I followed his gaze. A fishing boat was heading straight for us.

"Could you steer a boat like that?" I asked him.

"Oh, I could steer it all right, I go out fishing now and then with some friends, but I can't start the engine."

"Why not?" Always ask the obvious.

"Because . . . I can swing the handle all right, but someone else has to release the decompression lever."

"It's always on the right side of the engine," explained Thomas.

"Right side of the engine?" I queried. "Then we'll get one of those engines and we'll put it on the *left* side, eh?"

"He'll have a job, getting his fist up from the handle to the lever while the engine is still turning," observed Thomas.

"Then he'll have to be quick, won't he?" I replied.

"I can be quick," said Som, grinning. He'd understood.

"Then we'll do it," I said. "And Som will start his own bloody engine!"

We had found our Thai captain, and, although we didn't yet know it, we'd found our boat, too.

I waved my stick in the direction of the fishing boat. It was about thirty-eight feet long. Now it was being dragged, bows first, by four men and boys a short way onto the beach. "How much would a boat like that cost?" I asked.

Som smiled. "I don't know."

"Can you ask the skipper?"

Som hesitated before he walked slowly down the beach in the direction of the boat. I already knew that things like inquiring about the cost of boats are not done as directly or quickly as they might be done in the West. In the East it doesn't do for a potential buyer of anything to appear to be too eager. We knew that it would take Som a good half hour before he got around to asking the boat's skipper the cash value of his vessel.

Som was smiling when he returned to us about an hour later. By now I knew that the Thai smile didn't necessarily mean that the smiler was pleased, or had good news. "The owner says ten thousand baht for a used boat; fifteen thousand, maybe twenty thousand, new."

I did a quick mental calculation. There were about forty-two bahts to the pound. I stared at Thomas. "Ten thousand? Why, that's only about $500 . . . a thirty-eight-foot hardwood boat? Good God, a wooden boat of that construction in the States or England would—" I caught myself and grinned at Som, then at Thomas "—cost an arm and a leg . . . and I'm earning that much on that article that's coming out in *Yachting World*."

Like the legendary last of the big spenders, I turned to Som. "Ask the owner if he wants to sell his boat, cash down, tomorrow."

Som jumped up to do as he was bid. We were to find that like most Thais, I suppose like most people, he loved spending money as long as it wasn't his own.

Thomas said, "Steady on, you might be able to get one cheaper somewhere."

"Not the way things are going in Phuket, Thomas. That's a good boat. They're working in her, and they haven't offered her for sale. We'll get them to drag her right up on the beach and turn her over. Then you and me'll have a look around with your marlinespike, and if she's no rot, we'll buy her," I said.

"But," said Thomas, "before we take off in a boat for the Kra rivers, we need to go overland to look—"

I broke in: "We need a longtail boat anyway, to make the crossing. And before we go exploring by land, we need one to train our crew in." A tourist-toting longtail roared by the shore. As I watched the boat, I had an idea. "And while we're away, they can earn their own livings fishing or taking tourists out. They can keep half of all they earn, and the other half can go toward the crossing."

"What will you call her?" said Thomas.

I didn't have to think about it. "*Henry Wagner*," I replied.

Thomas nodded. My friend Henry Wagner had been the only person to take the trouble to come to the jetty on the day *Outward Leg* last sailed from America. He never lost faith in what I was trying to do.

And so it was that on the same day I found my motorbike, we also found our captain, our boat, and a means, at last, to say thank you to my friend so far away.

Back on board *Outward Leg* that evening, I sat in our cockpit in the moonlight and gazed over the tranquil waters of Ao Chalong Bay. I wondered to myself: Maybe the animist side of the Thais was right; perhaps, whizzing around Phuket and the Kra Isthmus on my motorcycle, I might indeed embarrass harmful spirits, so that they would flee from us, and take with them their bad luck. For sure, in the next few months, I felt, we would need more than our share of good luck.

Maybe the Buddhist belief in karma was right, too, I thought.

But I'd never had much "merit": Losing a bit less would make little difference. More important than my next existence (I'd deal with that when the time came) was getting a disabled crew in a boat across the Kra. The fact that we would probably receive little help made our challenge much greater, but it made my desire for success that much greater, too. Besides, by overcoming the Kra, might we not also help bring about a change in the everyday interpretation of the concept of karma?

If this was a possibility—and what dream is not?—if we, by our own efforts, could plant the seed of that idea into the heads of the fishermen and peasants, that the disabled need not be considered as flawed, that they can be useful members of society, then there was all the more reason, much, much more reason, for our endeavor than the overcoming of a mere physical or geographical challenge.

Now our challenge was spiritual.

I tried to interest a local branch of an international businessmen's organization in my ideas and intentions. They invited us along to one of their regular meetings. Thomas and I took Som (under protest that he would be "out of his class") along to interpret for us. After a long evening's speeches, including one by the governor of Phuket Province on America and South Korea, Thomas showed them some of our slides and I appealed to them for understanding, and for them to ease our way, if possible, especially on our coming voyage through the mainland isthmus.

The response was the kind offer by one of their members to act on our behalf with the Thai government in obtaining a lease of some land in Siray Island, on which to construct our shore base for Atlantis. We turned up to see the place reluctantly (we are not in the real estate business), and found that it was part of a swampy marsh. I took one look at the swamp and saw that it would take us three times as long to fill it in and make it reasonably fit to build on as it would to cross the Kra. The idea collapsed, and we heard no more from the businessmen's organization. It is not easy to explain abstract ideas to materialists. Our intent was to create an action, not to acquire a thing; to promote an idea, not to gain a material asset. How could they understand? They were not psychiatrists, nor were they navigators, or geographers. They were certainly not romantics. They were businessmen. There was no obvious gain for anyone in our forthcoming endeavor.

They were very busy. Phuket was well into a tourist boom. Everyone's mind was on building yet more hotels and bungalows, or wheeling and dealing in land by the beaches of the island. Land prices were skyrocketing. Few people could take their eyes off their plots of beachside land for more than a few seconds at a time. A few former peasants and many former tin miners were becoming dollar millionaires. Bulldozers and landfill trucks were everywhere, roaring and riding roughshod over God-given beauty to reshape it in the image of Mammon rampant. The whole island was drunk with the prospect of easy pickings from rich foreign tourists, arriving in greater numbers than ever now that Phuket Airfield had been extended.

For most people in Phuket there was little time to spare for the needs of a gang of cripples intent on some crazy prank. I got the impression that they thought perhaps we might spoil the view for the tourists. It might be all right for them to help us hide in some out-of-the-way marsh ground, but it was a different matter for them to help us to be out in the open, on the beaches, in the town, within sight of the sacred tourists.

Everything that was done for or by the Atlantis Society we did ourselves, or we paid someone to do for us, from my sparse earnings. There were no "free lunches" for us in Phuket, Phuket.

7

The Sea People

Our new boat turned out to be twenty years old. She had been built of a wood similar to iroko and almost as hard as teak, in Krabi, on the Thai mainland. The place was renowned for the quality of its timber and the skill of its boatbuilders.

She was an open boat, thirty-eight feet long from bow to stern. She was pointed at both ends, with a tremendous overhang at her bow. Her waterline length was nearly thirty feet. She had twenty-six ribs, four by fours on eighteen-inch centers. She was built like a battleship. The curve of her, from her high stem, with its long, high, bowspritlike stempost, decorated with sun-faded garlands, to her low, pointed stern, was utterly graceful. She put me in mind of a rather more than normally robust Venetian gondola. Unlike most of the more local fishing boats, she had been decked over with intricately joined duckboards from stem to stern. On her stern, balanced precariously, it seemed, was a gasoline driven longtail engine of uncertain vintage and, we would soon learn, reliability.

The boat's owner, sun-darkened and one of the *Chao-leh* (sea people), about my age, a very quiet, gentle man, told us that she had been used for fishing off the Similan Islands, which are about twenty miles northwest of Phuket. He wanted to move away from Phuket, he said, to other *Chao-leh* islands off the mainland coast, further south.

The next morning before dawn we started work on the boat.

The casual observer should not be fooled by the seeming languor of Thai coastal people. They worked, and they worked hard, but not when the sun was high. Most of their strenuous physical activity took place before 10:00 A.M. or after 4:00 P.M. Those were the times of their main meals of the day. Noon meant nothing to them except, if they could, to find shelter from the searing sun and rest.

With the help of a few friends and a cheap bottle of Mekong whiskey, the little boat owner and his *Chao-leh* crew of four men and a boy had the boat high and dry on the upper beach, after they had all traipsed onto the nearby headland to relieve themselves.

The year before, some do-gooder, Thai or *farang*, sociologist or plain old-fashioned philanthropist, had built a concrete public toilet in the middle of the village. It had never been used. Rightly, by their lights, the *Chao-leh* fishermen and their wives considered defecating close to where they ate and slept, and made love, to be anathema. It would for sure offend the spirits who guarded the village. On the headland the sun neutralized everything within an hour of its rising. It was a long walk, and took twenty minutes, there and back, but what was time? It meant a safer village.

Upon their return from the headland, Thomas and Som helped them to turn the boat upside down. I set to prodding around with Thomas's marlinespike. The boat's massive keel and side planks were all sound. There was no worm, no rot. They turned her over again. Only a few scuffs and splinters on her gunwales told the tale of the *Chao-leh* fishermen's many a long night at sea, rocking under the lee of the islands, silently, patiently tending their hooked lines.

We walked, all together, through the *Chao-leh* village at Rawai, and headed for a small store by the waterfront, to celebrate clinching our deal. The *Chao-leh* houses were all of wood, single-story, and were perched on pillars. In the shade underneath the houses, a layer of sand had been spread. On this sat the *Chao-leh* women, playing cards or laughing and joking at our passing.

I was curious as to why the old *Chao-leh* skipper wanted to move away from a beautiful place like Rawai. We sat at a long table, near a ramshackle beachside general store, under a shady palm tree. All along the shore, as far as a small headland a half-mile away, golden sand was shaded to beige by overhanging glistening palms. A long line of graceful longtail boats was drawn up, bows first, out of reach of the softly surging tide. To seaward, about two miles away, green islands gleamed in the sun above a cobalt sea that turned to turquoise over the reefs below the village. All around us small, happy, naked children played. Close to us, several boats were being prepared for the next night's fishing. It would be any regular package tourist's idea of good value. It was the very opposite of Düsseldorf.

I studied the little skipper and his crew. They were gentle and polite in a manner that had almost disappeared from much of the rest of the world that I had recently seen. Despite their obvious strength and their skills, there was nothing at all showy or aggressive about them, nor did I think there ever could be. Nor was there any obsequiousness in their manners.

Little by little, over our bottle of Mekong whiskey, their tale came out, through Som, Thomas, gestures, smiles, and grimaces. Their Thai was not good; neither was Thomas's or mine: We got along fine.

Although they themselves were line fishermen, their fellow villagers were mostly divers. Their boats worked the waters off the inshore islands, where the currents were strong and variable. First, long nets, sometimes a mile long or more, were weighted at the bottom with stones, and set down across an area of the sea. Then, with merely an air hose each, held in their mouths, the crewmen, stones tied around their waists, dived to depths of two hundred feet. In groups, they walked along the seabed herding the fish before them into the nets. When enough fish were caught in the net, they released the stone weights, and ascended to the surface. Sometimes, they said, they were below for an hour or more at a time. There were many cases among them of the bends, a diving sickness that leaves its victims half-paralyzed.

Behind us was a large corrugated-iron shed. A Chinese Thai supervised the tallying off of baskets of fish as they were lugged in from the boats by the *Chao-leh* men and boys. This, we were told, was the company store. It supplied all things the villagers needed—and, it seemed to me, many they didn't. The *Chao-leh* claimed that in Phuket town shops they could not get fair deals; the locals despised them, and they were grossly overcharged. They all bought everything at the village company store, including, when fishing was very good, motorcycles, refrigerators, television sets, radios, and tape recorders. They even bought electric rice pots, though few of them had electricity. They laughed as they admitted that they were all up to their necks in heavy debt.

Later, in conversation with the Chinese store owner, I commented on the baskets of snails I had seen at the back of the store. The snails were huge. Some were four inches long, fat and slimy. I asked him how to order snails in a Thai eating house. He laughed a peculiar Chinese laugh, the one that says, *"Hey, where you come from?"*

"No, they're not for Thai people," he told me. "They won't eat them. They're for export. Thailand sends tons and tons of them every day, by plane and ship, to Europe. They eat them there."

"Why don't Thais eat them?" I asked, all innocent.

"Mai dai . . . Cannot. Snails live in bathrooms. Snails very dirty. . . ." And again he laughed at the thought, probably of a fat Frenchman who had wandered around the store the other day, his beefy, hairy legs bulging in his ridiculous short shorts, now sitting elegantly with his latest mistress on the Boul' Mich chomping on some fat, rubbery snail that had been gouged, only days before, out of the washroom drain of some *Chao-leh* hut. I laughed with the Chinese: I for what I imagined he imagined, he for what he thought I couldn't imagine.

Chao-thaleh, or *"Chao-leh"* for short, the fishermen told us, meant "people of the sea" in Thai. There were four tribes of them living around the coasts of Phuket Island. They were not sure of their origins. They spoke four different languages, and between the groups the groups the lingua franca was Thai.

Some of them spoke Malay, and called themselves *Orang Laut*, which is Malay for "people of the sea." Others called themselves *Mohak*, and these claimed that their ancestors had come, centuries before, from the Mergui islands further north, off the coast of Burma.

The ancestors of all four groups, they claimed, were certainly in Phuket and other islands on the east coast of Thailand long before the Thais swept down from the north and conquered the area. For generations, until the 1950s, the *Chao-leh* had lived on the offshore islands around Phuket. Then, they said, mainland people came and bought them off their islands for small sums of money. In the 1970s (as tourism developed), they were forced by the new island title-holders to leave. In 1987 they squatted, landless, on a few beaches around the main island of Phuket.

Their main settlement was where we sat, at Rawai. The authorities, they said, wanted them all to move again, but this time to the same swampy area at Sillay Island that we had been offered as a shore base. It was inland from the fishing port near Phuket town. A school had already been built near the swamp area. The swamp had a narrow channel running through it from the sea, but the *Chao-leh* would not be able to live by the sea, as they had done for centuries. They all smiled sadly as they told us that. How would they sleep out of earshot of the sea? they asked.

Now a fish-breeding factory was being built further along their beach, where fish could be scooped out of tanks by willowy town-bred youths and sent to the icehouse to be packed for marketing. Behind the fish-factory site a little copse of trees had been bulldozed flat. There, the *Chao-leh* told me, in the shady glades among the now-felled trees, had been the home of their chief spirits. Now their spirits had no home. Now they would wander off and leave the *Chao-leh* to fend for themselves; defenseless against the avaricious landsmen.

The children of the *Chao-leh*, I saw in my mind's eye, would no longer kneel before the little spirit houses and pray for good fishing. Now they would squat before TVs and stare at ads for cornflakes and soap. Then the bright new world of the developers, market hucksters, and the practitioners of "make-believe" would be all theirs for the taking, and they would be, like so many millions of others, viewers not doers.

Slowly I hobbled back down the beach and flopped into our dinghy, and went back on board *Outward Leg* and sat and stared at the horizon beyond the islands for a good two hours, silent, as the sun sank over the *Chao-leh* village of Rawai.

8

A Bird

The next day, our boat paid for, Thomas and Som brought her round from Rawai and put her alongside *Outward Leg*. Our new boat was only a few inches shorter than our old. I clambered down into *Henry Wagner* (her name was not yet painted on her stern) for a spin around the bay.

Boating in a longtail was a new experience for me. I'd seen plenty of them about in Ao Chalong Bay, of course. The roar of their engines had broken my line of thought dozens of times a day while I had been writing *Somewheres East of Suez*. The way that longtail engines were mounted was beautifully simple. You got an engine, welded a square frame, like a gimbal, on which to sit it, and from the frame's center span welded a short shaft, a lug, protruding downward. The engine could rock in its gimbal and could move vertically. On the boat, in your sternpost, you drilled a large hole, and fitted into it a steel socket. Then your engine-gimbal lug was dropped into the socket, and there you were, with your engine balanced on your stern, yet able to be swung around horizontally, to change your heading, or swung up and down to raise or lower your propeller into or out of the water. Properly balanced, an engine and propeller shaft weighing together hundreds of pounds could be swung around with one hand by any strong-wristed, well-built, youngish *gorilla*.

Many longtail engines were simply car or truck engines that had been roughly modified by having a propeller shaft welded directly onto their flywheels. Some of these were enormous engines of a dozen cylinders and could drive a sixty-foot flat-bottomed scull at over thirty knots. These were the ones used by the cargo carriers of both the Thai coasts, and the passenger boats around Bangkok. They were also used by some of the pirates and smugglers of Southwest Thailand and in the Gulf of Thailand, the waters we were bound for.

Other types of engine used for longtails were general-purpose units, mostly diesel-driven, designed and built very ruggedly and simply for Third World farmers, to drive water pumps, rice mills, tractors, electrical generators, and a host of other machines. For longtail boats a reduction gear wheel was fitted onto the flywheel, which in turn, through a chain, drove a separate gear wheel on the propeller shaft. This gear wheel, we were to find later, was the Achilles' heel of the longtails on rivers. With all the chopping of the prop, and the changes of speed, the chain gradually wore away the teeth of the gear wheel. Then it would have to be removed or remade. That was fairly simple on the coast—but inland?

Most of the longtail diesel engines used in Phuket were built by a Thai subsidiary of my friends the Yanmar Company of Japan.

Yanmar had made *Outward Leg*'s more sophisticated engine and sail-drive propulsion unit. They had also helped me over some very sticky patches on our voyage, with a swift engine refit in Cyprus, and provision of replacement parts to some remote areas. I had good connections at Yanmar in Japan. I made up my mind to write to the people at Yanmar, tell them of our plans, and see what they might do for us.

We set off on our boat trials. Thomas let go of the lines holding *Henry Wagner* alongside *Outward Leg*.

Som surprised us. He put one foot on the longtail engine's steering handle, so that the propeller was stuck up in the air astern of the boat, grabbed, with his one hand, the engine starter cord, and yanked it. The engine didn't start (the gasoline variety rarely do at first pull) but at least he had turned it over. And a gasoline driven engine has no compression lever.

"Hey, maybe we don't need a diesel engine?" suggested Thomas.

When I feel something strongly, I sometimes break into pidgin German with Thomas. "*Mein lieber* Thomas," I said, "there's no way you're going to get me sitting in the *mittel von der* jungle in an open boot, *unter ein* hot sun, with maybe guerrillas around, and a dozen gasoline cans in the boat!"

Som, on his third try, got the engine started, and we were off, in the direction of Ko Lon Island.

It was soon obvious that the old gasoline engine would not be suitable for our Kra effort. First it took several pulls on the starter rope before it would fire into life, and then, whenever the sea splashed it, it spluttered and stopped. Someone then had to unscrew the starter plug, wipe it dry, screw it back in again, and, after several tries, restart the motor.

By now *Henry Wagner* was close to Ko Lon (*Ko* means island in Thai), which was about a mile off Phuket, and formed the southern monsoon protection for Ao Chalong anchorage. There was a good breeze blowing in the channel, on our stern, and, for the third or fourth time, as spray set up by our boat's propeller splashed onto the engine, it again spluttered to a stop. On the beach of Ko Lon several figures stood watching us approach. I knew Ko Lon was a Muslim island, and I made a mental note to wish them "*Salaam Alakeim!*" (the peace of God be with you!). It was an Arab greeting, but they all understood it, and it pleased them to be greeted in the language of their Prophet.

Som, with his shirt wrapped round his head now as protection from the hot sun, made to yank the starter cord again. I gestured to him to leave it. "We'll let the breeze blow us in to the beach. . . ." I hollered.

Som nodded, smiling, and made his way forward to drop our bow anchor. He moved well in the boat, despite only having one arm.

As the boat blew in to the beach, Som dropped the hook, quickly wrapped the anchorline around the bow sponson, and held it rigid. The anchor held, the boat's bow swung round into the wind, and faced offshore. Som, without needing to be told, then gently let out the anchorline until our stern bumped lightly on the sandy beach. He was a natural boatman, and I knew that I'd guessed right. Thomas, aft, had held the engine steering handle down, to hold the propeller shaft up, so that it would clear the beach.

No sooner had Thomas and Som pulled our stern up the sand a little way out of the sea, to secure the boat from floating off sideways, than a little dwarflike figure made for the engine. I was still sitting amidships, girding myself for the hobble back to the stern. In a low, rocking boat, decked over, there were no hand-holds at waist height. It was awkward—dangerous for anyone on one leg.

There was a rapid exchange of words between Som and the dwarf, now under our stern, while I tried to keep my balance on the still-rocking boat. The dwarf, with his shirt over his head like Som, took out our spark plug, and cleaned it. A moment later he screwed it back in again, leapt onto our stern, cocked up the propeller shaft, and with one mighty yank started the engine the first time.

As the engine roared into life and our propeller whizzed over their heads, the small crowd of onlookers on the beach shifted quickly out of the way.

I stood, or rather half crouched, halfway along the decking, braced to fall. The dwarf's back was still toward me. I realized it was, in fact, a small boy or youth moving like a grown man.

He was a sturdy little chap, no more than four-and-a-half feet tall, with a boxer's shoulders and hard fisherman's muscles. He stood with his feet braced well apart. His feet were small, with broad toes, splayed. He stood as if he were as much a part of the boat as her stempost. When she rocked, he rocked. When she jerked, so did he. I knew right away that whoever he was, he had spent his life in boats. Here was a born sailor. He might be twelve or so, from the size of him.

"Bravo!" I shouted stupidly. Then I remembered that he was a Thai. I racked my heat-numbed mind for a Thai equivalent. All I could think of was *"Dee maak ma!"* (Very good).

The stocky little figure turned round. In the shadow of the shirt wrapped over his head, I first imagined I saw a wide grin. Something opened again, and some noises came out. They sounded like grunts.

"Nah nah na ah!"

It didn't register. I was too shocked. As I said before, we disabled ourselves can find others' disablements shocking. I was still stupidly grinning. I was still starting to repeat my cheer . . . and I was stopped dead in my clumsy tracks.

The boy's shirt had fallen to one side of his face and revealed a . . . monstrous act of nature, or accident. My face must have fallen. I found myself straining to smile at a ruin of a lower face.

The whole of his lower head was a mess. His upper lip was huge: almost three times the size of his normal lip, and it was split wide apart. It pushed his nose up, so that I could look right into his nostrils. From under this monstrous protuberance a cluster of jagged, snaggled teeth stuck out this way and that. He reminded me of some monstrous underwater creature dragged from the depths of the ocean.

I half crouched there, half-frightened, staring at him like a fool.

"Na na nee nah!"

A vast orifice was wide open in a huge grin.

Recovering courage, perhaps scared of what it might find, my gaze strayed to his eyes. They were almond-shaped, smiling, above his little pushed-up Asian nose. I was already almost in tears. Then the thought struck me that above his nose he looked like a real Genghis Khan in miniature.

I must have grinned then; as I stumbled forward, balancing on my cane, he made quickly toward me over the deck and reached for my elbow to help me to the stern.

I usually shake people off, but politely, when they handle me, even when they are, in good faith, trying to help me. I've never liked being manhandled, especially by strangers. I suppose I've been alone too much.

But this one I couldn't shake off. He needed my elbow far more than I needed his hand.

As we reached the stern, to show him that neither of us should falter, and that I was not absolutely helpless and neither was he, I laid down my cane, shoved myself down, swung myself over, and landed shipshape on the sand. Then, sodden-footed, cane back in hand, I started to hobble up the beach. I could hardly see.

Thomas, Som, and the cluster of men were talking ahead of me. I did not want to call for help on the soft sand; sure enough, over I went.

Almost.

As my cane sank into the sand and I started to fall, our new acquaintance grabbed me and pulled me back upright, strongly. He stood supporting me and with that awesome jaw, laughing, or trying to, until I recovered myself. Then, with me holding on to his shoulder with one hand, we walked together up the beach, until we had rejoined Thomas and Som, where they stood in the shade of palms.

As we reached the top of the strand, I jerked my thumb at my companion. "Ask 'em what's his name, Thomas."

Thomas had his glasses off. He couldn't see well without them.

There was a long consultation. Finally the boy said, or grunted, what was meant to be Nok.

Som interpreted: "Nok says he's fifteen, but no one knows. Nok doesn't have any parents, he lives in the fishing boats. Nok says he got a big fishhook caught in his mouth when he was young. His name means Bird," he said, smiling.

Nok was doing his best to smile, too. It looked like a bombed ship's hull.

"*And a bird he shall be, by God!* Thomas, I do believe we've found ourselves a mate for Som!"

9

The Mercy of Allah

Henry Wagner needed recaulking. All the planks in a wooden boat work against each other as she moves in the water. To accommodate this working, flexible caulking—oakum or cotton strands mixed with putty and paint—is wedged in between the planks. It is a long, slow, monotonously finicky job, performed with patience, a hammer, and a specially shaped chisel. Given the importance of not having our boat suddenly open up and sink, our recaulking was best done by the people who would be using the boat. Besides, it was cheaper.

We returned from Ko Lon Island together in *Henry Wagner*, Thomas, Som, Nok, and I, to Ao Chalong. We dragged the boat high and dry and beached her. Then we turned her over ready for caulking and the space beneath her upturned hull became, for the next few days, Nok's home. There was little hardship in this for Nok. It was far better quarters than he was accustomed to. He was being well fed regularly, for once, he had one or two friends on the beach and in the fishing boats around, and occasionally he could joyride and show off on my motorbike along the beach. He had been much a pariah.

Besides the recaulking we also had to replace both gunwales. These are the wooden rails you step on, when you first go aboard, that run all the way along the boat above the planking.

Then we fixed wooden seats in *Henry Wagner* so she could assume her first guise for us—a tourist-toting ferryboat.

After Nok joined us, little by little his story came out. At first I was inclined to doubt his tale, just as I had done his little fib about his disfigurement; that it had been caused by a fishhook. I had known right away, then, that he had been making up a story; that he had a cleft palate. I had taken him to the Seventh-Day Mission Hospital in Phuket as soon as we landed. My dentist friend Dr. Nantje Twistre, a Dutch lady, had confirmed that his was indeed a cleft palate. We had made arrangements for Nok's teeth to be straightened, his mastoid to be treated, and for his upper lip to be surgically righted as much as possible.

But the tale that Nok managed to convey to us was confirmed, time and again, by his fellow-Muslim fishermen from Ko Lon. He had been born into a poor Muslim fishing family. The family boat, owned by someone else, as was usual in those days, had no engine; only a sail and oars. When he had been no older than six or seven years, his family had gone off to fish off Racha Noi Island, about ten miles to the south of Phuket. During the night their boat had been boarded by *kamoys*—pirates. Nok's father, mother, and two brothers had been murdered, knifed to death. Their bodies had been thrown overboard. Nok, asleep in the bilge, had been missed, and somehow escaped death. While the pirates rifled the boat, they were disturbed by another boat passing close by. The *kamoys* had jumped into their own boat in a hurry, and left Nok's family boat drifting. In the morning, when the southwest breeze had blown up, little Nok—alone—had sailed the boat back to Ko Lon Island. His family's bodies had never been recovered.

Since then, Nok had lived as and where he could, but mostly in line-fishing boats. On them he had worked mainly at night and had been paid mainly in food. He claimed to be fifteen, but I thought him younger, perhaps by as much as two years. It is difficult to gauge the age of an ancient ruin of a head on a young, sturdy body.

My motorbike with its sidecar was not easy for most bikers to ride, not even husky young ones. I had to really hang on to the handlebars; otherwise they would set up a tremendous wobble. I needed the strong arms that a lifetime of sailing had given me. On the road to and from town I could manage speeds of forty miles an hour and more, but I was always careful, especially on the bends. With all the construction work going on in Phuket, I never knew when a cement mixer, speeding along at fifty-five miles an hour, would not come roaring round the bend.

On one such occasion, when Som accompanied me into town, I pulled over to the verge to wait for a convoy of smoke-belching leviathans to rumble past. I turned my head away from the noise and smoke, and saw a small lad hobbling along on an old home-built wooden crutch. He was no more than four feet tall, dark-skinned, and dressed only in a ragged pair of shorts. His body was thin. His one good foot was bare. His features were plain, almost ugly. He looked about twelve. In the East he was considered even as low as the dust set down by the passing trucks.

As he limped closer, I saw that his right leg was much shorter than his left, and that it ended in a small claw foot where, by rights, his knee should have been. It dangled down like a baby's leg. As he swung closer, he smiled widely at me.

Here we go, I thought. "Tell him we'll give him a lift, Som."

"He's a Muslim," said Som. How he knew was a mystery to me.

"So what? So's Nok. You're a Buddhist. I'm a . . . a . . . *farang!*"

I gestured to the crippled boy. With a hop, a huge grin, and a flourish of his crutch, he bounced himself into the sidecar.

"Where's he going?" I asked Som. There was a quick exchange of Thai.

"He lives on the beach, between Ao Chalong and Rawai."

The road was clear now. I started the bike and set off. As we trundled along, Som, friendly enough toward the crippled boy, at my bidding asked him about himself.

Then he told me: "His name is Anant. He is fifteen. His family are poor. They are fishing people. Now they have no boat. He has no work. He lives by running errands for people." *On one foot!* "Sometimes he walks all the way into Phuket, and in that way he earns enough to feed himself." *Twenty-five miles in the heat on one foot and a crutch?*

"Does he know how to caulk a boat?" I asked.

"Yes." Som said it as if I'd asked him if the boy knew how to breathe.

"Tell him . . ." I glanced down at Anant. He grinned up at me. " . . . he's got a new job . . . thirty baht a day [$1.40] and his food three times a day."

The three of us, with one arm and two legs missing between us, trundled on to Ao Chalong in my three-wheeled magic carpet.

When we arrived at our boat, it was obvious that Nok and Anant knew each other, but very casually. Anant even understood, much better than Som, what Nok was trying to say. Now we had an interpreter for Nok. That would save us at least two hours a day, which until now had been spent puzzling out what Nok's noises meant.

"What does your name mean, Anant?" I asked him. He smiled widely at me and was silent.

I looked at Som, who spoke quickly to the boy. Som consulted his Thai-English dictionary that I had bought him that day. He was very proud of his new possession. It took him a minute or two to find the right entries, then he turned to me.

"It means 'the mercy of Allah,' " Som said, quietly.

To this day I don't know if Som was joking.

10

Crew at Large

Now, with five of us working on our Atlantis endeavor, it was time to set up a shore base. *Outward Leg* was far too crowded. We needed a place to work in when the monsoon rains poured down, or when the heat of the sun dictated that we should be under shade. We would need a place large enough to store our equipment safely, engines, dinghy, and such.

Stealing and burglary were too much of a problem in Phuket, but they did happen to the unguarded, especially on Thursdays. That was the day when, each week, the spirits that guarded houses went to heaven to consult with angels. Then the *kamoys* had their field days.

On the land side of a deep ditch at the top of the beach, close to where *Henry Wagner* lay, and opposite *Outward Leg*'s anchorage, there was a vacant, spacious, half-ruined one-story building. It did not seem to have been intended as a house; it was more like a long-abandoned restaurant. It had a half-gaping palm roof and a good concrete floor. Inside it was a great open space as big as a tennis court.

The place had been built some years before by a Greek who, for some legal reason, had lost it to the landowner. This was not a rare occurrence in Phuket. The landowner was an old peasant, now rich, who, in his expensive silk sarong, wordlessly watched every move we made, and every morning and evening carefully counted the coconuts on each of his trees. Not that I blamed him. Coconut milk and fish is a good diet for growing lads.

But he was willing to rent the place out to me for a pound or so a day, and so we moved in. Surrounded as it was by trees, I named the place the Bowery, in memory of old friends in New York City.

Inside of a week Som, with his one arm, and Anant, with his one leg, helped by Thomas now and then, had fixed new palm leaves to the whole extent of the roof, and so made the building rainproof.

A couple of miles away, close by the temple at Wat Chalong, was a rubber plantation. On it worked friends of our boys. One of them whose nickname was Meow (Cat, and he moved exactly like one) hailed from a village in the Kra, on the banks of the River Trang. He was a quiet young man of twenty-one. His pay at the plantation was very little—five baht (25 cents) for a kilo of rubber collected, drop by drop, from the trees. I took him on as general shoreside assistant (he was very prone to seasickness), on condition that he taught our lads what they needed to know about thatching a palm roof and building a small wooden bridge across our stream, but didn't do it for them. This suited Meow very well. The Thai word for "work" is *ngan*; so is the Thai word for party. Now work could really be party time.

In a few days the boys and I built a bridge of coconut-tree trunks wide enough for my motorcycle, over the deep ditch in front of the house. We put into the house two hammocks, three mattresses, and the stove from *Outward Leg*, and there we were, with a large, cool, beachside residence, shady workshop, and storage rooms.

There was one snag with our new base. Local legend had endowed the place with "evil spirits." The Thai boys were afraid and would not sleep in it, but preferred to spend their nights beneath the boat on the beach. Something drastic was needed. I persuaded Thomas to convince the boys that I had magic powers. In my own land, he told them, I was a mighty shaman.

I rode into town, and bought some white cotton thread and Chinese crackers. All our lads silently watched me as I tied the cotton all around the house in the shape of a six-pointed star, with firecrackers on each point.

That night, as the moon rose over Ao Chalong, and feeling

very foolish but not daring to show it, I stood in the center of the star, holding the *Admiralty Pilot for the Malacca Strait* in one hand, and my walking stick in the other. As my awestruck crew gaped at me from a safe distance, in a sonorous voice I pretended to pray, to frighten away the evil spirits. Thomas surreptitiously fired the crackers, and they popped and banged all around the house.

I didn't know what to shout at the lurking spirits. The first thing that came to my mind was Shakespeare's sonnet "When in Disgrace with Fortune and Men's Eyes," so I shouted that. It seemed to do the trick. The boys, after our ceremony, had insisted that we place a bowl of water and a can of sardines on one of the house rafters, in case any good spirits came to the house hungry. Then they slept happily inside the house, and we heard no more of evil spirits. I had a new name now; *Captain Keng*, "strong"!

Nok, once he was through at the hospital, worked on *Henry Wagner* every day in the cool hours of the morning and evening. His teeth had been straightened. His lower head was now much more shipshape. He still couldn't speak, but it was all a vast improvement. By the time our house was finished, he had recaulked the whole boat, and, with Thomas's help, replaced her gunwales and oiled her sides, to protect her wood from the heat of the sun. Six wooden seats and an iron-piping frame, covered with yellow plastic fabric for a sun shelter, were built and fixed into our boat. Her name was painted on her stern, and Nok and *Henry Wagner*, looking brand-new, were ready to tout for the tourist trade.

Our friends at Yanmar in Japan and in Thailand had rallied quickly to our cause. They had even sent an engineer all the way down from Bangkok to make sure our new engine was balanced correctly. Now they sent a handsome new eleven-horsepower diesel longtail engine. It was Nok's pride and joy, and sat on our boats' stern. From it projected a wicked-looking shaft, fourteen feet long, and on the end of it, gleaming in the sun, was a huge three-bladed brass propeller. We soon had the decompression lever changed for Som.

The launching of any longboat, whether newly built or refitted, should always be a festive occasion, and so it was for our boat. We went into town and bought new garlands of yellow and red silk to place round her bow, a present to please her own resident spirit. A thousand (yes, a *thousand*) firecrackers, on long lines, were also draped around her bows.

Early one morning in November, we all stood around the boat, at the water's edge: Thomas, Som, Nok, Anant, Meow, and I. With the aid of a cheap bottle of Mekong whiskey, we procured the help of six men from the village. I lit one of the firecrackers. We all heaved up on the boat and pushed her, bows first, into the sea. The firecrackers banged and cracked and popped loudly, to scare away any evil spirits, and *Henry Wagner*, the expedition vessel of the Atlantis Society, was launched and afloat. That time I quoted the whole of Kipling's poem "If." If that didn't scare evil spirits away, nothing would.

Nothing has ever been wasted in *Henry Wagner*, and certainly no time. Her postrefit hull and engine trials were held on her way to her first day's work taking tourists out from Naiharn Beach, about six miles from Ao Chalong. Our trials were a success. Flat-out, our engine made more than thirteen knots, and her hull planks leaked no more than could be expected the first time out after sitting on a beach for two months.

On the way to Naiharn Bay all three boys, and Thomas, too, tried their hand at steering, and it was clear that, with the engine carefully balanced, they would have few problems in calm seas; but in heavier weather the two smaller boys would have to be relieved at short intervals. Little Anant's quick mastery of steering with our engine, while balancing on his crutch, with the boat moving at speed, was a wonder.

I suppose, writing of our first passage in our boat in her new guise, I could describe the beauty of the scenery: green, green islands, golden beaches, a small fleet of handsome charter yachts and gallant cruisers at anchor, the cobalt sea deeps, the turquoise stretches over shallows, the lovely hills of Phuket, the scarlet-and-gold roofs of temples peeking over the palm trees. But this is not the purpose of my tale, and so I tell you about our lads, their faces alive with delight because they were moving in something they had made come alive themselves. And the three of us with crippled limbs creeping and crawling and hobbling, each of us, slowly and carefully around the boat, as she moved and rolled, exploring every handhold, noting every drop at each and every movement of the hull, and conquering with smiles and gasps and laughter our own fears and trepidation. This, and not the surrounding scenery, is what my eye and mind dwelt upon.

On that day, when *Henry Wagner* first arrived at Naiharn Bay, Som wanted to beach the boat at the quiet, almost-deserted end.

But I insisted that she should go as close as we could get her to the Yacht Club Hotel—the only one on the bay—and probably one of the fanciest beach hotels on Earth.

The high-tourist season had not yet started. There were few other longboats for hire, from Ko Lon or Rawai; both Nok and Som had a few acquaintances in them.

Thomas and I sat ashore by the hotel for an hour or two, until, suddenly, a couple of beach-bag-bearing *farang* tourists (*bless 'em!*), stopped by the boat, spoke to Som, and awkwardly clambered on board *Henry Wagner*. Soon our boat, with Som at the engine steering her, and Nok and Anant tending the anchor, took off on her maiden voyage as a tourist ferry, for a trip to God knows what island.

As we mounted a small bus to return to Ao Chalong, I said to Thomas, "Well, that's that. They're on their own now, sink or swim, until we return from the Kra. They've plenty of food in the Bowery, they've a stock of diesel oil, they've fishing hooks and lines. It's make or break. If they do all right, we'll know we've a good crew we can trust. Otherwise . . ."

The little bus was bumping along. "Otherwise what?" asked Thomas.

"Well, otherwise . . . oh hell, we'll have a crew anyway. What choice do we have?"

The three lads were back at dusk, all smiles and laughter. Thomas and I were packing our bags for our motorbike exploration of the Kra, due to start next day. The boys were cockahoop. They'd had two trips out from Naiharn Bay, at two hundred baht a trip ($10). They'd made more money, in one day, than they had ever hoped to make in one week, together or singly, in their lives.

Som, of course, was in charge of the accounts. He paid out equal shares of 50 percent of the take. The other 50 percent went into our expedition kitty, $10 towards stores for the Kra crossing. This was manna to me; it was treasure to the lads.

"The tourists," Som said, "did not notice our . . . disablements. If they did, they made no comment about them."

"All the same if they had done," I observed, "as long as you got the money."

It had been, crowed Nok, "*Na aah aah nah!*" "My best day's fishing *ever!*"

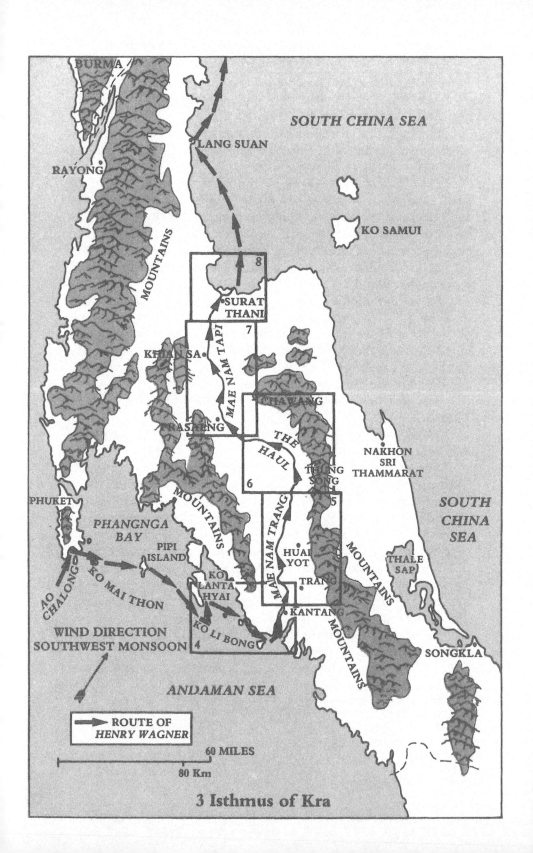

3 Isthmus of Kra

11

Rubber-Stamp Tango

I must explain why, on our crossing of the Kra, we were so *poor*.

Thailand was a country whose government, while spending vast sums trying to attract foreigners—and their money—to its shores and beaches, also insisted that most *farang* residents leave every three months to renew their visas. They had to either get another visa at a Thai consulate abroad, or activate the second part of their existing double-entry visa. A double-entry visa meant that foreigners were allowed to enter Thailand twice, for two consecutive spells of ninety days, as long as they left again before the first ninety days were up, and had a non-Thai stamp in their passports to prove that they had done so. Then they could reenter Thailand for another ninety days.

Future generations will hopefully find it very hard to believe that this continual senseless shuffle of dozens—hundreds—of human bodies, from here to there and back, hundreds—often thousands—of miles, merely to get some ink impressions onto some bits of paper, was accepted, in the main, by the owners of those bodies, but such was the case.

It went on, this rubber-stamp tango, as I called it, every day and every night of the year, and as I write, it still goes on. Most *farangs* who resided in Thailand usually went to Malaysia, because it was nearest. The Lord only knows how much time and money, which would otherwise have been spent among the ordinary Thai people, were wasted on chasing rubber-stamp impressions.

Every Thai official I tackled about this said that it was "so that we can keep tabs on who is in the country." When I suggested that the same thing could be done by having each *farang* report to a local immigration office every three months, their only reactions were smiles and, "Well, that's the rules."

None of them ever said that this practice also provided a continual subsidy for the Thai airways and Thai railways, both government-owned transport monopolies; nor that, under this system, there were very many likely rake-offs by corrupt people at the borders of Thailand and inside other countries, too.

We had been told that our first visa period expired on the twenty-eighth. It was now the twenty-sixth. We would do the 360 miles or so to the Malaysian frontier at Padang Besar on my motorbike. We could be there in two days at a steady speed. We could get our passports stamped, then return immediately into Thailand, with the second of our doubleentry visas activated. Then we could explore the rivers of the isthmus on the way back to Phuket.

Simple, we thought.

As soon as we crossed the bridge that connects Phuket Island to the Thai mainland, it was as though we were in another country. There was much less traffic. *Farangs* were much rarer on the mainland, especially *farangs* on three-wheeled motorbikes. Everywhere we trundled, we were stared at. Everywhere we stopped, we were surrounded by curious Thais, old and young. The further we traveled from Phuket, the more their curiosity.

Along well-kept, almost empty roads we traveled through Phangnga (pronounced Pangnah), a small town surrounded by almost vertical limestone mountains exactly like those in Chinese pictures. Their bases were hidden in mist, their summits crowned by clusters of trees. Then on through Krabi, another small town, where we stayed a while to watch boatbuilders constructing craft exactly the same as our own *Henry Wagner*. We marveled at old men's skill with adzes and huge planes, and at how these vessels were almost wholly constructed without the use of electrical machinery. There seemed to be no one under the age of sixty using hand tools, and there were few power tools.

We had a cheap lunch of noodles and hightailed it south along the coastal road for the port of Trang, to reach there by nightfall.

At every town, every village we passed, it was obvious that most of the shops and businesses were run by Chinese-Thais. Later, on our boat passage, we were to find that the ethnic Chinese were, above a certain level, the key men. There were no supplies, no service at all, above a very simple level, that would not, somewhere along the line between its source and us, pass through Chinese-Thai hands. Perhaps it was just as well; all the Chinese we were to meet were industrious and intelligent. "Can do" seemed to be in their bones. But always at a fair price. A fair price usually, after much careful bargaining. If agreement could not be reached and the deal fell through, the Chinese were not offended; and once a bargain was agreed with them, they kept it—always.

In Kantang, a port at the mouth of the Trang River, which we pulled into just before dusk, there were no *farang* visitors in evidence, even though there were sandy beaches close to the town.

Thomas and I found a food stall in a park above the river, and watched darkness enwrap the town. We ate a fresh fish supper for the equivalent of 40 cents each.

In Kantang we slept in a Chinese-owned hotel—a great, rambling wooden building, filthy inside and out, and noisy from the fish-toting trucks in the street outside. There were dust-encrusted but very fine Chinese pictures on the walls.

In the morning the Chinese hotel-keeper engaged us in conversation. He was a stout man of about sixty, whose smile reminded me of a small statue of Buddha I had inspected in a shop in Phuket.

His English was halting; our Thai was sparse. Through him we engaged a small longtail boat to take us some way up the river. A couple of hours' boating, during which we covered about twelve miles upstream, showed us that the river, even where it branched off into a maze of waterways, was wide and deep.

The hotel owner accompanied us and tried his best to sell me some land on a high bluff at a river bend, above a small village of wooden houses on stilts. "Ver" good. No have flood. One *rei* eighty-five thousand baht [$4,000],' he declaimed. A *rei* was about 1,900 square yards.

The view, over flat, riverside swampland was . . . pretty. "Yes, good, but we don't want to buy land, we only want to see the river."

Later, on our trip in *Henry Wagner*, we found that the going price for a *rei* of land on that particular bluff was in fact eight thousand baht ($380).

By noon we were back in Kantang. If we were to be at the Malaysian frontier, 180 miles away, by the following day, the date our visas expired, we would have to hurry. It was hard going, uphill, in the rain, for our old motorcycle, over the central mountains of the Kra Isthmus, but we made it to Hat Yai, the nearest Thai town to the frontier, by late evening. We stopped only to buy gasoline and to be briefly and courteously inspected and waved through by soldiers at Thai army checkpoints at both ends of the mountain passes.

Hat Yai was a bustling frontier town, notoriously full of Thai prostitutes who catered year-round to hordes of male tourists, mostly from south of the frontier, mainly from straitlaced Singapore.

The morning saw us at the Thai frontier checkpoint thirty miles from Hat Yai. We were turned back. "Not have," said an official, "export license of motorcycle. Go from Thailand cannot."

"But we're only going over to get a stamp!"

"No can do. Must have export license. Government rules!" Smile. He was about thirty years old, well built, and handsome.

I stared at his plastic name tag. Patping. He had a paratrooper's parachute badge on the breast of his uniform shirt.

"Can we walk over?" asked Thomas in Thai.

"Walk over can," allowed Patping.

I butted in, speaking English, "But it's a mile to the Malaysian checkpoint. It's blazing hot," I tapped my prosthesis with my stick, " . . . and I'm on one leg. . . ."

"*Mai pen rai*. It doesn't matter. It's the rules!"

"Taxi can catch across?" Thomas suggested to the official.

"Here no can do. Must return to Hat Yai. Catch taxi there."

Back we went, the thirty miles to Hat Yai, to park the bike and find a cab. By now it was blazing-hot midday. After an hour's search and bargaining we found a taxi driver who would take us across without it costing me another leg. Back we drove to the Thai checkpoint. No problem now that we were in a taxi. The driver was known to every official we encountered. On familiar terms, in fact. Straight through we went, all bows and smiles. Across a mile-long dreary stretch of sun-scorched scrub, past a low frontier wall, topped with barbed wire, to the Malaysian immigration checkpoint.

No problem. It felt good to be back in the dear old Commonwealth. In five minutes we had been entered into Malaysia, at a window under a notice that read PENALTY FOR SMUGGLING DRUGS IS DEATH (good idea) as three polite little men scrabbled through the contents of our pockets.

Within ten minutes we had been driven a hundred yards along the road into Malaysia, our taxi made a U-turn, and we passed again through the Malaysian checkpoint. Now we headed once more, over the scrub plain, back toward Thailand.

12
A Fly in the Ointment

There are no prizes for guessing who was at the window of the Thai immigration checkpoint.

Right first time: Patping.

Above his window was a notice saying that long-haired and improperly dressed people would not be welcome in Thailand.

I thanked the gods of the sea that Thomas had submitted to my exhortations to have a short-back-and-sides only a week before.

Behind us a group of Buddhist monks, orange-robed, with sandals and shaved heads, and without smiles, patiently waited. While my eye was on them, my mind wasn't. It was on flashed images of the prostitutes in the hotel lobbies in Hat Yai the night before. If they were properly dressed, I pondered, God only knew what improper might be.

Smiling at us as though we were long-lost friends returned from afar, Patping took our passports, inspected the Malaysian stamps, fingered each page, then pressed his rubber stamp as per the rules.

"Entry permitted fourteen days only," he stated.

My mind whirled in a turmoil. "Fourteen days! But we're on double-entry visas! They're each for ninety days! Look, our first visas expire on the twenty-eighth. That's today!"

Patping smiled wider. "Yes, have twenty-eighth today, but must use second visa *before* twenty-eighth! Now can have only tourist visa for fourteen days!"

"But . . . but we've come over three-hundred-sixty miles . . . a motorbike!"

Patping smiled even more widely. "Have many buses, trains, planes in Thailand." Smiling still, he gently handed us our passports and retired to the inner depths of the office, to be replaced by another, older official. I started to tackle him about our problem. "No can do. Mister Patping say, I no can do."

Hot, perspiring, aching all over, we clambered back into our taxi and drove once more the thirty miles to Hat Yai. The road would have turned blood red had it been able to listen to the language issuing from the back of our taxi.

We could remain in Thailand only two weeks! Then we would have to return to Malaysia, and obtain new visas! We would not be able to do it on the motorbike. It would take too much time, and anyway we would now have to go to Penang, the nearest town in Malaysia with a Thai consul. It would take us weeks to get an export permit for my motorcycle. There was no alternative to an expensive air flight except for a long journey by bus and train. We would have to fly from Phuket to Penang at great expense of time and money. We knew that to obtain a visa in Penang meant a wait there of two days in a hotel that would eat into our expedition funds. *We would be poor in the Kra!*

By the time we had recovered our motorbike and covered a sixty mile trek north from Hat Yai, I had also almost recovered my composure. I was pleased that we were back in Thailand, even though we'd been absent for a mere ten minutes.

"Not a bad country, this, Thomas," I told him. "The officials on the whole are not too officious. Many of them even try to be helpful. . . ."

It shows how colloquial Thomas's English had become after three years in *Outward Leg*: "There's always a bloody fly in the ointment," he said, "even in Thailand."

"First fly I ever saw with a paratrooper's badge," I rejoined.

We were on the coast road heading north. Between us and the Gulf of Thailand was a line of sand dunes, shaded by palm trees and sometimes cypresses. Under the trees nestled at the sea's very edge was village after Muslim village of fisherpeople. To our left was a brilliant emerald sea of rice paddies stretching away almost to the western horizon. In the distance the low mountains of the central Kra range loomed, blue and gray and very mysterious. A fly in the ointment? I thought. Some ointment!

We headed north up the coast and then through the mountains to Thung Song, a small town at the headwaters of the River Trang. We little knew how much those two names would come to mean to us within only a few weeks.

The Thai word for river is *khlong*. But that can also mean canal. Each natural main river is called *mae nam*, and that means "mother of waters." We were going to head up the Mother of Waters Trang: in colloquial Thai, *Mae Nam Trang*. We had a hotel room, clean and cheap, in Thung Song, spent a dull evening there, slept well, then took off to explore the pathways by the River Trang.

There were very few roads across the river. Most of the approaches to the riverbanks were by earth tracks, either through jungle scrub or rubber plantations. Fortunately their earth and clay surfaces were hard and dry now the rainy season was passed, and we managed to bump along on my motorbike, but painfully.

We reached the banks of the River Trang at five places, all at villages whose inhabitants stared wide-eyed as we approached.

The last spot where we managed to get to the riverbank was near the house where Meow, our shoreside assistant, had been born. It was in the bush, about ten miles northeast of the town of Trang, almost on the river. His family and a dozen friends and neighbors were there and pleased to see us. They lived in a small, almost empty concrete box of two rooms. There was no paint, no plaster, and no decoration in the house except for a calendar that showed His Majesty the king of Thailand in full-dress uniform. There was no furniture. As I could not, because of my prosthesis, sit on a floor, Meow's father lugged in a bag of rice for me to sit on as their honored guest. We had taken them some cans of fish and meat, which were accepted by Meow's father. He wore a sarong and bowed low and smiled and held his right wrist with his left hand as he accepted each can from me. Then we rode down to the river to sight it before the swift nightfall.

The current was nowhere strong—never more than two knots—and the river shallow and narrow, between high banks. We were approaching the start of the rainy season. My inspection of weather records in Bangkok had shown that the very first monsoon rains on the Kra were heavy for a few days, but in mid-

June a drier period began that lasted for about a month. If we were at the mouth of the Trang at the start of the rains, we would stand a chance of making our way against the current during the lighter monsoon period. If there was not enough water, we could wait for more rain, and so head on again, as the river level rose. The trick would be for us to get *Henry Wagner* to the Nam Trang headwaters by late June, get across the divide, the watershed plain, in the middling monsoon rain in mid-July, when the streams in the plain would be flooded, and so pass into the Mae Nam Tapi, which flowed down to the Gulf of Thailand, before the main monsoon rains became too heavy and made of the rivers roaring torrents. If we could not get to the far coast of the Kra by late July, we might be in danger of flash floods sweeping down the narrow river from the mountains above the watershed plain.

We returned to Meow's family, bearing a bottle of cheap whiskey, and made our farewells. That evening, not wishing to encounter our land-selling friend from the Kantang hotel, we found a hotel in Trang, musty and fusty but with some marvelous thirties art deco in the dining room and a friendly staff.

The next day we trundled off, two hundred miles, back all the way to Phuket, and rejoined our three crewmen in our base at Ao Chalong.

While we'd been away, they had not done so well with tourist trips; the able-bodied competition had scared them away. But they had fished, and made a few hundred baht at that. They had covered their expenses and fed themselves. Nok and Anant had kept an eye on *Outward Leg* for us. No one could have got on board her at night. Around Phuket Nok was renowned as a fighter. No one had ever bothered to teach him the Buddhist precepts of non-violence; he was a Muslim:"*An eye for an eye . . .*" Our boats and Anant were safe from marauders who now and then, as it suited them, might find it convenient to forget, for a night, their own religion's teachings.

We made arrangements with Meow that he would, when we had notified him by cable that we had reached Trang, ride my motorcycle all the way from Phuket to his house, and meet us there. We would stow the bike in our boat there, if the river was deep enough to allow for its weight, and use it for our shoreside transport. If not, Meow could accompany us across the Kra on roads parallel to the river wherever he could, and meet us at our stopping places. It was a tremendous responsibility for someone who knew little but hunting, rubber-collecting and land work, but I trusted Meow, so long as he did not have any of his multitude of friends around him, or enough money to get hold of whiskey.

We were conveyed by air, Thomas and I, 1,250 miles, to Penang and back, a day or two later, to renew our visas. It cost us half of our money.

By Easter we had all our gear prepared for the Kra attempt. We watched for the southwest rain monsoon. Sure enough, by late May it was upon us. Carefully, every morning and evening, we scanned the sky for signs of the expected break in the rain.

"When's D-Day?" asked Thomas. The monsoon break was still absent. I was deep in writing a passage. I thought he meant the anniversary of the Allied invasion of Normandy in 1944.

"June sixth," I replied, absentmindedly, and returned to my writing.

And so it was that Thomas had three days' supply of canned food stored on board *Henry Wagner* on the evening of June 5. But there was yet no sign of the break in the rain monsoon.

There was no sense in taking the canned-food stores ashore again. We waited and waited, and waited, until finally, on June 18, we could wait no more. We all piled wetly into *Henry Wagner*, and were ready to set off to sea, at dawn, heading for the Kra. Now it was make or break.

PART TWO

. . . THAT . . .

O wad some Pow'r the giftie gie us
Tae see oursels as others see us!

Robert Burns, "To a Louse"

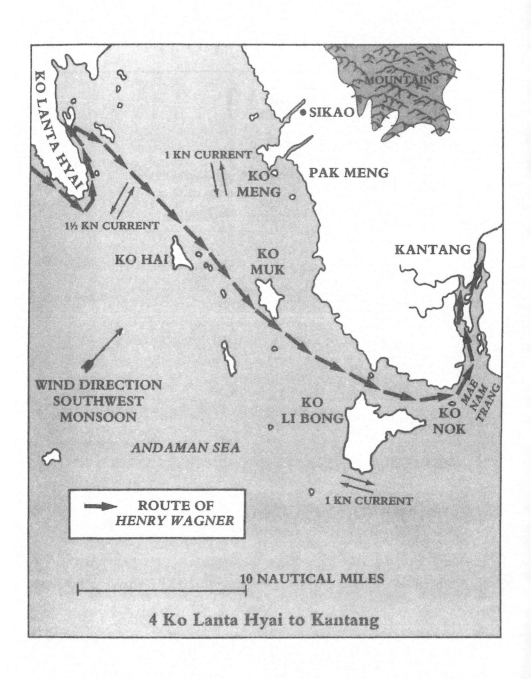

KO LANTA HYAI

MOUNTAINS

• SIKAO

1 KN CURRENT

KO
MENG

PAK MENG

1½ KN CURRENT

KANTANG

KO HAI

KO
MUK

WIND DIRECTION
SOUTHWEST
MONSOON

ANDAMAN SEA

KO
LI BONG

KO
NOK

MAE
NAM
TRANG

1 KN CURRENT

→ ROUTE OF
HENRY WAGNER

10 NAUTICAL MILES

4 Ko Lanta Hyai to Kantang

13

Departure

On any voyage there's usually some crisis, major or minor, at the start. Ours seemed then a small one: Thomas, lugging the engine on board, dropped his spectacles and trod on them. Luckily he was wearing shoes, or he might have had a wounded foot as well as nearsightedness to deal with. Without the glasses he could see clearly only as far as six feet. Further than that, he said, "all was fuzzy." I told him we could delay sailing by a few days while he replaced his specs in Phuket, but he would have none of it.

"I don't need them so much at sea, and I can probably get replacements in Kantang or Trang."

That seemed reasonable enough. We had, after all, four other pairs of perfectly good eyes in the boat. While Thomas steered, someone else could keep watch for him, for rocks or floating debris in the sea. I could con the boat with my good, ocean-accustomed eyes and my hand-bearing compass.

I had intended for us to depart from Phuket in *Henry Wagner* on June 6, and to make short passages through the Bay of Phangnga and along the coast over a matter of two weeks, to explore the bay and the coast before heading into the River Trang about June 20, when, according to my calculations, the break in the rain was due to start. But now we would have to make our way as directly as we could from Phuket to Kantang, in long daytime hops between islands.

Henry Wagner's first sea passage took us, through continual

monsoon rainstorms, roughly one hundred miles across the width
of the immense but shallow Bay of Phangnga. For people more
familiar with Western waters, this was about equivalent to crossing
the western English Channel in October or, in North America,
crossing the Bay of Fundy in September.

The monsoon rains poured down outside the boat, and with
all the stores and expedition gear stowed on board *Henry Wagner*,
as well as five people, our quarters were cramped, especially when
the boat was under way and our rubber dinghy, nine feet long,
was stowed in the bow.

Our boys had a wonderful way of being able to make themselves small on board. This they did mainly by squatting on their
haunches, even when the boat was lively, to work at low levels,
where most Europeans would have had to bend or sit down.
Thomas had learned to squat, too, and even, like the Thais, move
along while squatting, with a ducklike waddle. Even when the
boat was rolling over thirty degrees each way, and pounding like
the hammers of hell, they could keep their balance while they
squatted. Not Anant or I, of course. But we two legless wonders,
to salve our regret at not being able to squat, could console ourselves that our missing legs also saved a bit of room.

On a beach, or at anchor, our yellow plastic sun and rain
shelter was a blessing. So also was our collapsible-forward canvas
dodger. This worked like the hood of a perambulator, on a collapsing frame. Our two framed shelters didn't keep us altogether
dry, but they stopped most of the rain from falling into the boat.
We were always damp. But before we set off from Ao Chalong,
southeast, we collapsed the forward dodger and unshipped the
midship awning shelter from its frame and stowed it low in the
boat. Better to be wet than dead. The forward dodger obscured
clear vision ahead, and also added to our rolling moment; our
midship awning weighed about a hundred pounds. In a boat draw-
ing only a foot underwater, working her way through heavy beam
seas, the less weight aloft, the better, in case an extra-heavy sea,
aided by that weight, capsized the boat. If that happened out of
sight of other boats, with all the weight we carried, we would
overturn and sink like a brick. Then Anant, unable at that time
to swim very far, I, who couldn't swim at all, and probably Som,
with his one arm, would die. Thomas and Nok might stay afloat
long enough to be sighted, eventually, by some craft, and picked
up. It was that simple.

All the way across the Andaman Sea and the wide-open mouth of shallow Phangnga Bay, while we were underway, we had to suffer the rain pelting right down on us. Anant's main job was to pump zealously and bail the rainwater out of the boat as fast as it bucketed down. We could have dismantled the midship awning frame, too, to get even more weight down low in the boat. But we left it in place; it was very useful for Som, Anant, and me, all missing a limb. While the boat rolled and jerked in heavy seas, even while we moved about her in harbor, we could use the frame as a convenient handhold. Som could hang on to the frame with the stump of his arm, and so, even, could Anant, standing on top of our midship storage boxes, with the stump of his leg. I could hold on to it, of course, with both hands, to take the weight off my own stump in its prosthesis. I weighed up the risk factor in leaving the midship awning frame rigged against the convenience factor, and decided to leave it in place.

We could not carry a sail for the same reason: We had no keel or deep ballast to counter the capsizing moment of a sail. One of the frequent sudden blasts of wind would have blown her right over. It would have to be motor all the way.

Older people love their comforts. I had tasted a few weeks of comfort, though a mite too warm and humid for me, in our Ao Chalong "bungalow." Now I was back in a heavy sea in a bouncing boat, my life once more in discomfort and jeopardy.

Why should I take the risk? Why voluntarily be continually sodden or broiled in heavy rain or burning sun in an open boat? As we crossed the Andaman Sea at right angles to the strong southwest monsoon wind and heavy seas, coming all the way at us across the Indian Ocean, I asked myself those questions time and time again.

As our boat lurched off one sea and onto another, and yet another, I already knew the answer: *There was no one else I could ask to do it for me.* It needed to be done; faith could only be truly proven by the laying of life on the line. The doubters might only be convinced by proof: Proof demanded risk.

I reflected that I could be quite content, certainly more comfortable and happier, perhaps, now I was in my sixties, to sit in some charitable organization's office somewhere, perhaps in a cooler, drier, more temperate climate, and organize charity for the disabled.

But it's not so much charity that most semiactive disabled

people need. It's hope. And hope means examples for them to gain faith in themselves. If we wished to pass on to other disabled that faith in themselves, so that their hopes could rise, we had to show them that it was possible for them to *shift for themselves*. We had to prove to them that we ourselves had faith that they were able to do it. The only way we could show that faith was by taking great risks and doing it ourselves. But we had to aim very high indeed.

Audacity can shift mountains. Big mountains need true audacity. But the truly audacious must be prepared to pay, if necessary with their lives, for their own temerity. Like mankind's reach for the stars.

We in *Henry Wagner* had no billions behind us, no cheering crowds, no frantic media on the shore, as we set off into the darkness of the Andaman Sea. We five cripples (I use that word intentionally) including Thomas, without his spectacles very near-sighted, had an old wooden boat, an engine, and in our midships "treasure chest" three sea charts, one road map of the Kra, the scraps of three religious beliefs, six days' supply of food, and $776-worth of Thai money.*

Most of our passage across the Andaman Sea from Phuket to Kantang was what weekend yachtsmen (no disparagement intended) would consider rough. Landsmen would say it was a wet misery. We two ocean rovers, and our Thai fisherlads were accustomed to that sort of thing. Our boys seemed to think that it was "all in a day's work." Heavy white-topped seas rolled and heaved. Because the southeasterly direction of our course cut directly across the paths of huge waves and the hard southwest wind, our little boat heaved and rolled and jerked like a mad thing. She jerked so violently on one occasion that a forty-pound anchor, carelessly left untied but jammed behind a hull-stringer, was flung

---

*There were a few other things though, and these may interest those who like to know the ins and outs: one 15 hp outboard engine, one dinghy, rubber, 8 ft long, the first ever made in Thailand, by SeaNomad Company, Phuket (supplied at generous discount), one Yanmar gasoline-driven generator, output 12 volts or 220 volts, one single-ring gas stove, one small butane gas bottle, one compass, one sextant, one altimeter, six plastic 5-gallon diesel-oil jerricans, two oars, one ax, one sledgehammer, two spades, three shovels, three handsaws, one 1-ton chain-hoist, one radio receiver, one VHF two-way radio (donated by *Multihulls* magazine, USA), one handheld VHF two-way radio, one diving mask, one underwater harpoon gun, one samurai sword, one 70 lb hunting bow and set of arrows, one teakettle, two sets of knives and forks (our boys would not use them), five plates, five tin cups, five tatty mosquito nets, five worn blankets, and my laptop computer and printer for keeping precise records.

right out of its stowage over the side. On top of the seas she rolled, and her leeward gunwale would often be only a half-inch from the surface of the moving waters.

As I gazed, as I could hardly avoid doing, at our gunwale for what seemed an eternity each time that happened, I found that inside myself I was very much at peace. A half-inch away from certain death I had no regrets at the course my life had taken, and I was certain that what I was about now was the right thing.

When our gunwale rolled so close to the sea that water lapped on board, then, at my signal, the lad at the helm would shift it over, to veer the boat slightly off the wind, to turn her stern more into it, so reducing the risk of our capsizing. But to hold our course, we could only do that when the risk was too inordinate. Otherwise, if we veered too much to the east, and if our engine should fail, we might find ourselves being powerlessly pounded in shallow waters by monstrous rollers onto the open coast of the Thai mainland.

14

The Bay of Phangnga

Our sea passage was not all open ocean and rolling misery for me.
There were several islands on or close to our course. Behind these
islands we could seek the lee, take shelter from the mountainous
ocean swell. There is no shame in seeking lee whenever you can.
God placed islands for sailors to shelter behind.

To the north of us, the whole way across the width of the
bay, the scenery was like a fantasy. Island after limestone island
rose out of the blue waters, emerging from the morning mist, or
shining golden in the late-afternoon sun between rainstorms. It
was a sight of heaven's sea.

We knew that a few tour operators in Krabi touted boating
trips to a couple of the more easily reachable islands on the strength
of them having been the filming location, a few years before, of
part of a James Bond film. As I gazed from our rolling, rocking
craft at the sheer beauty of the Phangnga islands, I reflected on
the shame that such utter glory should be connected, evidently,
in many minds with trite yarns of greed, sex, and violence. Surely,
I thought, anyone who took that trip solely for the James Bond
connection would be committing extreme blasphemy? Surely they
would be spitting in the face of God?

Our first island was only twenty miles from Ao Chalong.

We sought the lee of Ko Mai Thon to find some respite from the rolling and rocking of our boat, so that we could more securely lash down gear. Besides, as we reached it, noon was upon us, and the monsoon winds are always strongest in the afternoon and weakest in the very early morning. We would stay at Ko Mai Thon until the following dawn.

Ko Mai Thon was a low, round, palm-covered, coral-fringed islet, no more than perhaps one thousand yards right around its rocky shore. On its lee side was a tiny beach, no longer than twenty feet, between rocks. Above the tiny beach was a small wooden hut.

In the lee of the islet there was less wind, but little shelter from the ocean swells; the islet was so perfectly circular that the swells merely curved right around it in two separate waves, which met on its lee side and caused a jumble sea, in which one anchored Thai trawler now rolled heavily. No deep-keeled sailing yacht would ever find any comfort behind Ko Mai Thon, regardless of from whence blew the monsoon winds.

Now *Henry Wagner* showed the sense of her design and build; her wide beam and shallow draft, which were the result of centuries of experience in these waters. Nok, whose trick it was, simply dropped our stern anchor and upped the propeller as she approached the shore, and as she touched, Thomas and Som leapt over the bow onto the beach, hauled our bow three feet or so up the sand, and there we were, as they say, home from home and high and dry, on solid land.

Before two minutes were up, our heavy yellow awning was lashed on its frame, our dinghy was over the side, our forward dodger was up, our rice pot was on our one-ring gas stove, and a half hour saw us well fed, dry, and in shade. In the daytime tropics, in an open boat, those are the things that matter.

No one but a fool or a *farang* works outside in the tropical afternoon, if it can possibly be avoided. The rain had stopped. The sun beat down. In the heat of the early afternoon we all rested in the shade. As the sun declined, the boys fished from the rocks on the shore. It was a wonder to me to watch how Anant managed to scramble with such agility on his one good leg, wielding his little wooden crutch. He used the crutch as if it were a live part of him. It was like watching a brown crab use its pincer to climb over some obstacle.

But except to exercise the boys' limbs, their fishing expedition was futile; the current rushing around the islet and the swell and spray soon sent them back to our cozy beach. An hour before dusk Thomas and Som donned diving masks and, using hand harpoons, speared the main course of our supper.

When the boys returned, they accompanied me as I explored the beach and the islet.

The sole inhabitant of the hut was an ancient, sitting staring at his collected copras. He must have been about eighty years old. He was deaf and dumb and had a walleye, so it was difficult to gauge who was the object of his gestures and grunts. He made us understand that the only fresh water on the islet was what he collected in an old iron oil drum from the monsoon rains. In the driest part of the dry season, he gestured, the islet was deserted. No other *farangs*, no tourist boats, had ever, so far as he knew, visited the islet.

The population of Ko Mai Thon was pleased at my invitation to sup with us. Toothlessly he grinned, crouched in polite humility, and rushed back to his hut. Minutes later he was out again in a clean sarong. Despite his toothlessness and ceaseless smile, he managed to eat like a horse. He was wordlessly merry, but polite in his way. After the meal he belched and patted his belly, gently rose, and left us quickly.

Our next sea passage took us some twenty-five miles to Ko "Pee Pee." Its real name was Ko Phiphidon. But tour operators and their *farang* limpets, their minds as narrow as lizards' gullets, seemed to have thought it wasn't naughty enough. Throughout Thailand this stupidity by tourist touts, large and small, persisted. The inevitable result was that in many minds worldwide, Thailand was considered to be not much more than one great brothel, instead of the beautiful land that it is. For the Mammon-rooters, the name "Phiphidon" would not serve. It sounded, perhaps, almost a little classical. Something more enticing must be thought up. So some dollar-chasing greedy guts, to the shame of his race, breed, and generation, whatever they were, allowed this fragment of celestial beauty on Earth to be renamed "Pee Pee."

We made our way into a lovely, deep fjord between high cliffs, beached the boat, and walked up the sand. Apart from a few sheltering Thai trawlers, their crews asleep on deck, we were the only visitors. I took my hand from Nok's shoulder and surveyed the scene.

First I raised my eyes to the hills. Great, tree-covered limestone outcrops reared lovely, rounded summits to cloud-flecked blue skies. I dropped my eyes, perhaps in humility, before this magnificent prospect.

The first thing that caught my eye amid all this beauty was a rusting, bulbless, fluorescent light fixture dangling from a palm tree. It looked as if it had been swinging in the wind for at least a year. All along the strand, in the shade under the trees, although it was the depths of the nontourist season, were rickety beach stalls, their ripped Cola signs blowing like distress signals in the wind. Each stall had a person, young or old, in attendance, sitting idly behind its counter. Every single stall was surrounded by mounds of old paper wrappers and plastic bags trapped by the breeze and heaped against the palms. Amid the garbage a dozen mangy dogs guarded their rubbish and snuffled.

"Let's go back on board and anchor out, Thomas," were the first words, I think, I said on Ko "Pee Pee."

I didn't have to explain to Thomas why.

Even as I spoke, loud pop music blared out from a stall nearby. It had taken the stall attendant, a sturdy-looking young man wearing a Hell's Angels T-shirt, time to organize the music. We turned back toward the boat, and he realized he had been too slow; his face dropped from a beaming smile to a pouting sulk.

Our Thai boys' eyes had already lit up at the prospect of a cold drink. I bought them a large bottle each—but the Thai brand, not the foreign. No point in encouraging nondomestic blasphemy. The garish advertising of the home-grown variety was bad enough, in any case.

Then we returned to *Henry Wagner*, pushed her bow off the beach, clambered on board, started her engine, and made our way half a mile to seaward, but still inside the fjord, almost out of range of the violent nonsense noise, and nearly out of sight of the sloppy litter.

We departed Ko Phiphidon on the morning of June 20. It was to be our last encounter with what I named "Farangistan," the main tourist track in Thailand, for several weeks and hundreds of miles. We did not know if we should be sorry or not to leave what must have been, only a short time previously, before tourism developers clapped their rapacious eyes on it, one of the world's loveliest isles.

15

The Edge of Nowhere

Once we departed Ko Phiphidon, we were in waters almost completely unknown to Western sailors. Even to our Thai boys, they were unknown waters. Phuket inshore fishing boats did not often reach into the coastal waters of the mainland. We found that the sea charts I had available, British and American, were both out of date and, especially in inshore areas, grossly inaccurate. On them rocks and even islands were shown where none existed, and we sighted reefs, banks, rocks, wrecks, and islets where nothing but navigable sea was indicated on our charts.

I waited for false dawn before I made up my mind about heading out for the next leg. The morning, as we broke cheerfully out of the fjord at Ko Phiphidon, showed a good, clear blue horizon above the Andaman Sea, to the west. The weather signs were good for us to make the longest leg on the open sea of this passage: the fifty miles or so from Ko Phiphidon to the lee side of Ko Lanta Hyai. Our chart showed a passage round the north of Ko Lanta Hyai, between it and the mainland, but when we neared the place where it was supposed to be, all I could see through my binoculars were white breakers. I decided to give the northern passage around the island a miss and head around its southern point. It put another fifteen miles or so on our passage, but it was far safer. We could not afford to risk disaster; thousands and thousands of youngsters we had never seen were with us.

Nok, on the helm with Som, stared at the sight of the faraway breakers and the steamlike mist rising from them in the morning sunshine. Without looking, with one toe he tapped poor Anant, who crouched half-asleep still, in the bilge. "*Noh Nai Noh*," he grunted. "Nok not like . . ." They always spoke of themselves in the third person. It avoided offense in a culture with five different ways to say "I."

For once I understood Nok. "Dead right, *amigo*," said I. "We'll give that one a miss."

Even as Nok mumbled to me loudly, and I, unthinking, replied to him in Spanish-English, Anant threw himself into his only job when the boat was under way in heavy seas: his almost incessant pumping of bilge water out of the boat. Wooden-planked open boats will almost always leak to a degree in any kind of seaway. No harm done; a bit of salt water is good for the wood, and a bit of exercise never hurt a healthy lad.

Som was the most cerebral of our Thai crew. He had spent some years in secondary school and could read the Roman alphabet almost as well as the Thai. His English was enlarging and improving daily. Certainly he was doing better at his English than I at my Thai. He did his best to keep his fair share of tricks at the helm, but with only one arm, in heavy seas, it was tiring and painful for him. Then Thomas or Nok would double up with him, or even relieve him early from his hour's stint. But he kept himself busy always.

Nok could neither read nor write, having never been to school for more than three days in his life, but he was one of nature's small-craft seamen. On board *Henry Wagner*, in his work, he never put a hand or a foot wrong. His balance was as sure and firm as a champion boxer's. So long as I didn't dwell on his face too long, it was always a pleasure to watch him move, even when the boat labored in heavy seas.

When Nok stepped on board a boat, he became part of her, even, it seemed to me, as the keel or the plank fastenings were. When Nok was on the helm, I always knew, without turning around to look, that it was he who was steering. As he stood there, his square-toed feet wide apart on the tiny, sharp stern, it was as though he could feel the nerves—the intention—of the oncoming seas through the soles of his feet, and knew at each and every roll which way the boat would next be thrown, and could adjust the helm in time to meet the growler. It was as though his heart beat in rhythm with our boat's movements. Nok was probably the neatest and steadiest helmsman I ever encountered in almost fifty years of seafaring. He was also one of the strongest lads, for his small size, that I had ever seen.

Nok's main job, apart from steering with, or without, Som, was maintaining the engine clean and keeping its integral fuel tank topped up. To see him balance on the stern, when the boat was hove to (stopped) for the fuel tank to be refilled, holding a heavy fuel can up with one hand and gripping the engine with the other, pouring the diesel oil into the tank with only a few drops spilled, was an acrobatic wonder.

Anant was the youngest on board. That made him, by Thai seamen's lights, inferior to the rest. His job was to do all the menial chores: pump the bilge, light the stove, clean the rice bowls, dive for tools lost in the bilge. He was too small, and on his crutch too unbalanced, to steer for longer than ten minutes at a time in any heavy kind of sea. After his first attempts, although I was much impressed by his agility on his crutch, I asked Som to keep him off the helm. I could not let Anant lose face by telling Som he was too small or weak. I had to say that there were too many small jobs to be done inside the boat.

I could in no way interfere with the delegation by the other Thai lads to Anant of all the messy little chores. If I had done that, all three Thais would have been offended, even Anant himself. They would have considered that I had tried to upset the natural social order. I would have made Som and Nok lose face, and I would only have confused Anant. He knew exactly what was expected of him. He was happy day and night. He made little innocent jokes of his own devising, and sometimes practical jokes. To even suggest that Anant might move up one iota out of his small, dark refuge would have propelled him, I was sure, into the uttermost depths of exposure to face-losing misery.

In a little open boat trying to get across a heavy sea, I had more profitable things to think about than attempts to counter the ingrained effects of five thousand years of social order. I did the only sensible thing I could do, and let our three Thais get on with it in their own way. There was little friction between them. A bit of argument now and then, but nothing that was not soon forgotten. I think they started to look up to me when they realized that I was consciously leaving them to sort themselves out.

Our differences in religion were never, I think, mentioned, except perhaps in passing, and then only in good humor. Our two Muslims, Nok and Anant, appreciated my forbidding pork (a safe precaution anyway in the tropics) or alcohol in any form on board *Henry Wagner*. Our Buddhist, Som, appreciated, I think, both Thomas's and my respect for all forms of life, unless it was something dangerous, like a snake, or a pirate, or plain pesky, like flies or mosquitoes.

When they learned from Thomas that I had lost my leg through the effects of a wound sustained in fighting against Thomas's country, and that I didn't hold any ill-feeling about it at all against Thomas, Som's respect for me increased a thousandfold. I got the impression, after a while, that Nok and Anant waited excitedly for me to stab my German friend and throw him over the side one dark, starless night. That, Nok told me through Anant, is what he would have done.

As for their attitude to girls, our Thais were very much the same as any other boys who had been brought up in their social background. Anant seemed to think they were funny but nice. Nok, far more mature, and in his Muslim soul a male chauvinist, thought of them as desirable fair game. Som, nineteen and uncomfortable about sex, as are, I suppose, many nineteen-year-old boys, was shy about them. Before their admiring gazes (for he was handsome), he seemed to melt and back away, smiling, into shadows. None of our lads seemed to think that their disablement was any drawback as far as their relationships with girls were concerned. No one had ever told them to. They had no packaged pop heroes, strong-limbed and lithely proportioned, to continually shame them, as many disabled kids had in the West. It was a pity, we all thought, that we had no disabled girls with us, but neither did we have a toilet.

16

A Priceless View

Back in Phuket, when I had mentioned Ko Lanta Hyai to *farangs*, even some who had lived in Thailand for years, no one knew anything. The Phuket natives spoke of it as though it were primitive and perhaps a little dangerous.

We found it to be neither. We came to a green, lush island, separated from the low-lying mainland coast by about three miles of strait cluttered with islets, banks, and rocks. The island rose to a height of about a thousand feet. The main village of the island, Lanta Palace, was on its eastern side almost completely hidden from seaward by palm trees. The only sign of the village's existence from out in the strait was a lofty radio mast, and a tall, thin minaret rising from amid the palms.

Nok and Anant were nervous (as I was to a degree) of our reception, and as we approached were strangely silent. The sight of the minaret, as we neared the village anchorage, reassured them, and they became again almost their usual lively selves.

The disabled sailor's main problems begin when the boat pulls into harbor or anchorage. This is especially so when he is no longer young and the weather is both hot and humid, or rain is pouring down. It can be a torturous hell for him getting ashore. For the many of you not familiar with false legs, let me explain. If anyone dares to say that in telling you about these things I am complaining, I shall haunt them, my marlinespike in one hand, caulking mallet in the other, for the rest of his days.

Those of you who are a mite squeamish can skip this next bit. My false leg has two parts, jointed at its knee. When I want to walk on it, I have to kick the lower part forward, and bear down hard on its heel, to prevent the knee from collapsing as the prosthesis takes my weight. My stump (about half my original upper limb) fits into the top part of my plastic leg and sits on top of its socket, on its rim. Because of the sharpness of the plastic socket rim, I first have to encase my stump in a thick woollen sock. You can imagine, perhaps, how that feels after about half an hour when the outside air temperature is 105 degrees Fahrenheit. By the time I have been wearing my leg for ten minutes, my stump is perspiring so much that the sweat soaks through the sock, and I have a wet, slippery stump working up and down within a hellishly hot socket as I walk. The temperature within the stump must be 130 degrees. The top of the socket, as it rubs against my skin, chafes it, and I wind up with a rim of red rawness, sometimes bleeding, right around the top of my stump.

If I do not use my prosthesis, if I leave my stump free and use two crutches, then I find it difficult indeed, and even dangerous, to clamber into a dinghy, or negotiate slippery wet steps on jetties, or broken-down decks on piers.

If I am not complaining, why am I telling you this? So that perhaps it will catch the eye of some bright spark in the prosthesis-manufacturing business, and perhaps lead him to come up with some simple ideas for solving the problems. Enough of this. I'll cut a long story sideways and tell you that by the time I got into and out of our dinghy under a blazing-hot sun, to the top of the steps slippery with seaweed at Lanta Palace pier, I was just about flying with pain and discomfort. I felt as if I had bitten my nails to my elbows.

On the end of the half-mile wooden pier there was a tiny customs office, a toilet (a hole in the deck behind a sheet of corrugated iron), a bathroom (a bucket and an oil drum), and a shabby little coffee shop, but no Coca-Cola signs. There were no signs of tourists or tourist-oriented activity, no sign of "Farangistan." We were back in the real Thailand.

The coffee shop had good shade, very good coffee, a shy, smiling staff of three young women and one ancient, and the most beautiful view I have ever seen from any catering establishment anywhere in the world.

Immediately I forgot the oppressive heat, the clinging humidity, all my pain and misery. Nok swung back on a cold bottle of the local brand of cola. Thomas and the Thais waited patiently as I stood stupefied, and stared in wonder.

I could see for about eighty miles. In the distance near and far, all along our eastern horizon, across a cerulean strait, a handsome land rose up, through the green of palm-tree glades and the plantations, through meadows and pastures of celadon and chartreuse, up, up past the almonds, ochers, sables, and cobalts of high barren rocks to the summits of mountains, stretching away north and south as far as the eye could see, shining pure gold and silver in the afternoon sun. The mountains of the Kra! On the other side of those mountains was the South China Sea. Our adversary was *beautiful!*

Closer to where I stood on Ko Lanta Hyai, in the strait, a dozen or more needlelike islet rocks, white, silver, and green, reared above the sea. As my gaze dropped, closer, across the green shallows close to our shore, I saw that they were alive with tropical fish of every hue: yellow jack, golden goatfish, scarlet-and-gold butterfly fish, blood-red and blue gobies, duck-egg-blue parrot fish, bronze batfish, and thousands upon thousands of rainbow-colored angelfish.

Recovering myself, I painfully stepped closer to the edge of the pier and looked over, down at the water. Although the seabed was under a good thirty feet of water, my view of it, for hundreds of feet all around, was clear. There were growths and coral of every description: bronze, ivory aphrocallistes, a hundred different-colored zoophytes, and red, gold, and white corals. There were razor clams, long-horned Scaphoda, azure sea snails, golden-green chitons, spiral wentletraps, deep black abalones, thorny oysters, and lovely yellow, golden-brown, and purple bivalves.

Above, double-crested cormorants flew, while in the distance I saw, to my utter surprise, two ocean frigate birds, hovering, crucifixlike, above the waters of the strait. I thought, What a pity Thomas can't see all this!

I always remember with gratitude and pleasure our stop at Ko Lanta Hyai. When longtail ferries, with a roar of ear-shattering noise, arrived from the mainland and disgorged wet vegetables, small children, and chickens, the helmsmen and crew joked with our lads, and were pleasantly disposed to us two *farangs*, without seeking any evident advantage. Their burdened passengers, as they politely stepped around us, were merry. Everyone was pleasantly disposed, even when sudden monsoon showers sent rain bucketing down.

On the pier there was little cover. A bevy of maidens, graceful and lithe, waiting for a ferry, giggled and sought the shelter of the coffee-shop kitchen. Men and boys stood in the rain and let the water stream down over their bare chests and down from their bright sarongs, over their sandaled feet, smiling and joking quietly all the while. The older men were husky; all had their heads covered, Muslim fashion, with little white caps, a few, probably of distant Arab or Indian descent, were bearded. They silently smoked their damp cigarettes and cheroots.

I stayed at the coffee shop, drinking coffee and staring at that wondrous view of the Kra mountains, while the others went into the village to look around. My excuse for not going was that someone had to keep an eye on the boat, at anchor fifty feet away from the pier. The truth I hid was that walking was too painful for me.

A customs sergeant from the pier office came and sat with me, and told me that we were the first foreigners to arrive at Ko Lanta Hyai for many years. He spoke a little English.

"How many years?" I asked him. He had roused my curiosity.

He dropped his head on his beribboned chest and thought for a while. "Forty-two years," he replied in Thai. "I saw them when I was a little boy." He smiled, and held his hand, palm out, about three feet above the deck.

"Who were the last ones?" I asked. He replied something like "Neephom Haijaiey."

It took me a good fifteen minutes to work out that he meant the Imperial Japanese Army! They had left in 1945.

The boys and Thomas returned from exploring the village, each bearing a plastic bag of sticky rice and bits of roast chicken. We all returned to *Henry Wagner*, weighed our anchor, and sought a quiet place to rest for the night. Years of calling at fishing ports have taught me how rudely fishing boats can wake everyone near them when they set off or return in the middle of the night.

About a mile to the north of the pier was a tiny sandy islet, with a low hill. I decided we would shelter behind it for the night. I was wary of possible boarding by intruders, but we were still within distant sight of the pier, and the customs sergeant had promised to ask the night policeman to keep an eye on us.

In the comparative coolness of the late afternoon our crew

went ashore on the islet, to fish and run (hobble, in Anant's case) around. They caught small fish, enough for supper by the light of our gas lantern. Then, arranging our shelters so that the least rain would find its way into our boat and onto us, we all turned in.

It must have been about one o'clock when we were all awakened by the bump of a heavy body leaping on board.

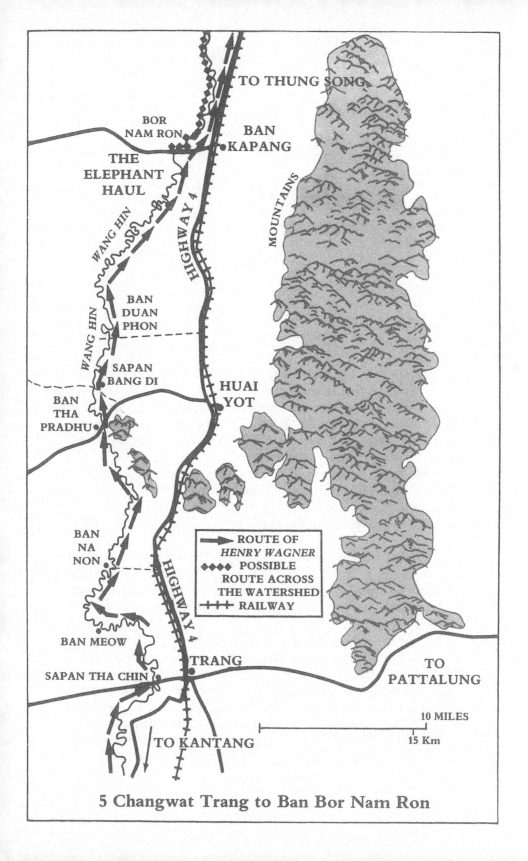

TO THUNG SONG

BOR
NAM RON

BAN
KAPANG

THE
ELEPHANT
HAUL

WANG HIN

HIGHWAY 4

MOUNTAINS

BAN
DUAN
PHON

WANG HIN

SAPAN
BANG DI

HUAI
YOT

BAN
THA
PRADHU

BAN
NA
NON

HIGHWAY 4

ROUTE OF
HENRY WAGNER
POSSIBLE
ROUTE ACROSS
THE WATERSHED
RAILWAY

BAN MEOW

TRANG

TO
PATTALUNG

SAPAN THA CHIN

10 MILES

15 Km

TO KANTANG

5 Changwat Trang to Ban Bor Nam Ron

17

Aground

My sleeping berth in *Henry Wagner* was on a narrow coconut-fiber mattress on the deck of the forepeak, right up forward in the bows. I woke with a start, to see a figure looming above the foot of my berth. Already my hand was on the hilt of our samurai sword, which lay along the side of my berth. I was ready to draw it silently from its greased sheath.

The figure was crouching over Anant, who lay asleep in the port passageway, between the boat's side and our treasure chest amidships. Locked in the box was everything that would be attractive to thieves, such as VHF radios, compasses, binoculars, money.

Even as I started to slowly pull out the sword from its sheath a light suddenly burst from the stern, and Nok's voice grunted loudly, "*Mnamna! Mnamna!*" I understood him enough by then to know that he was calling out "Captain!" That was our lads' name for me.

Then everything happened all at once. Thomas was up in a whirl of movement, our engine starter handle in one hand, and Som had grabbed our hand lamp. In the handlamp's glare I glimpsed Nok. He was holding our seventy-pound hunting bow, its bowstring pulled right back to his shoulder, an arrow already strung, aimed directly at the intruder—and dangerously close to me.

There was a swift interchange between Som and the intruder. While they talked, I stretched myself and peered over the side, to see a medium-sized fishing boat lying alongside us. In it one old man's face showed under the moon. He smiled. It was the Thai smile that said, "You caught me!"

"He says he needs some fresh water, Captain," said Som.

As Som spoke, he held the beam of his flashlight on the intruder. He was a stocky man with big shoulders and a deep chest. He was dressed in a T-shirt and khaki shorts. In his belt was a long fisherman's gutting knife, blade down. I guessed his age at about forty.

"Where's his water container?" I asked.

Som, smiling, relayed my question to the intruder.

"In my boat," replied the intruder, smiling.

"Why didn't he bring it?"

"I thought you might lend me one of yours," he replied, weakly.

"*Kee kwai* . . . bullshit," I started to rejoin, but thought better of it. My boys knew as well as I did that no one went from one boat to another looking for fresh water without a can or a bucket. It simply wasn't done. It would be like breathing through your ears. I spoke in English: "Give him water, Som. Thomas, tell Nok to keep an eye on him and keep him covered. As soon as he's off the boat, we'll get under way." I peered down at Anant; he had slept through the whole episode. He was still snoring like a dormouse; his little crutch clutched in one fist. He looked utterly defenseless.

"Where're we going?" asked Thomas as soon as the intruder had jumped onto his own boat. The man made no attempt to push off from our boat, but crouched muttering with his ancient companion.

"By the pier. There's a policeman on duty there all night. He'll watch us. We'll be better off among all the noise from the fishing boats than out here. We stand out here like a sore thumb."

As soon as Nok started our engine, rain poured down as it only can in the southwest monsoon, and we searched our way through the rainsheets, to our former anchorage off the end of the pier. There we spent a wet, but peaceful night. I stayed awake because of the rain; I was soaked to the skin anyway, and cold.

By five in the morning I'd had enough. Weakly, as day was breaking, I woke all our crew, and we shoved off for the port of Kantang, at the mouth of the Mae Nam Trang, the River Trang.

* * *

Ever after that incident at least one of us was wide awake at all times day and night, rain or shine, in *Henry Wagner*. South Thailand, in a boat, was no place to be unwary of knife-toting, silent strangers coming alongside in the depths of the night, or at any other time.

We left Ko Lanta Hyai in a rainstorm, using our hand-bearing compass to find our course. But by the time we had cleared the south end of the island, the rain had fled inland and the sun had his gleaming razor out to shave the morning. The seas were rolling as ponderously as ever, even in the dawn before the wind woke and tightened his braces. It was a blessing, again, to be able to pass behind islands in calm water now and again.

There were a few fishermen's bamboo and wooden shelters tucked cozily under cliffs on the lee sides of the islands we passed, Ko Hai, Ko Muk, and a dozen others. But it seemed that none of the islands were inhabited permanently, except for Ko Li Bong, a large, low delta island close inshore, right off the mouth of the River Trang.

On my sea chart there was a passage shown between Ko Li Bong and the mainland, but with no depths indicated. It was a blank stretch. We had tired of the incessant pounding in heavy seas. We were anxious to fetch Kantang before the full heat of the noonday sun. I decided we'd feel our way inside the passage and try it. Once we were in the lee of the island there would be little sea. *Henry Wagner* drew only a foot; if she touched, we could always shove her off. Besides, a low offshore island, only a foot or two above the sea level, usually indicates a soft bottom, clay or mud, between it and the main shore.

We braced ourselves, slowed our engine to half-speed, headed in, and found, most of the way through, a good channel deep enough, probably, for an oil tanker fully loaded.

The scene at the mouth of the river was dramatic. Out to seaward, as I peered past the southern tip of Ko Li Bong, the white-topped seas of Andaman marched onward toward us and the river bar. All across our sea horizon, in a wide panorama of almighty majesty, the dark blue and ponderous seas reared, hovered, crashed, and boomed, in a crescendo of steamy vapor, onto the shallows where the river met the sea. As the seas battered the bar, they recoiled in great blue humps. Each time a sea arrived, there was a pause, a silence, and then a massive emerald iridescent wall of water rose up, changed to turquoise, and crashed again, spouting silver spray into the blue sky, high and dense enough to hide the horizon.

Only a hundred yards away from the drums of the sea gods we, in flat, calm coffee-brown water and warm, dry sunshine, held our boat against the swift river current and, as we rigged our yellow awning, silently grinned at each other, and congratulated ourselves on reaching our river safely and on outwitting the heaving ocean for the moment.

Nok, on the helm, and anxious to reach his first strange port, headed at a steady speed upstream into the maze of the Trang Delta. He was a good helmsman, as I have said, and he kept an eagle eye out for any hazards or obstacles. I had few qualms in leaving him to steer while I looked around.

The banks of the Trang Delta on all sides were very low, only inches above water level, and overgrown with mangroves. Anant, grinning, excited as Nok, nudged my elbow, and pointed to the north. Across the coastal plain we could clearly see, between the palms, shimmering in the miasma rising from the riverside swamps, the higher buildings of Kantang town.

A quick sounding with our bamboo pole showed that we were in a deep channel. Upstream of us there were no buoys evident, nor any other kind of navigation mark. I turned to look at Nok; he returned my gaze, expectantly. He wanted me to let him open her up.

I scanned ahead quickly once more, and I nodded my head.

Nok grinned. He loved steering at speed. The bow rose as she picked up speed—and we shuddered and growled our way to a grinding halt. We were aground, hard and fast on a sandbank.

18

The Unwanted

Nothing was said. When these things happen to people born and bred in boats, it very rarely is. All I did was bow my head, shake it, and groan to myself what a fool I had been to order faster speed. Then I grinned to myself. There was no harm done to our boat. The river bottom was soft. I knew the tide was about half up, and that sooner or later it would overcome the river current and lift us off. I wasn't in so much of a hurry. Kantang wasn't my first strange port of call. I must have been in ten thousand of them.

They say that time and tide wait for no man. But neither does the excitement of young people at the prospect of new worlds to see and conquer. Before I'd even lifted my head, all four of our crew were over the side, thigh-and waist-deep, with shovels and oars, scrabbling away at the sand, to clear a ditch so that our boat might be heaved off.

As every good skipper knows, some lessons have to be taught, and some lessons have to be learned. Some lessons can be learned the easy way, and some the hard. How to overcome impatience must be learned the hard way: So it must be taught the hard way. I lowered myself under the shade of our rigged awning, and let them get on with their sweaty, energy-wasting shoveling for a good ten minutes.

I knew that the river current would never allow them to dig a ditch out of that sandbank. As fast as they dug it, it would carry suspended sand back into it. On the other hand I was, on the bottom line, responsible for our predicament. The only way I could excuse myself from my error would be by relieving them from arduous toil. That meant that first I had to let them toil arduously. It was, like many skippers' necessary maneuvers, a shabby trick in the short term, but to a good purpose in the long run.

In the deep channel, only feet away from us, local craft passed by. Some of their occupants were so surprised that they even forgot to smile, and stared at us goggle-eyed. "Farangs *in a longtail?*" they seemed to be wondering. "*Whatever next?*" No one offered any assistance—not that we needed it.

Sure enough, after a few minutes our crew tired of shoveling liquid sand. Now they tried another tack. They would push the boat off with the engine. As Thomas, Som, and Anant gripped the gunwales and prepared to shove mightily, Nok hopped onto the stern and started our longtail engine. He swung its propeller shaft and pointed it forward, along the starboard side of our boat, and lowered it, whirring down into the water, where it promptly sat on its metal guard, on the sand, and stirred it mightily, like an eggbeater. Our boat, her keel solid on sand, shook with the vibrations of the engine, and, so I imagined, with laughter at their efforts.

I remained silent. Let them learn that the propeller would not push the boat off; it would only stir the sand around and drive more of it against the boat's hull.

A few more minutes of heaving and grunting and pushing and shoving left them all silently staring at me. They had excused me. I was exonerated. Now they needed me again. We were fair and square again. Our slate was wiped clean.

"Right," I told them. "Now you can set out our bower anchor, off load the dinghy, pile all our heavy weights in it, and dump the fuel cans over the side, but tie them to our boat first!"

All four of their sweaty, red-eyed faces lit up.

No sooner said than done, and in five minutes our boat was afloat—just—and held by her anchor. Gently, slowly, because I wanted this lesson to sink in, I wordlessly eased out the anchor line myself, inch by inch, as though I were begrudgingly paying out cents to a creditor, until our boat was clear of the sandbank. No youngsters can feel cockier than an old man does when he's shown that his knowledge beats their strengths.

Then, as Thomas hopped up onto our stern to start our engine, our boys off loaded the dinghy once more into *Henry Wagner*.

All except the outboard motor. Nok had clamped it to the dinghy sternboard. Now he stood, waist-deep in the river, holding himself against the current, grasping the dinghy painter. He looked up at me, in silent expectation.

Our dinghy, with its twelve-horsepower outboard, could reach twenty knots at full speed. For weeks, Nok's ambition had been to drive our dinghy on his own. I had let him practice driving it with myself, Thomas, or Som. It had been necessary, to quell Nok's natural speed mania. He was light and too harum-scarum for me to let him drive it alone at high speed.

Now Nok had me over a Thai barrel. I had made him lose face before his companions by telling him to speed up our engine and so making him run our boat aground. I now owed him the opportunity to regain his lost face. It was quite obvious, from the way he held on to the dinghy, what form he thought that opportunity should take. His almond eyes spoke volumes. The other two Thais knew perfectly well what a struggle was going on in my mind, what silent exchanges were being made between Nok and me. They gazed at us, dumb, waiting for the tension to break.

I broke first. "Okay, Nok, put the outboard gas tank in the dinghy. Nok drive it. Follow us into Kantang. Nok take it easy. Nok *rawang!* Nok be careful! Nok *cha-cha* . . . Nok slow down when dinghy turn. . . ."

Nok's eyes lit up like a mosque on Friday. Vigorously he nodded his head, his grin almost as wide as the river. Before I'd finished my warnings, he had the fuel tank connected to the outboard, the starter cord jerked, and the engine ticking over. Then he was off, in expert order, slowly chugging forward, holding the dinghy against the river stream.

Anant crabbed to *Henry Wagner*'s bow and weighed our anchor, and we were once more under way, at half-speed up the river. Nok was doing all right in the dinghy, keeping his speed the same as ours, hanging, like a grinning limpet, on to our course. Then he started to weave the dinghy this way and that a little. I didn't mind that; he was a boy, after all. We can expect lads to bend rules a bit. There'd be something wrong if they didn't.

Heading in to Kantang, I was content. We had missed our dallying in the Bay of Phangnga, but we had reached Kantang on time, on June 20, and now we were back on our original schedule. From now on, for two weeks or so, the rainfall should be less, and that should give us a better opportunity to get to the head-waters of the Trang River before the monsoon downpours re-commenced in earnest.

We rounded the last bend in the river before the town, and all bedlam was loosed. There was a great scarlet-and-gold Bud-dhist temple on an island in the middle of the entrance to the port. In the extensive shade below the trees in its grounds were crowds of orange-robed monks and brightly dressed worshipers. In the river, right before us, there were dozens of small boats fishing in the middle of the channel, huge, fast trawlers rushing their way among them. There were barge-towing tugs and dozens of longtail ferries crammed with people crossing the fairway, and behind it all like the backdrop of some Conradian film, was the waterfront, dirty white and black, crammed with gaily painted fishing trawl-ers. Above their masts, tall minarets and incongruous radio towers pointed to a monsoon-clouded sky.

I was far too busy keeping my eye out for hazards moving and fixed, and for a good place to berth our boat, to watch out then for Nok. Thomas, without his glasses, could see only six feet at the most.

For a disabled crew, a good, convenient mooring place is ten thousand times more essential than it might be for an able-bodied crew. Preferably the disabled should be able to step directly onto dry land, and not to have to overcome high obstacles or very soft or broken surfaces.

But in an unknown port, anywhere in the East, for *farangs* to beach a boat on a shore would be asking for problems. Thais, old and young, had great curiosity. Whenever they had the oppor-tunity, they would clamber on board without a prior word, and look around our boat, usually asking how much each thing cost. Apart from the continual disturbance and lack of any privacy (embarrassing at times when a prosthesis must be doffed or donned), there was also the problem of sorting out the well- and ill-intentioned visitors.

The solutions, awkward as they were for us, were to anchor our bow off, and have a stern line to pull the boat onto the shore, so we might get down onto the beach over our stern, or to anchor right off and use a dinghy to go ashore. The second solution was the best, because with a stern line on the beach there was always the risk of tripping someone. Playful youngsters or prankish drunks would be bound to pull it, and bump the boat; or let go of it and send us drifting around to our anchor in the busy, crowded harbor.

We were lucky. I sighted, right in the middle of the water-front, a small, shady park above a high river wall. The park was alongside a restaurant on stilts, which overhung the water's edge.

We made for the park. Anant heaved the anchor over the bow, and Thomas somehow maneuvered our stern around. Then he jumped into the river with a line, and tied it to a park rail, and there we were.

Except that our dinghy, with Nok in it, was nowhere in sight.

We squared up the boat. Still no sign of Nok.

"He might have stopped off to look around somewhere," suggested Thomas.

"Nok find girl. He give she ride," suggested Som. He interpreted this into Thai for Anant. Anant grinned hugely and rested his crutch on the gunwale.

We waited, and waited, and we scoured the harbor with our tired eyes, against the hot, bright afternoon sun. As the evening shadows began to lengthen, I started to be concerned. As the sun dropped, I sent Som ashore to tell the local police that Nok was missing, and get other boats out to search for him.

Even as Som climbed the ten-foot wall to get over the park railings (our way of getting ashore), and we prepared to get our boat under way to search for Nok, a fishing trawler, its siren hooting at us, worked its way inshore and stopped only an inch from our stempost.

In the evening twilight I stared and stared. There, on the deck of the trawler, his tragic eyes making him look like a sodden spaniel puppy, stood Nok. I glared at him. But I thanked Muhammad, God, and Buddha that he was safe.

But there was no sign of our dinghy—our pride and joy— the very first inflatable boat ever made in Thailand!

19

Legion of the Lost Ones

The crew of the fishing trawler crowded the deck as she nudged up closer to our bow. Nok flung himself over her rail and landed lightly on our foredeck.

"Ask Nok where our dinghy is, Som," I said, quietly.

Nok seemed barely able to make any of his usual noises. He hung his head. His ragged shorts dripped water onto his bare feet. He looked as if all the steam had gone out of him. His little body shook, and I realized that he was snuffling, crying.

Even as Som asked my question, a crewman shouted something, and three others, grinning, lifted our dinghy, minus the outboard, into sight above the bulwarks of their ship, and flung it over the side bodily as though it were a feather. Our dinghy flopped on the water next to our boat. Thomas jumped over our side to secure the dinghy painter on board *Henry Wagner*.

"Where's the outboard engine, Som? Ask them."

There was an exchange between Som and the fishermen. Som turned to me. "Say no have engine. Pick up Nok sitting on dinghy upside down."

"Where, for Criss . . . crying out loud? Ask them where they picked up Nok."

Another rapid exchange. "Out in the sea. The river take him

onto bar at mouth. They see"—he pointed his arm stump at the fishermen—"Nok have big trouble. They swam over and pulled him and the boat away from the big waves."

I saw Buddhist tattoos on one fisherman's arm. I dived into my pocket, turned to Thomas and handed him a five-hundred baht ($25) note. I nodded toward the four fishermen who had thrown us our dinghy. "Mate, give those four this for their trouble. Tell them it's for whiskey tonight!" (It was about two days' pay for the four.)

Thomas made to hand the money up to one of the fishermen, but he smiled and wagged his head. *"Mai pen rai!* It's nothing!" he shouted. The fishing boat took off with a roar for her unloading berth, and grazed our bowstem with her stern as she did so. That was nothing. We could expect that in a harbor as crowded as Kantang.

Surprised but pleased by that unknown fisherman's gesture, I turned again to Nok. I was tempted to rail at him, but the fisherman's gesture had reminded me where I was. I must not shout, I must not lose my equanimity, no matter what the provocation. If I did so, I would lose face. I would lose the game. This was Thailand.

"Give him a drink and some food, Som," I muttered, and hobbled aft to stare over our stern at the trees in the park on the shore. Now it was almost dark. The trees were packed with thousands upon thousands of small twittering birds. There were so many of them that the noise of their chatter almost drowned out the clatter of traffic rushing to the fish wharves nearby. I thought the birds were starlings, but I couldn't see them very well because of the descending darkness and the dampness in my eyes.

Whether they were tears of anger, frustration, loss, or relief I still don't know. All I could think of was how the devil we crew of cripples were ever going to tackle the tremendous challenge ahead of us, to get *Henry Wagner* up the mysterious River Trang, over the watershed divide, and down the River Tapi. How were we ever going to impress even the locals, let alone reach to the four continents of the world to stir people's minds? We couldn't even get a hundred miles without losing an anchor and an outboard engine!

I sniffed, blew my nose in my fingers, shoved my doubts aside, and forced myself to cheer up. In my mind I nicknamed the little park ashore "Gethsemane." Then I forced myself to face facts. I turned and gazed over our old wooden boat and our puny, flawed crew, and I wondered where our Golgotha would be. I wondered where we would ever find the sum of intelligence we would need to tackle the Calvary ahead of us. Then I remembered that in such things heart and guts and patience and compassion were far more important than anything learned. I'd seen illiterate deckhands prevail, time and again, where university graduates, not to speak of dons, had collapsed into quivering, defeated wrecks. Heart, guts, and patience, God knows, our Thais had in full measure. They'd had to have them. Without them they could not have withstood, for most of their wretched lives, the demeaning attitudes of many of their fellow beings.

There is no place to get to know companions more intimately than in a small craft on a voyage. Very little can be hidden in those tight confines. Thomas had been shocked at how continually demanding in small things our Thai boys had been.

I had half listened to him. He was much nearer their age than I. But the forest isn't obvious when you're looking at the trees. It was not easy for him to see much of the full scenario of our Atlantis endeavor.

My stump was burning. It always does when strong emotions affect me. (It does now.) I reckoned to myself: If our Thai boys had seemed to be demanding, if their attitude seemed, to our ocean-accustomed eyes, to be all "I want" in little things, could I blame them? Som might have asked me for a few baht at the end of each day. He might have asked me time and time again to sacrifice my precious hours of rest teaching him a few more words of English. Anant might have whined until I caved in and bought him a cheap little tape player; Nok might have sulked and looked pained until I let him drive my motorcycle and our dinghy; but good God, what were their demands compared to mine?

I wanted nothing less than their whole being. I was demanding of them all their strength and nerve and sinews; even asking them to risk losing their lives if need be. I wanted every minute of their waking day and their nights. I wanted to persuade them and inveigle them, stir them and pound them, and forge them and mold them into three of the most unlikely heroes that the world had ever seen. I wanted to grab their minds and their bodies and their hearts and their souls, and their skills and their delight in life, and fling them before all the powers-that-be in Thailand and the world. I wanted to shame all the fortunate, unaware, healthy, able-bodied

beings, all the rich and the lucky on this earth of ours, into rec-
ognizing and respecting these three raggle-taggle strays from the
Legion of the Lost Ones, not merely for themselves, but for all
their fellows everywhere in the world.

It was not our lads who were demanding; *it was I.*

If there had been any lack of foresight or intelligence, I decided, or if there were to be any disaster, or hurt, or death, any
blame must lie firmly with me. I should never have allowed Nok
to go off alone in the dinghy in those fiercely flowing waters, in
that hard wind. Grimly, smiling Thai-style, I rejoined our lads.
If they could still smile when all hell broke loose inside them, so
could I. I was learning. I even managed to pat Nok gently on his
shoulder with my right hand, without the others noticing.

Later, at supper, as we sat and squatted around our treasure
chest, the top of which was our dining table, Nok's tale came out
bit by reluctant bit. He had been speeding and weaving the dinghy
about. He had forgotten to check the outboard-engine fixing
clamps, as Thomas and I had taught him; at full speed, almost
twenty knots, he had made a sudden right-angle turn, and the
engine had jumped up off the stern board, and fallen into the sea.
Worse, Nok had forgotten to fasten the lanyard that secured the
engine through a hole on the dinghy stern board. As the engine
had zoomed up in the air, it had taken the dinghy stern with it
and dragged the boat right over. Nok had dived over and over
again to find the engine, but of course the river water had been
far too clouded with mud. When he had stopped looking for the
engine, the dinghy had been swept away downstream, almost out
of sight, carried by the river current, even against the breeze. Nok,
a strong swimmer, had then, in a panic, set out after the dinghy;
by the time he had caught up with it, it had been almost at the
sandbar, where the seas pounded so mightily. By that time he had
been so ashamed of losing our engine, and so afraid to face his
mates and me, that he had wanted, he had determined, to die.
Luckily he had been sighted by men on the fishing boat, and two
of them, brave souls, had jumped into the river, dragged Nok
and our dinghy clear, and had brought them into port.

Nok knew, roughly, where the outboard engine had been
lost. I told Som to organize a local boat to go and drag the river
with a wire, to see if they could find the engine. Maybe they could
hook it, or send a good diver down to recover it.

We didn't need to organize anything. Word was already out

in Kantang about what had occurred. Several drag boats went out that very night. They dragged for the engine the whole time we were there, two days and nights, it was said without success.

Jumping ahead: When we reached sixty-two miles upstream, about two weeks later, word reached us that our engine had been found. For reasons that will be clear later, we could spare no one, or the time, to go back to Kantang to collect it. So far as I know it's still there, and it can stay there. Who cannot *lose* cannot *win*.

But we could not wait in Kantang for the dinghy outboard to be found. Heading for the unknown in the southwest monsoon period, we were slaves to the weather. Given the records of previous years, this dry spell should not last more than a week—perhaps ten days. We had to press on while we had less rain.

On the other hand we needed some power for our dinghy. No one can row a lightweight, roundish inflatable for very long in strong river currents without the risk of coming to grief. Even in a mild current, a rubber dinghy will tend to whirl round and round unless it is vigorously paddled by two strong people, both with two arms *and two legs* each. (The center of gravity of a leg amputee is much higher.)

I had seen the longtail engines that were used to propel dugout canoes. Some were tiny things, only a couple of horsepower. But there were five-horsepower models that were not too cumbrous for our dinghy's stern board, and yet were powerful enough to push it, though slowly, against the river currents. We determined to find one the next day.

That was one of the better resolutions we came to on this trip. With the shallow depths of the river, the outboard would have been all but useless. The fivehorsepower longtail, the "jigger," as we called it, was able to reduce the amount of water needed beneath the dinghy to a mere four inches, and would be a godsend.

The cost of the jigger, $380, was very close to half our available funds, but that was probably cheaper than having the river dragged for a week or more. We didn't know the dragger boats were working on (*it was said*) a "no results, no payment" basis.

But having to buy the jigger meant that we could not afford the money for replacement spectacles for Thomas. We were working on too narrow a margin, and we had no alternative. The rhythms of the monsoon would not pause for us.

Thomas did not place his own welfare before others'. He was

one of the Old Brigade, as I termed it, or perhaps, God willing, one of the New. His eyes, half-blind or not, were on the horizon, and his mind was over it. I'd had little need to teach him that; it had been inside him when we met. His lack of far sight would be a handicap, but what's one more among four? We other four had good eyes. We could see for him.

20

Kantang

The moment we had arrived in Kantang, the rains had stopped. The modern explorer would put that down, I suppose, to expert planning. I put it down to God's grace. As I told Thomas, "He had to do something to make up for all those heavy seas, and all those nights with the rain pissing down on us, and the lost anchor and the bloody drowned outboard!"

Despite the heat and humidity and the mosquitoes at night, our stay in Kantang was easy and pleasant. We decided to stay where we had first berthed, in front of the park and beside the overhanging restaurant. The morning after our arrival in Kantang we clambered onto the beach, and up a ten-foot wall and over the park rails, into the cool shade of the trees.

There were a few con men in the Garden of Gethsemane. But they were Thai con men and smiled at us. Thomas and I pretended that we neither spoke nor understood Thai. These Kantang charlatans were very amateurish, compared to some I had encountered from Valparaiso to Vladivostok, Dallas to Durban. Pristine, pure, and unassailed, we made our way into the restaurant and ordered coffee.

Most people, I suppose, when they go into a restaurant with a charming and interesting view over a busy little port, relax and enjoy the coffee, the cuisine, the drinks, the shade, the service, and the view. Not only those delights for us disabled small-craft voyagers; at any rate not on our first visit. We went mainly to size up the amenities. Was there a freshwater supply on tap? Was there a toilet? Was it (for us legless) a sit-down toilet? Might there even be a staff shower? Could we use it for a small fee? Was there a night guard, who might keep an eye on our boat? Was there, perhaps, an electrical socket, where we might, for a small fee, plug in a cable for our light on board? Was there stagnant water on the river shore under the restaurant, which might cause a plague of mosquitoes if we lit a light on board?

The riverside restaurant in Kantang had all of these amenities, so, apart from the mosquitoes, it was ideal for our purposes. Besides, the meals there were so cheap that it was less costly for us all to eat there than to eat on board: about $4 per meal for all five of us.

Kantang was a busy place on water. Ashore there were very few cars. The traffic was mainly fish trucks, bicycles, motor-cycles, and bike-rickshaws. The pavements were crowded with pedestrians. There were Chinese merchants in blue cotton suits, their collars tight around their necks, Muslim women in sarongs, their heads covered, Arab seamen in djellabas, Thai fishermen in their peculiar baggy trousers and homemade collarless shirts, old men, looking opium-besotted, asleep on low wooden platforms, and a hundred street stalls selling God only knows what varieties of herbs, spices, and mysteries.

Kantang's waterfront reminded me of the Chinese parts of Singapore in the immediate postwar days. There were rows of wooden shops, fronted by huge letters of Chinese script in scarlet and gold. Under the signs, blacksmiths, goldsmiths, silversmiths, coopersmiths, toolmakers, barbers, bakers, pie-makers, bird-catchers, fishtank–makers, coffin-builders, cycle repairmen, herbal druggists, and cloth merchants all plied their trade. The depths of the shops were dark and mysterious, and joss sticks glowed dimly in the smoky gloom.

I knew all this wouldn't last (the tourist touts would see to that), and I regretted it. I wished that future generations might see the wonder, and the striving, and the misery and pain of life as it has been lived in the East for past ages. I knew that by the time Nok and Anant were a few years older, it would all be gone. (I stopped to let Anant, on his crutch, limp past me.) They and their children risked being subliminally seduced by smart-ass, money-mad, sold-out technocrats into thoroughly believing how charming and quaint and primitive life before them always had been, and how much easier and more convenient and cleverer their miserably alienated existence was.

"God help the future generations!" I prayed. "And punish, hard and quick," I clambered over yet another stretch of broken pavement, "the greedy, electronic-chiphearted money-grubbers who are wheedling their way into absolute control of all human activity!"

We all stopped in our slow progress along the pavement. Nok and Anant had bought, from a chubby little woman at a street stall, something odious-looking and sticky in a plastic bag. Now they were peering and ruminating over a stall full of Thai and Western pop-music tapes. There was a lot of pop-music tape piracy going on in Thailand. I silently wished good luck to the pirates. Anyone who stole from squalling sound vandals couldn't be bad at all.

I studied our boys for a moment, then returned to my thoughts. I consoled myself that when all this world we know and have loved is gone, perhaps all the more unpleasant parts of life would be over, too, so maybe it would be a good bargain, to exchange reality for make-believe. Or would it? Would the ever-growing trust in practitioners of make-believe be our human destiny? Would only catastrophe halt it?

We passed out of cool shade into searing heat. I shook myself out of my depressing view of the future and returned to the present and to more important matters. I doled out a few baht for a bag of sticky rice and a live chicken.

Up the street we found a five-horsepower longtail engine. It was gasoline-driven, but we found that acceptable. We already carried gasoline for our lost outboard and for our electrical generator. In any case, the gasoline engine was air-cooled, and simplicity should be the watchword when choosing equipment for an endeavor such as ours. By noon we had a longtail shaft fitted by a local blacksmith, and by lunchtime it had been bolted to our dinghy stern and tested in the harbor.

Thomas wanted to try out the new jigger. I wouldn't let him. I insisted on Nok doing it, so that he might regain his face before the others. Nok was pleased at this, and gave everyone in the harbor a superb performance of small-boat handling. The dinghy was nowhere near as fast as it had been with the outboard, but nevertheless Nok managed to get about six knots out of it in still water, and maybe a knot and a half against the full current in midstream.

I was pleased. Having a mobile dinghy meant that further inland we would not have to moor *Henry Wagner* on the riverbank at villages or landing places. We could anchor her off in the river, and so be a little less vulnerable to roaming tigers, slithering snakes, enormous cockroaches, yelling kids, or even, perish the thought, violent intrusion.

Two days after *Henry Wagner* fetched Kantang, we set off up the Mae Nam Trang, the first of our rivers, to conquer the Kra.

21

Different Strokes

There had been another reason for our two-day sojourn in Kantang. A month before, I had sent to the Thai government Geological Survey Department in Bangkok for satellite photographs of the Kra. One of the very few courteous and well-written letters that I ever, in my life, received from a government agency anywhere, had told me that the photographs should arrive in Kantang, at the post office, around June 18. They arrived on June 21. Considering their potential importance to us, their cost was most reasonable: $15 each, for six pictures.

Excitedly, followed by a taggle of ragged market urchins, Thomas bore the tightly wrapped cardboard cylinder, about as thick as your arm and all of four feet long, to our boat. It was too precious for him to throw it from the shore to my waiting hands, as he would any more mundane package back in Phuket. Like an Olympic prize, he held on to it until he could place it carefully into my shaking hands. Anyway, he was half-blind now, and couldn't see far enough to throw it.

Henry Wagner was now really a part of the late twentieth century. Now we had space science on our side. Now we were modern explorers. In my mind's eye I saw rows of large, well-fed men in offices as big as football fields, all watching six computer terminals each and talking ten-to-the-dozen into microphones as the latest state-of-the-art trillion-dollar rocket shot into space to carry a thing of wonder—a photographic satellite—

hundreds of miles above the surface of our planet. And all so that this roll of pictures could be delivered to *Henry Wagner*. So that it could reveal to us, without any effort or strain on our part, all the previously hidden mysteries of the Kra Isthmus. We had a tool in our hands that probably no previous Kra-crossers had ever had. We had the superiority of modern technology. We were at the pinnacle of evolution. We and space science were the tops! The survey maps of the isthmus we already had would have been, in other circumstances, laughably inaccurate. They had been prepared by the Royal Thai Survey Department, Supreme High Command, "for civilian purposes." Perhaps the inaccuracies were intentional? This we were beginning to wonder already, in only the five short miles between the sea and Kantang.

In stern-faced anticipation, our boys gathered around me. I fumbled at the tight wrappings of the cylinder. I was far too Western and clumsy. Nok gently relieved me of the roll and, delicately, with his sharp fishing knife, slit it open in one graceful sweep of his blade. The roll of pictures unwrapped itself like a slashed onion onto our treasure-chest lid. The photographs were wide and long, and produced on best-quality paper. There rose from them, as they lay upside down on the box, a whiff of clean, air-conditioned efficiency. Trying hard to keep my hands from trembling with delight and pride at these achievements of the human brain, I turned over the top picture.

It showed a few patches of mountains and rice paddies from between monsoon clouds. The rest were all the same. There was hardly one yard of our river depicted in the whole caboodle.

I glared up at Thomas. He threw me a warning look.

My throat suddenly tiny and dry, I leaned over the pictures and peered at them, and to the boys' utter mystification, ummed and ahhed over them, like Moses over the tablets (and probably for the same reason), for a full minute. Then, rapidly, silently, as though I now had command of the wisdom of the ages, I rolled them up and stowed them away in our treasure chest. I stiffened my upper lip. No sense, at this stage in the game, in undermining our Thai lads' almost religious belief in the efficacy of modern technology . . . even less sense in my losing face. Better to stay silent and head out blind. Some things in the East are more important, even, than sight.

To bear great disappointment, to know intense anxiety and

concern, and not to dare to let them show; those are by far the worst of a skipper's burdens.

Our first day's run upstream from Kantang, for about eighteen miles, was straightforward and simple, compared to what was to follow.

Kantang was the only settlement bigger than a few huts and fewer houses that we were to see along the whole lengths of the rivers Trang and Tapi, right across the Kra, until we arrived at Surat Thani a month later. All the other sizable villages or towns had been set back miles away from the rivers, on higher ground, because of the perennial flooding at the height of the monsoon rains.

At Kantang the River Trang was about three-hundred yards wide, and it kept this width, and a deep channel, almost all the way up to the first road bridge to cross the river. That lay around eight miles southwest of the city of Trang. That bridge carried desultory traffic first to the town of Sikao and then, up the main west-coast highway, to Krabi and the north. We also knew that at the first bridge the stream suddenly shoaled and was only about one hundred feet wide.

A good half hour before we were due to set off, Nok, smiling his Thai "Forgive me and I'll forgive you" smile, was hanging on to the helm. I let him keep the helm as long as he wanted to, so that he could further regain his face after the outboard-motor de-bacle. It was only fair to him—and to us. In the event, Nok steered the whole of the first day's leg, all the way to Saphan Tha Chin.

Kantang came to an abrupt halt at a mangrove swamp about a quarter of a mile upstream. As we set off at full speed in *Henry Wagner*, with all six of our flags flying, I watched the shore. One minute there was the crowded waterfront market, the next minute there were fine old Chinese-style rich merchants' houses overhanging the river, the next, open-sided godowns (warehouses), next a small shipyard for fishing trawlers, and then nothing but mangrove swamp on one bank and savannah-type bush on the other.

Even as we rounded the first bend above the town we almost collided with our first obstacle. As we roared round the bend at full speed, we had about two-and-a-half seconds to size up the obstruction and decide what to do. It was a thick bamboo fish trap built almost right across the river, like the frame of a fence, except that instead of wooden palings, it had a small-gauge fishnet suspended from it. Its horizontal middle beam was just about the exact height of my head above water level. On our side of the channel, the deep side, the outside of the bend, there was a gap, no more than eight feet wide, between the end of the fish-trap structure and the bank. Over the gap hung a big tree, its over-hanging branches swept by the river current.

During our stay in Kantang I had practiced hand signals with our boys for an hour or so. It's no good shouting and bawling simple orders for repetitive actions, like "starboard" or "port" or "cast anchor." For one thing it's unpleasant to have someone shouting all the time; for another it probably wouldn't be heard when most needed over the noise of the longtail engine. Better for the watch skipper to have a preset system of hand-signaling in emergencies.

My signal for "Head that way" was simple. I pointed my finger at where we should head for.

It couldn't be mistaken, because I never pointed my finger under any other circumstances, and especially at someone. As I said before, it was considered, in Thailand, to be an extremely impolite thing to do.

I pointed my finger: There was nothing for it but to head straight at the overhanging branches of the low tree. Nok didn't hesitate; he steered at full speed straight for the tree. We crashed bows-on into at least three branches as thick as your wrist. Under our weight of one-and-a-quarter tons, impelled by our speed of eight knots, they snapped off with loud cracks, and left *Henry Wagner* enwreathed like a Roman victor in a harvest of greenery, but she pressed steadily onward. Four other thick branches scraped over the whole length of our gunwales, but by that time everyone, including Nok, was lying flat in the bottom of the boat, so no bodily harm was done.

We eased our speed, and opened our eyes wider, all of us. I sent Som ahead of *Henry Wagner* in our dinghy, to signal when we approached a hidden obstacle.

Som had already mastered starting and stopping the jigger engine with his one hand. He did this by holding the jigger steady, one foot on the helm bar, and pulling the starter cord with his one hand. To scout the rivers ahead for hours on end every day, under blistering sun or in pouring rain, was to be Som's unenviable job from then on, for much of another thousand kilometers. With one arm.

22

Different Folks

Now we were forcibly reminded of one of the Achilles' heels of the longtail engines. Because the engines were general-purpose units, which might be adapted to many different uses, no water pump to cool them was provided. On boats, because the engines were on gimbals and had an infinitely variable attitude, in other words because they had to be swung around every which way, to steer the boat, it was impracticable to fit the usual type of cooling system. Instead, at the outboard end of the long shaft sleeve, about a foot forward of the propeller, a funnel like scoop was fixed, and from this, running the whole length of the shaft, a hose, which eventually connected to the engine cooling-water inlet. As the propeller shoved the boat forward, the funnel scooped up water that, by the pressure set up by the boat's speed, was rammed all the way up the hose. But there was a snag about this arrangement: When the boat's speed was slow, there was less water pressure, and the water failed to reach the engine. That rapidly caused severe overheating.

Our only solution to this was to disconnect the cooling-water hose, scoop up river water in a bucket, and pour it directly into the engine cooling-water inlet—a thousand times an hour.

But that could not be done by the man (or boy) steering the boat. He was already fully occupied in holding the helm steady. The heavy engine vibrations made that enough for anyone's strength. And at the same time he was peering ahead, searching for obstructions in the river, making rapid adjustments at bends and turns.

That meant that someone other than the helmsman had to keep the engine cool whenever the boat's speed was lower than three knots for any longer than three minutes. The "coolie" had to scoop water out of the river in a can, poise himself over the engine, and pour the water steadily into a tin funnel stuck in the inlet pipe. To do this, he had to share the stern platform with the helmsman and the engine. The stern platform was triangular, about two feet long on all three sides. Across this tiny coffee table of a space, the helmsman swung the noisy, shaking engine on its vertical trunnion and its horizontal fulcrum this way and that continually. To watch our "coolie" at work was to see a display of coordination, balance, grace, poise, and delicate footwork that could be performed properly and efficiently only by someone who had spent hours in the cool of the evening, at every opportunity, or every spare day of his life, playing Thai kickball with his mates. No *farang*, except perhaps a super muscled ballet star, could hope to do it. No one-armed or one-legged person could hope to do it. That meant it must be done by Nok, while Thomas or Anant (if the going was easy) steered. I was Thomas's eyes, for every minute he was at the helm. And I was far too ancient for agility. Besides, with the best eyes in the boat, I was needed to sight hazards long before the others could.

The sum result of all this was that for most of the way upstream, and right across the Kra, wherever the going was tricky and slow, Thomas steered our boat. But much of the time, when the going was good, and we could make speed and cool the engine automatically, Som, Anant, or Nok took over the steering. But if it comes to accolades, who steers a craft is not the crowning issue. There are long ranks of ocean captains, of vessels big and small, who have not laid a finger on a steering wheel for decades.

The Trang riverbanks changed from mangrove and swamp to tall reeds almost high enough to block the view of distant mountains. There were huts, sometimes single, sometimes in clusters, in clearings between the reeds. The looks of them made me feel, at first sight, as if we were all living ten thousand years ago, they seemed so primitive. I was amazed to think that we were still within ten miles of Kantang, and that we had satellite pictures and a laptop computer in the boat.

But when I managed to get a closer look at a few more of

these huts, I realized that the woven rattan and bamboo of their walls and roofs showed a standard of workmanship that would leave many a modern factory worker looking like a clodhopper. Later we were to find that simple, isolated riverfolk made practically everything they owned with their own hands, and that everything they made was beautiful because it was so functional and practical. As for some of their boats and paddles, many an art gallery, it seemed to me, would give a year's endowment to get such works between their walls.

We passed a settlement of sturdy houses on a small, steep outcrop of limestone, and I recognized the spot where our Chinese hotel owner from Kantang had tried to sell us land. It did look pretty in the early forenoon sunlight, but I thought to myself, If the view of the river from that land is worth so much, then how much is the view of that land from the river worth? I suppose it was a sailor's way of thinking.

The river was well cluttered with tiny dugout canoes (pirogues would be more accurate a description) much of the way up to the first bridge. It was wide and breezy, and, apart from our continual lookout for sudden obstacles, very pleasant after our recent rough sea trip. But for our loud longtail engine's noise, we could have been passing this way ten millennia before. We could have been ancient Egyptian or Arab traders seeking our way across a mysterious land, searching for a way through the distant mountains to the China Sea and the fabulous treasures of the empire of Cathay.

Now Nok and Som, out in the open under the sun, had their heads covered with their spare sarongs. They fitted exactly into my imagined time warp. It was as if they were living long before the first Portuguese or Venetian mariners ever even heard the name Siam.

But the boys' head coverings were not for show. They were for protection against the searing heat of the sun. We were to find that the hotter it became, between the high banks of the Mae Nam Trang, the more clothing our Thais wore. The several layers of loose clothing they wore formed an insulation against the heat. When there was no cooling breeze (which was most of the time), it was less hot under all those clothes than it would have been in a bare skin. That's something else for us Westerners to relearn; our forefathers knew it, by reasoning or not. Another reason for the lads wearing loose clothes was to protect themselves, to a degree, against possible snakebites, and certain assault by squadrons of wasps or mosquitoes.

Very, very few of the local pirogues had engines. They were mostly paddled, and skillfully too, by women old and young. It seemed that they used the pirogues to get to and from the market in Kantang. Heading upstream, to avoid the swift current and to take advantage of the shade cast by overhanging trees, they clung very close to the bank. When we passed them at slow speed, they ran their pirogues under the low trees, right up onto the bank, and hung on to a low twig or branch for dear life until our wake had slopped them around, and then died again. We always slowed right down for them. There would have been no sense in us leaving a wake of offended people astern of us.

Heading downstream, the pirogues stayed in the middle of the river, to take full advantage of the current. Then, for the effort of a paddle stroke or two every minute they seemed to be flying along, as if they were being towed by some obliging dolphin.

It took about three hours for *Henry Wagner* to reach the first bridge across the River Trang and return, it seemed, to the twentieth century, if only for a fleeting moment.

Soon after the bridge hove into view, almost as we passed under it, a large bus, obviously a luxury-class tourist-toter, rumbled over it, heading north. Looking up, I had a mere glimpse of pale faces behind dark window glass.

I found myself trying to imagine what must go through the mind of a tourist whizzing over the Khlong Mae Nam Trang in an air-conditioned bus. I wondered if, as the corner of their eyes caught a glimpse of the brown muddy waters of the stream, they realized that it would be perfectly possible to launch and provision a small boat there, and with luck, sail all the way to the Teddington Lock on the River Thames, or Houston, or Sydney?

I wondered if this difference, between the landsman's and the ocean sailor's view did not speak whole volumes about two completely different outlooks, that of the voyager and the tourist? I bet to myself that if the tourists ever thought of such things at all, they would more likely imagine that Singapore or Bangkok airports were more closely connected to London or Houston or Sydney than the muddy-brown water of a narrow, shallow, remote *khlong* under a little obscure bridge, but if they did, I concluded to myself, they were dead wrong. We are all part, one of another, the waters tell us so.

Immediately beyond the bridge our river split up into a five-armed maze. We knew, from our previous exploration, that the turn to take was the first to starboard. The narrow channel under the bridge held back the current, so that immediately upstream there was almost-still water. No sooner had we cleared the bridge than *Henry Wagner*, her speed then unimpeded, shot forward at about ten knots and, unable to turn fast enough with the longtail at such speed and at such a sharp angle, smashed straight into the far bank opposite the turnoff.

Nok stopped our engine right away, and there was dead silence, broken now and again by the faraway barking of a dog, the cheerful chirp of some bird, and the haunting howl of a monkey.

There was simply no point in getting excited or angry over things that could not be avoided. Shouting and screaming never got any boat off anything. All I said, as Thomas and the boys piled over the bow to shove us off again, was, "Watch out! Don't forget the snakes!"

The branch stream we followed was not much wider than the boat. There were a couple of bamboo fish traps built across it. These we had to dismantle to make a gap wide enough to pass through. Then, when our boat was upstream of it, we moored up, returned along the bank to the fish trap, and rebuilt it, to leave it whole. (Try that with one arm or one leg!) These few traps on the first day's run were a foretaste of what was ahead: By the time we had pushed our way 180 miles upstream, and reached Thung Song, we had dismantled and repaired parts of *234* separate fish traps.

Now the banks of the River Trang were, on both sides, steep, and on average thirty feet high. Little breeze reached us through dense scrub or high trees. At two in the afternoon, as the second bridge, at Sapan Tha Chin (Bridge of the Chinese House) hove into view, I checked our temperature gauge inside the boat. It showed 112 degrees Fahrenheit. Our humidity gauge showed 98 percent.

Suddenly the long, curved roofs of a temple, scarlet and gold, glittered above the treetops. We knew that wherever there was a riverside temple, there would be a landing stage, so that worshipers arriving in their dugouts would not have muddy feet when they cast off their sandals to enter the temple. The temple landing stage was where we would spend the night, safely tied up, under the benign, watchful eyes of Lord Buddha.

We passed old, rambling Chinese and Thai houses, each with intricately carved roof gables and eaves, we ran under a small, low road bridge with only inches of clearance over our heads, and emerged once more into the hot sunlight. I stared and stared at the riverbank ahead.

I sighted, about two hundred yards away, under shady trees on the bank, the expected temple landing stage. Above it, high on the bank, in the shadows of the trees, was what I at first imagined was a swathe of golden flowers. Whatever it was stirred gently, as though wafted by a slight breeze.

We drew nearer, slowly and carefully, watching and wondering. A cloud overhead slowly shifted:A patch of sunlight reached the bank and lightened the shadows under the trees.

There were no flowers, at least not as we thought of them: They were monks, about three-hundred of them.

23

The Prophet

As we reached the temple landing stage at Saphan Tha Chin, I saw that most of the shaved-headed, orange-robed figures looking down on us from the shadows were youngsters. Their ages must have ranged between eight or nine years to the late teens. With them were three or four burly, mature monks maybe in their thirties, and one incredibly tiny ancient monk. In his robe and sandals, wielding a staff, he reminded me of pictures of Mahatma Gandhi.

Nok stopped our engine's racket as soon as Som and Thomas were on the landing stage with our mooring lines. Som murmured to me, "They're apprentices. They live here. They come to the river every evening to wash." Som must be our spokesman and go-between. Among our crew, only he was a Buddhist.

"Oh," I said, "are we in the way? We can shift out to anchor if they want to use the stage. . . ."

Som smiled. "They will not stop anyone coming to the temple. They cannot send you away. It would be against their rules."

"Tell them to come on down, Som. We don't mind them washing round the boat. In fact, if they want to, they can use our dinghy to bathe from, as long as you don't mind steering them around for a bit."

Som grinned. He spoke rapidly to the burly men, who seemed to be teachers in charge of the boys. They smiled at us the Thai "We'll be around" smile, and walked away toward the temple buildings. Then Som spoke to the boy-monks in general. Immediately the vast majority of the boys lost all their dignified monkish demeanor, and before we knew what was happening, the whole landing stage was crowded with yelling lads, and ten or twelve had already leapt excitedly into our dinghy. Only one or two remained at the top of the bank, to keep the old monk company.

Then followed one of the most hectic, rowdy hours I have ever known in a small craft (and I've known some). The apprentice monks laughed and yelled and joshed each other as soon as Som ran them in the dinghy far enough away from the temple grounds. Whenever the dinghy returned to the landing stage, the waiting crowd silently splashed the arrivals with water, while lads in our dinghy beat the river with our paddles, to wet those on the stage.

Even Nok and Anant, both Muslims, hopped into the dinghy to join in the fun. But Nok, his eyes gleaming with excitement, bursting to tell me something, surfaced near the boat, scrabbled up to the gunwale, and shouted something at me. It sounded like "*Na ni! Na ni!*"

Thomas grinned and said, "He's telling us it's drinking water. Fresh water! He's never seen a freshwater river before!"

We were just out of the range of the sea tide. Ever after that, Nok, before he stepped over the side, would stick his finger in the water, wherever it was, and test it, to see if it was salt or fresh.

The crowd of boy-monks all behaved exactly the same as would boatloads of lads of the same age at any other place anywhere in the world. It was a fine late afternoon, the sun was shining but not too hot. I fancied, watching all the lively antics, that Buddha and Allah must be either holding their ears or having a quiet chuckle. As the sun dropped and the action around our boat slowed down, we showed a few of the older lads the two Western magazines we had on board. One of the burly teachers had reappeared. He saw his pupils looking at our books. He may have thought that they were copies of *Playboy* or *Penthouse*, who knows? He almost tripped over his sandals as he rushed down to the landing stage, to see what they were looking at. He may, or may not, have been able to read English, but when he saw the pictures the lads were so avidly inspecting, in our copies of *Nautical Quarterly* and *Yachting World*, of sailing yachts and motorboats, he smiled a Thai "relief" smile and told Som that those were the first nonreligious books that these lads had seen since they entered the temple, and some of them had been there for years.

The ancient monk was gently helped down to the landing stage. His helpers had a large, leatherbound book with them. They brought it on board *Henry Wagner*. It was a visitors' book, and the first date in it was 2450—the Buddhist equivalent of our 1908.

By signs and through Som they gave Thomas and me to understand that we should sign the book. We did so, and they told us that we were the very first foreigners ever to sign it, except for one. They showed us his name. It was written, they said, in Japanese, and it belonged to a colonel in the Imperial Japanese Army, who had signed in our year 1944.

The ancient monk, they said, was the secretary to the abbot, and through him that dignitary had sent word for us *farangs*, Thomas and me, to go to the temple and join him for tea.

Normally I would never go anywhere from a small boat in which I was on voyage unless all my crew were also invited. They needn't have gone. It was the invitation that mattered, not the function. My contention was that if they were fit to face the ocean with me, they were fit to be invited anywhere I went. *Love me—love my crew!* But this seemed to me to be a special occasion; the landing stage belonged to the temple, and the abbot had been kind enough to send word that we could stay as long as we wished. I felt I owed him the small courtesy of a visit. Nok and Anant wouldn't mind in the least us going to talk with the abbot; they were Muslims.

Thomas helped me up the rough steps in the bank, and I, at the same time, assisted the ancient monk. We crossed over a large open space, and passed the temple charnel house, where bodies were cremated and their spirits sent on their way into their next existence. Then we passed by a long, wooden barracks like building where the apprentice monks lived. It had three stories, and was plain, with rows of tiny windows so that there was about it something of a prison. Then we passed a beautiful temple, all carved wood, brilliantly painted, and several smaller ones, similarly decorated, until we came to another plain, unpainted wooden building on stone stilts. It reminded my sailor's mind of a sailmaker's loft in the old days.

Clumsily I clumped up a narrow outside staircase. At the top I excused myself from doffing my shoes. On my prosthesis, without its shoe, I cannot walk well, and there is little shock absorption. If I take off the shoe on my good leg, then it's worse, because my real foot is an inch lower than the false. The ancient monk smiled and nodded his head, to show that I was excused.

We were shown into a spotlessly clean room. It was all teak, unpainted, and looked polished. Except for a couple of scrolls on the walls, a few cushions on the floor, and an incense-burner, the room was almost bare. There were large windows all around the room, with wooden shutters, but no glass. Those away from the sun were all open, and through them came the sounds of monks chanting and birds twittering in the trees nearby. In one corner of the room an old monk, even more ancient than our companion, sat on a low wooden stool. By his side sat two small apprentice monks, studying scrolls.

I bowed to the abbot, for this is who he was. He smiled at me and gestured me to sit on a cushion near him. I cannot sit down on the floor without poking my false leg straight out in front of me. To display a foot so prominently while sitting in company was considered, in Thailand, to be almost obscenely insulting. I tapped my false leg with my walking stick, and grinned at the abbot.

The abbot gestured to one of the small boys, who disappeared through the shadows at the end of the room, and came back bearing a rickety but serviceable kitchen chair, Western-style. As I sat on it, I found myself wondering when it had last been used.

Tea was then served in tiny pots of delicate bone china. It was very good green tea, aromatic and slightly bitter. Our conversation was a halting one, carried on in slow Thai, the abbot using a few English words.

The gist of the abbot's speech seemed to me to be that while he admired the way we were trying to help our boys, he was concerned that we might be trying to change their karma.

I said very little. I thought a lot. I could not throw overboard my own spiritual ancestry. The gist of my reply to the abbot was that perhaps to try to change the lot of millions of poor kids looked as though it was my karma. If anyone's life had unfolded so inevitably, surely it was mine?

The abbot cocked his eye at me and studied me quietly for a while, but he said no more about karma. He did look at me closely at one stage, though, and said that I should be very careful of my health, that there was a danger that I should be sick soon. He said perhaps I would have an accident. There seemed to be something very mysterious about him when he said that.

I shrugged it off, and slapped my chest and laughed (or coughed, I forget which), and gave him to understand that I felt as fit as a fiddle.

The abbot gave me a Thai "So you think you're special?" smile. I gave him a positive grin. As we stood to depart, the abbot asked us if there was anything he could do that might ease our way.

I told him that I would appreciate his getting the word upstream that we were on our way, that we wanted nothing from anyone, but while we did not seek assistance, we would appreciate being let pass along their river in peace.

At this the abbot nodded, and our audience was over.

"Many a good tune played on an old fiddle," I said to Thomas after we left the temple and returned to our boat.

"How old do you think the abbot was, then, Tristan?"

"You . . . ! I meant me!"

24

Hooked

Thomas had said very little at the powwow with the abbot. Just as well, I thought. He'd already been thrown out of a monastic school in Bavaria for not wearing socks, he said.

We slept soundly that night, in silent peace by the temple steps. We also slept dry, and while that was a comparative pleasure, it was to me also a concern. It had not rained since we had arrived in Kantang four days previously. A semidry period was to be expected, but not a drought. If rain showers did not replenish the river waters, there would not be enough depth for us to get very far upstream. Yet the river might be deep enough now, with the remnants of the previous rains, for us to pass a fair way upstream. We must get a move on. Besides, the sooner I could manage to burn our boats behind us, the better. Rightly or wrongly, as on any expedition as weak, desperate, and poor as this one, the sooner I could get to the point of no return, the more committed I could keep myself and my crew. Now, in my mind, the braces were off, the shirtsleeves were rolled up, the belt was tightened.

We cast off from the temple landing stage, and pulled out on our anchor until we were midstream. Even as Thomas reached for the engine starting handle, I heard a strange noise from the direction of the temple. It reminded me of the ululation of Arab women at wakes for their dead. Puzzled, we all stared up in the direction of the sound. We saw that all the little windows of the lads' barracks were alive with waving and shouting boymonks.

Then, as our engine sprang into life, we could hear them no more, but we watched their farewell, and waved to them, until *Henry Wagner* passed around the first bend in the river, and they were all out of sight and gone.

The river in front of the temple was deep. The current was about three knots midstream, but as soon as we passed the bend, the river narrowed, and the current speeded up to about five knots. Also, as we passed around that first bend, we came to our first fallen tree.

We moored the boat under a shady willow and inspected the obstacle. It was a large tree, about eight feet thick near its roots. The roots had been undermined by the swift current, and torn out of the bank when the tree had fallen. The tree was about eighty feet long from roots to twig tips, and it had fallen not across the river, but askew it, so that its branches were downstream of its roots.

Bear in mind in what follows that the temperature out in the sun, between the high banks of the river, was around 115 degrees Fahrenheit, and the humidity was 98 percent. There was no breeze. This was not at all unusual in the weeks that followed.

Our plan was that we would break out our axes and saws, and lop off the tree branches far enough away from the bank so that when they were dragged loose, out of the way, we would have a clear passage just wide enough for the boat to pass through.

But this was Thailand, and our crew were Thais. And the Thai word for work is the same word as for party: *ngarn*.

First Anant's tape player was switched on, and jolly-sounding Thai songs were played. Then they set up our little stove and put on the rice pot. Then they rested while the rice cooked and fists beat time to the music. Then, replete with rice and fish, the lads rested in the shade for an hour or so, and dozed a while. I waited.

The action didn't start with a bang; it was more like a whimper. First one, then the other of our crew (Thomas first, always) roused himself, casually picked up a saw or an ax, then made his way slowly, almost lackadaisically, it seemed, along the riverbank toward the fallen branches. It would take a practiced eye to know that their seeming reluctance to set foot in the river, or to set to hard work, was not caused by laziness. They were conserving their strength in the heat and continually watching for snakes and scorpions and other dangerous creatures.

Soon Nok with his ax, and Anant with his meat cleaver, were bracing themselves against the strong current flowing under the treetop, and lopping away steadily.

At this first tree Thomas and Som, with a large two-ended handsaw, tackled a thick branch, which when it was cut through was too heavy to be pulled clear by hand. We rigged up our chain hoist and lashed it to a nearby tree. I sat in the shade of the tree and sweated and yanked the oily chain, to work the hoist. Anant repurchased the ropes for me. I pulled the branch clear in an hour, slowly and steadily.

When a passage, only seven feet wide, was finally clear between the tree trunk and the riverbank, we hauled our boat through using our long bowline, to avoid the risk of hitting a sunken branch with our propeller.

We didn't know it at the time, but we were through the first of *eighty-four* full-size fallen trees obstructing the River Trang along its length from the sea to its headwaters. In some stretches of the winding river there would be a fallen tree around each and every bend. In some stretches it would take us five days to move as many miles. Some of the fallen trees would be only as hard to shift as that first one; some would be far more difficult. Some would be a few feet in girth, a few as much as twenty feet. Some would take an hour or two, some would take as much as three days of hot, strenuous labor to cut a passage. We had no machine tools. It was to be all, as we sailors say, "Armstrong's Patent System."

I would, at times in the coming weeks, have given my other leg for an electric winch or gasoline-driven saw. They would have made our passage ten thousand times easier. But we could not afford such luxuries, and anyway, the lack of them would prove our point more effectively: how useful and persistent disabled people can be.

I very much doubt, given the same conditions and work, if a crew of urban-bred people could have lasted for very long in *Henry Wagner* in the Kra. The hot, muggy climate would have slammed them down for a start, I'm pretty sure. The food—rice, rice and more rice—might have allowed Oriental city kids to subsist, but Westerners would have suffered badly from the lack of solid substance, except for canned beef and sometimes a scrawny chicken.

There is no boasting about our toughness here, in recounting what we did. For anyone to have gone into an endeavor such as ours knowing how it would be, with urban-bred disabled kids, would have been an action close to "intent to murder." But the only way we could demonstrate our point was by overcoming the "impossible." There was no other way that might be as effective and convincing.

In the coming weeks, at every single fallen tree we were to encounter, at every rocky rapids with tons of rock ahead for us to shift, at every complicated fish trap, every hot, miserable shoal bank, every fierce, narrow channel with the river water rushing through at speed, I would study the skinny arms of our crew, I would study Som's stump, and Anant's half-leg, and Nok's wounded face, and Thomas's small build and squinting peer, and I would suffer the torments of the damned.

But then I would remember others, like Gye, sixteen years old, back in the dust of the temple at Ao Chalong, on his rusty old cart and him with no legs, holding his arms outstretched for alms, forcing his smile through his pain and his shame, and the millions of other amputees and born-awry kids of poor families throughout the world, despised, hidden, derided, and I would rouse myself and know that what we were doing was right, and that that tree, that rock, that shoal, that obstacle, would be overcome by us, on our own, unaided, or we would die in the attempt to overcome it. I knew our lads, and I knew that for them, too, it was now all or nothing.

The faces on our lads, when our boat passed through what had seemed an impassable blockage, were wonders to behold. But we had no time to stand and gloat; by then the afternoon was almost half over. We hoped to reach the place we knew as Ban Meow that evening, before dark.

Off we shoved and on we pressed, clearing here a log jammed in midstream, there a fishnet strung from a line slung across the river, and here again an array of hooked fishing line hauled clear of the stream.

As we approached one of these hooked lines, I stretched out my arm to lift it clear of our helmsman, Nok, who was standing immediately behind me. We were making about five knots at the time.

Anant, using a paddle, had cleared the fishing line over the high bowstem. It scraped and zinged its way aft toward me. I reached out my right arm to pass it over Nok—and got a fishhook deep into the base of my right thumb. The fishing line was trying to drag me aft and off the boat, and the hook was mining into my hand.

Nok had seen what had happened and stopped our engine. Thomas somehow hopped up out of our galley with the meat cleaver and cut the fishing line on one side of the hook. Then Nok drew his knife and cut the line on the other side. Blood streamed from my hand. The hook was about a half-inch long and deeply embedded.

Nok started to dig around the hook with the point of his knife. The pain almost made me jump overboard. "Leave it," I groaned, "until we can get it extracted properly. Get to Ban Meow before dusk!"

So we pushed on upstream into the waning light.

As the sun dropped over jungle scrub and palm trees, and *Henry Wagner* rounded yet another bend, I recognized Ban Meow's landing beach. Suddenly a wave of nausea overwhelmed me. My eyes failed me. Everything blacked out, and I was dimly aware that I was falling into the bottom of our boat.

25

Ramblings

It had taken until almost nightfall that day to reach the place we called Ban Meow. The tiny scattering of wood and bamboo huts had no name that we could know. Thai peasants, anxious to keep away harmful spirits, do not advertise real names. This was a place where Thomas and I had reached the River Trang on our motorbike. We knew it was nothing much: an old wooden ferry punt, that was pulled along by line over the river, a sandy beach, a bluff, overhanging palms, a few small huts, poverty. Meow had kept his word and brought our motorcycle from Phuket, but of course I could not know this.

Ban Meow was the place in which I recovered consciousness and sobriety of mind three days after lapsing into a deep fever. A nursing woman—from Thomas's description a comfortable soul —had been fetched on our motorcycle from a rural clinic some miles away, and had removed the deeply embedded fishhook from my hand, all unknown to me. I am told that she had spoken some English, and that I had conversed with her soberly and lucidly while she had probed and prodded for the hook, but I recalled nothing of the whole episode.

Some rubber-plantation workers had been paid off in the district. There had been drunken singing on the riverbank while I lay comatose on board the boat, but I knew little about it. It was as though I had been dead drunk myself. In the hamlet there had been dancing and laughter, I was told, while my crew had sat quietly around me, and had raised water and later chicken soup to my lips and had tried, vainly, to feed me, and had waited patiently for me to stop perspiring freely and shivering at the same time.

What I did recall clearly I was silent about.

I had watched the ancient abbot from the temple at Sapan Tha Chin somehow board our boat one evening without climbing or clambering, and I had greeted him with cups of Lipton's tea, and heard him tell me, somehow in perfectly good English, that I must not leave with the wrong impression. I must not think that he had said that Buddha was against what I was trying to do. I remember clearly being surprised that neither the hem of his brown robe nor his feet were wet, even though we were anchored midstream and Thomas was away somewhere in the dinghy.

"The Lord Buddha," the abbot told me, "taught us to practice the four *brahmaviharas* [rules]—*metta* [give alms, respect all life, help children], *karuna* [be peaceful[, *mudita* [live a hardworking life], and *uphekha* [be generous]—which mean a Noble Way of Life. He taught us to look upon people more fortunate than ourselves and recognize that they are more fortunate due to their good deeds in the past. We should not envy or resent them, but we should wish that they continue to be fortunate. The Lord Buddha has laid a bridge between the fortunate and the unfortunate, not division or envy."

I replied, "But I am truly not, nor ever have been, envious of anyone. Quite the reverse; I wish that many, many people could live a life as full and as rewarding as mine has been. That's why I am trying to inspire some of the crippled, by our example, so that they, too, can live full lives. We are not emulating anyone; no one has ever done this before. That's why I chose this challenge; I have no desire that we should win over anyone else but ourselves. I want only to counter the derision that is the lot of so many. I am no hero. But I cannot accept that people—and especially young people—are being condemned to live life and never reach their fullest capacity. And if we can persuade more fortunate people to think better of unfortunates, are we not helping both the fortunate, in their thoughts about others, and the unfortunate, in their thoughts about themselves, to live a more Noble Way of Life?"

The abbot had smiled, silently nodded—and faded away; but I had not seen him climb the riverbank.

* * *

Then, on the morning of the third day, I was well again, fresh
and lively, completely recovered as if the fever had never been. I
was pleased that Meow had brought the motorcycle, but indignant
that there had been no rain and the river had dropped two inches,
and that everyone else in the boat was not up and about as the
sun rose above black mountains, seen through blue palms across
the steamy gray swamp to our east.

Our crew rubbed their eyes, but no one mentioned the abbot's
visit, and I knew then that it had been a dream.

Apart from the bout of fever, I was in fairly good shape,
although my lungs suffered in the early-morning humidity, which
was never once less than 99 percent. On our hygrometer it was
often over 100 percent. Even in the early afternoon, when the sun
was at its hottest, the humidity on board never dropped below 90
percent.

I had, ever since Phuket, a small but growing sore on the top
of my one foot. That had been caused by the rubbing of a wet
shoe. Now it was red-raw, and no scab would develop to heal it
in that kind of humidity. All I could hope to do was swallow daily
an antibiotic pill, and try to prevent flies, mosquitoes, and other
insects getting at it.

In the days that followed, as we struggled upstream, and cut
our way through fallen trees and thorny bushes at the river's edge
to ease our way past rocky rapids, we all sustained scratches, some
deep, some mere flea bites. Our Thai boys seemed to have little
problem healing their sores and scratches (and they had enough).
It was as though their constitutions contained some form of natural
antibiotic that we Europeans did not have. Neither Thomas's nor
my cuts would heal in the high humidity. By the time we reached
thirty miles upstream from Ban Meow, Thomas was one mass of
running sores on both arms and legs; I was covered with them all
down my right side, as I worked, hacking and lopping, with a
machete on that side from the bow of our boat, along the banks.

On the first day's run up from Ban Meow, where the river
seriously shallowed, we made twelve miles in twelve hours.

Thomas, alone, had left Ban Meow a few minutes ahead of
Henry Wagner and, courageous and foolhardy, had gone on ahead
in our dinghy to somehow, half-blind as he was, reconnoiter the
river. He had left too quickly, and was unprepared. He left behind
the handheld VHF radio. When he reached about three miles ahead

of us, somehow, probably by hitting an underwater rock, his longtail shaft had snapped clean off at the engine joint. Not knowing if we were still making our way upstream, and not being able to sit and wait for us, in case we were stopped for some reason, he started to paddle downstream. In his circumstances imagination could run riot with concern about possible risks or disaster. The rubber boat might have struck a sharp object and been deflated, leaving him stranded in the jungle in that awful heat. He might somehow have broken one of his legs. These dangers were very real. If we more far-seeing cripples in *Henry Wagner* could not get to him, he could very well die. A snake might bite him. Guerrillas might stumble across him. By the time he did encounter us again, he'd had about enough of paddling like mad to get off obstacles like jagged logs, boulders, or fallen trees, which he couldn't see until he was practically upon them. From then on we made it a rule that never again would the dinghy go out of sight of *Henry Wagner*.

As Thomas wearily came alongside *Henry Wagner*, we tied up to the bank. The question now was whether we should all retreat down to Ban Meow and wait for the dinghy engine to be fixed, or whether we should not. I decided we should not. I was never going to retreat on this river, I swore to myself, except in a coffin. Thomas had reported that the way ahead lay clear for at least four miles. He and Som went downstream to the rough track at Ban Meow, while Anant, Nok, and I pressed on ahead slowly. In the day it would take them to get the engine fixed we moved on upstream as far as the spot where Thomas's longtail had snapped. There we awaited their return upstream.

As *Henry Wagner*, jerking with the engine vibrations, moved steadily in a generally northerly direction, so the banks of the river rose higher and higher. It was as though we were in a dark, deep trench, with strange, primeval-looking tropical plants crowding the banks, and sudden rustles, as though large creatures were hurrying through the undergrowth. Soon the banks were twenty feet and more high, and this would be the case all the way up the river, for more than 90 miles.

Now and then there were huts or small wooden houses near the river, and then we would see people, sometimes women in sarongs who washed clothes or small children in the shallow pools at the river's edge. Very rarely was there no one somewhere on the banks: a buffalo-herder, or boys fishing, or people merely idling away the hot afternoons in the shade of a tree. Then we would envy them, for they had a breeze, however slight, that we in our narrow, hot, humid trench could never feel.

All the way upstream on the River Trang, snakes and lizards were plentiful. In the mornings and evenings startled birds, as they wheeled, almost darkened the patches of sky between the over-hanging trees above us.

Sometimes youngsters, hearing the noise of our engine from afar, would flock down to the riverbanks and stand and watch us, all smiling at the music playing on Anant's cheap tape machine. Thomas and I had brought along some of our old classical tapes from *Outward Leg*, but these sent our Thai crew either to sleep or off the boat. Mostly Anant played Thai pop music, and to this day, when I hear it played at some roadside coffee shop, I see him, in my mind's eye, his crutch laid aside, his stump drawn up across his lap, half-lying in the hot, damp bilges of *Henry Wagner*, pump-ing, pumping his way, singing softly to the music, all the way across the Kra.

26

Rapids

Som was Thomas's eyes ashore. With him along, communication was easier, too. They returned to the boat the following morning. The river twisted and turned back on itself so much that we could hear the sound of their longtail engine almost two hours before we sighted them. The shaft had been repaired and reinforced with extra welding where it joined the engine. The Chinese who had sold us the longtail had generously refused to accept any money for the repair. With some of that money, Thomas and Som had bought another live chicken. It turned out to be a tough old cock, but we would need every scrap of protein in its stringy body.

Two miles further upstream we came to a bridge with one solitary house by it. We stopped for the crew to stretch their legs and to look around to see if there might be a coffee shop nearby where we could obtain more fresh supplies. They found one about quarter of a mile along the narrow road.

Our boat lay in the shade of a big tree, and I was resting. Suddenly there was a bang, and as I opened my eyes, I saw that a policeman, fully uniformed, had jumped on board, his pistol clattering at his side. He looked as though he, too, had just woken up. Very unusually for a Thai, he was frowning. I had my leg off. My raw stump was exposed.

"*Bye nye?* Where are you going?" he demanded brusquely. Smiling is not in the policeman's role.

Even as he challenged me, Thomas and the crew appeared

on the riverbank. I was still gathering my wits. "Where are you going with this boat?" he repeated. He looked confused, as though he was in shock.

In my doze I'd forgotten I was in the East. I must have been dreaming I was back at sea. I thought, "What a bloody stupid question; where's he think we're going, stuck between two high banks, in a river this narrow, pointing our bows upstream?" I pointed at the bridge and along the road. "Coffee shop," I told him. (It's the same word in Thai.)

The policeman stood staring at me, wide-eyed, for a full minute. I smiled at him. There was a silence you could cut with a knife. Then, seeing the irony of my silent reply, he broke out laughing, until his face was as red as my foot, and all our crew joined with him, and he left in the best of moods, shaking his head at the crazy, crippled old *farang* in the boat. But he did promise that he would phone the police in Huay Yot town (about twelve miles back from the river) that we were heading upstream.

A mile beyond that bridge, although the policeman hadn't thought to mention them to us, we came to our first rocky rapids. There was a flat ledge of limestone right across the river, about twenty yards long, over which the water, six inches or so deep, rushed. The limestone was comparatively soft, for rock. That meant that we could, using a long crowbar and a sledgehammer, break off lumps of it, as much as two or three pounds at a time. In that way, working steadily for ten hours a day, for two days, we gouged out of the rock ledge a rut about six inches deep and five feet or so wide, just enough for the boat, unloaded, to be hauled through by hand. The whole time we watched warily for water snakes.

Then, we unloaded the boat of all movable gear—about a quarter of a ton of it. This was all piled onto the dinghy, except for the fuel cans, which were towed astern of the boat. Then the dinghy was dragged over the rock ledge, and anchored.

It was *Henry Wagner*'s turn next. Unloaded, she drew about two inches less water. She was half-dragged, half-floated along the channel we had carved in the ledge, until she floated freely upstream of it. After that, we reloaded all the gear onto our main boat from the dinghy.

That was the first of *thirty-eight* portages over rapids between the mouth of the River Trang and its headwaters.

I know that you will forgive me for reminding you of the

high temperatures and humidity, and that, between us five, two were small boys, three of our limbs were missing, one could not speak, one could hardly see six feet ahead of him, one of us was over sixty, and two of us were under fifteen.

At the end of each awful day breaking stone on the rapids, we retired downstream a few yards to moor the boat. It was difficult for intruders, ill-intentioned or not, to approach us there from the riverbank. After we had eaten a simple rice and canned-fish meal, you may depend on it, we slept like dead men, even though the high-pitched noise of a million crickets in the long grass by the boat was almost deafening.

Our boys were cheered by our having broken through the rock shelf. You would have thought they were on the shores of the Gulf of Thailand already. I said nothing, there was no point in discouraging them after all their hard labor, but I reminded Thomas that, after a week's hard going from Kantang (apart from my three fever days) we were still only eighteen miles or so from the Andaman Sea. There was still about another hundred miles as the crow flies to the Gulf of Thailand. We could count on 180 miles ahead, minimum. At the rate we were moving, it might take us another ninety days to get across the Kra.

"Can you take that?" asked Thomas, looking me in the eye.

"I've got to, haven't I? Besides, what else would I do? Go and do what old sailors are supposed to do? Sit in a bar or on a park bench, remember the past, be a silly old bore to everyone younger, and when they avoid me, feel sorry for myself?" I leaned down and wrapped my foot rag over my instep. Its colors were like those of a temple roof, all green and scarlet and glowing gold. It was oozing pus. "Hell, I can do that here!"

"You should let me take you into Trang and get your foot fixed, Tristan," said Thomas.

In my mind's eye I saw thousands and millions of kids, all over the world, mostly on crutches. They couldn't afford wheelchairs or plastic legs. They'd never even seen the outside of a rehabilitation clinic, let alone the inside. No one had ever told them that they had it in them to move the world, if they only shifted for themselves. What they needed was fire in the gut, not merely money and three square meals a day. Given the fire, the money and the food would come to them, all right.

They were always with me, those kids, even though I had seen only a few hundred of them, and met even fewer. They had been with me for four-and-a-half years, ever since I had left my New York hospital under a cloud for having organized a wheelchair race around the ward corridors. I had sworn to them then, the ones who were there, white, brown, and black, that I would shift opinion about them or that I would die in the attempt. There could be no going back on that for me. If I did not keep my word on that, I would be, to myself, as a dead man anyway.

It was all too involved to tell Thomas. In any case he knew most of the tale already. "No way," I told him. "If I do take off for treatment in Trang, the people there will probably see money lying in bed. They'll try to keep me in their hospital for days, if not weeks. Our lads will lose heart. They're already homesick. We must get to the divide. Besides, I can't stand hospitals! We must get to the Thung Song area. Then we'll see. Then they'll know that there's a way forward and that it's not all rapids and fallen trees and fish traps. If we can get to the divide all right, they might even imagine we can succeed without them, and be eager to remain with us. If I don't stay with them, they'll be off. They'll flee the scene, and quite right, too. So would I if I were in their place. I can make allowances for them, God knows, but I can't make them for myself. No! I'll stay with the boat until we're at the divide, even if my bloody foot falls off!"

It was sometimes very strange to be on a primeval river, and to be suddenly reminded that we were living in the twentieth century. Most of the time, when our engines were stopped (which was more often than not), there were few sounds but those of our axes chopping, or our saws grating, or our heavy breathing in the hot, damp air. Then there would be nearby jungle or plantation noises: the whisper of a tantalizing breeze ruffling the leaves of trees far above our heads, the rippling of water as it babbled over huge boulders waiting for us to shift them. Then would come, in the less-hot hours, the chirrups and howlings of birds or the mocking of monkeys, or the chirping of crickets, or even the sound of mysterious human voices from somewhere behind a thicket of thorns. Sometimes we could come close to a track, and we might hear the strange noise of a motorcycle popping away. Then we would feel like spies from a time-travel machine. On a half-dozen occasions we came to road bridges, and I would gaze in amazement as a car or truck trundled over it, and I would find myself staring at the vehicle as though it had landed from Mars.

A curious thing was that although word of our coming flashed, somehow, ahead of us upstream, and the local inhabitants crowded onto each bridge to see us pass under, and motorcyclists and even buses and trucks stopped for people to watch us, never once did I see a car stop on a bridge. Their drivers' errands, it seemed, were too vital for them to even notice an old wooden boat crawling inch by inch up a narrow, insignificant stream so far below them. I first noticed this distinction between car drivers (or rather, people affected by cars), and others was at the bridge at Sapan Wang Hin (Bridge of Rocks) at Ban Na Non.

That bridge was crowded with people, for it was late afternoon, and marginally cooler, when we appeared round a bend of the river. Even from afar, even without being able to distinguish the faces lined up above the bridge rail, there seemed to be an air of excitement, anticipation, about them. About fifty yards below the bridge a fallen tree, right across the channel, had blocked our passage. It had not been a very girthy tree, and in an hour's pulling and hauling with our chain hoist and a few minutes of lopping of branches, we soon had it shifted far enough out of the way to be able to pass. This time our boys worked like Trojans, with few stops for cooling off in the river. They were under observation from the bridge, and if there's anything any boy likes more than showing off before his peers, I've yet to come across it. At Sapan Wang Hin I was so impressed and pleased with their performance that I wished we could have an audience of boys and girls wherever we might have an obstacle.

Then, as we cleared the tree and hauled our boat partly over a shallow sandbank, to deep water directly below the bridge, I saw why there had been an air of anticipation, even of excitement, about the people on the bridge. All the way across the river, on the upstream side of the bridge supports, was a piled-up mass of trees and branches, reeds, rubbish, part of a wooden house that had been swept downstream in some previous flood, and even, washed up on the mudbank by the shore, half the hull of an ancient rice barge. That old hulk at Sapan Wang Hin was the only indication I saw above the temple at Sapan Tha Chin that this part of the river had once been used for navigation.

As we waited for our tea water to boil (we boiled every bit of river water we consumed), and as the Thais on the bridge above us smiled silently at our boys, Thomas gazed at me from his steering perch on our stern. He was nut brown, with filthy, bloody bits of rag tied around his elbows and knees. The only thing that distinguished him from the Thais was his fairish hair and bird beak of a Bavarian nose.

His nose, I knew, was the subject of much favorable comment by Thais. So was my own honker, come to that, for Thais admire big noses. They told me they thought it was a sign of good breeding, and very handsome. They might have been dissembling, but I don't think so. We knew for a fact that many desperately poor Thais sold one or two of their ribs, which, when extracted, were shaped by cosmetic surgeons in Bangkok into nose bones to be inserted into the faces of richer people of the cities.

It was five o'clock. The sun would swiftly disappear in an hour, then we would be in complete darkness.

"We'll look over the obstacles before dark," I told Thomas. "We'll sleep better if we know exactly what is before us."

But we didn't. At any rate I didn't, not after what we found.

27

The Bridge at Ban Na Non

In the telling of how we passed the bridge at Ban Na Non, I shall be as nontechnical and brief as the tale allows me to be. Technically all that was involved was a river, about eighty feet wide between high banks, a longtail boat, weighing about a ton and a quarter unloaded, a quarter-ton of cargo, a bridge about sixty feet high, against which was piled, to a height of about three feet above the river level, around *five hundred tons* of old lumber and debris.

To move our boat past that obstacle, we had a one-ton chain hoist, four hundred feet of nylon line, one hundred feet of one-inch steel chain, three anchors, there anchors, three 3-limbed people, one a small boy, and two 4-limbed people, one half-blind and one a speechless half-grown youth.

The debris piled up against the bridge at Ban Na Non almost completely blocked the river, except for little trickles of water gushing through the mess. It was like a dam. Its base was locked in place by a huge tree trunk, half-buried in the sandy bottom. Behind it, upstream, the water level was six inches higher than downstream.

Our task was to clear a way for our boat to pass through or over the mountain of debris. By the time we had cleared away the top layer of jetsam, and uncovered the half-sunken tree, it was clear to me that there were only two ways for our boat to pass. One would be to dynamite the junk, and the sunken tree with it, out of the way. But that, even if we had dynamite (which we hadn't) would have endangered the bridge structure. The only other way was to get our boat over the junk heap. There we had a saving grace—the bridge. If we could lift and hang our boat from the bridge, we would be able to swing her through, suspended inches over the biggest junk, and then, one bonus on top of another, we would have the boat in deeper water for at least a few miles.

In theory it sounded good and fairly easy. As I told the lads what we were about to do, it all sounded cool and reasonable; we had a one-ton hoisting winch, and enough lines to lift the boat. But in practice, as we first unloaded our boat onto a dry sandbank, then got the winch up onto the bridge girders, twenty feet above our heads, and then sent one-armed Som up to hang on by his toes and wind its chain, and levered our boat up so we could get lifting ropes around her hull, it was a different matter, of heat, sweat, flies, more sweat, and more heat.

We had to secure two holding strops for the winch on the bridge, so that when the time came (when we ran out of chain and unwound it), we could shift the winch from one strop to the other. Each time the hoist chain reached the end of its working length, we had to secure the boat up tight to the bridge girders, using our mooring lines to take her weight, then wedge her up securely using old tree branches and such, from the heap. Then the hoist chain was unwound agonizingly slowly by Som, sweating away, and then the whole process would start all over again. It took about an hour to lift our boat three inches, and we had to lift her up almost two feet. It was almost a full day's work to get our boat's keel above the junk. Then we worked into the night, by a light provided by our little generator, to swing the boat forward ten feet or so, until she was lying, bows down, on top and athwart the sunken tree trunk, ready to be slid down into the water. That we managed to do by midnight, and by 3:00 A.M. we had all our gear stowed away on board, and collapsed into well-earned sleep, with the boat floating in a good two feet of water behind the "dam." It was the first time in days that we'd had more than two or three inches of water under our keel.

That we had won our greatest victory so far there was no doubt. There was even less doubt that we had achieved what surely most expert observers, engineers, doctors, seamen, anyone with any knowledge of effort and weights, angles, and strain, must have surely considered, looking at our crew, to be well-nigh impossible.

But there's more to life than technicalities. We had also uncovered further another "fly in the ointment." To say that the people on that bridge were friendly and hospitable, polite and helpful, would be easy! Truly I would ten thousand times rather write that. I am severely tempted to write that. But I won't, because it is not true.

Many people have never even considered their attitudes to others less physically fortunate than themselves. Practically every single disabled person, old or young, male or female, in this world will tell you that they encounter evidence of this fact on just about every occasion that they are among able-bodied strangers. Some —in the poor countries almost all—are so inured to lack of consideration, to disdain, to derision, that they accept them as facts of life, like their own breathing or sleeping. They are as natural to them as the mountains, the sea, or the deserts where they live. They are as natural to them as pain, or heartbreak, or death itself.

In telling you about the attitudes of the people at Ban Na Non, and the majority of the people in the parts of the Kra that we witnessed, I am not complaining, I'm accusing. I'm accusing parents and schools and temples and religions and anyone who purveys knowledge of failing to instill into those peasants when they were children the idea of compassion, the idea that other people are not merely objects for our curious observation; the idea that we are each responsible for the other, for good or ill, that "No man is an island, entire of itself," that we are part of all that we have seen, and above all, the idea that it works both ways.

It would be nonsense to think that because I tell you the truth of the attitudes toward us of many Thais that we encountered that I do not like or respect the Thais, or think they are in any way more callous or inferior to the people of any other nation.

When one whole limb and half your guts are missing, there is less room left to harbor illusion. I have no doubt that many, many genuinely good people give of their time and effort unstintingly to help their less fortunate fellow creatures. But these are not the people I am trying to reach with this tale of our crossing of the Kra. I am after much more slippery fish—those who have hardly ever thought about their attitudes to their fellow beings. I would rather just one of these, reading this account, find some disabled person and really, for the first time, without thought of any reward, moral, spiritual or material, *help him*. I don't mean merely throw money at him, I mean *help* him. Go out and spend *time* with him. Find out his particular difficulties. Show him how things might be done that the disabled never thought possible. Dive into the mud, headfirst! That's the only way that miracles can happen. Shout it from the rooftops!

Those were my aims in the Kra, and those are—must be— my aims in the telling of this tale. I will use any means I can to change attitudes toward the disabled. And if I must shame people into changing, by telling them the truth, then so be it, I'll do that, too, for *change there must be!*

28

Cap of Shame

Some rose-bespectacled souls might say that those Thais on that bridge might not have been looking upon us as disabled people at all, but rather as foreigners and strangers doing a strange, hardly understandable thing. They might ask: "How could those peasants understand the ramifications of what you were about? How could those peasants know that the world, from Vancouver to Victoria, would one day know about them?" But that is no excuse. Those people were not blind; between us we had two legs and an arm missing, and half a lower face, and they knew it, and they laughed at us and poked fun at us, and that's what mattered.

They had not been verbally discouraging in the least. They had smiled the while, throughout our whole performance. Like any good audience, they had laughed on cue. Each time little Anant, trying to stumble over a log while balanced on his crutch, had fallen into the river or onto a hard rock, and when I, with my false leg collapsed under me, ended up jammed between two logs, halfdrowned and cursing bitterly, they had roared with rippling laughter. They had found Nok's attempts to speak things of uproarious mirth. They had waited, silently, to hear him try to call out something to me or Thomas or Som. Then they had, to a man and woman, almost split their sides with loud laughter or sputtered girlish giggles. Thomas's nearsighted fumblings they found hilarious. Som had got off scot-free. With his stump he'd been hanging on while he worked the hoist chain below them, out of sight.

Both Anant and Nok, inured long since to derision, and being in a strange place, among people of a different religion, had grinned back apologetically at the peasants, while I had silently and grimly attacked the job of lifting the boat over the obstacles as though those rocks and tree trunks and balks of rotted timber and stinking masses of debris represented the gross, unthinking, knee-jerk inhumanity in those people's laughter.

I remembered thinking to myself, as I caught a blinding glimpse of their silhouettes against the searing sun on the bridge high above, that in a month's or a year's time they'd still be on that bloody bridge, smiling or not, while we, God willing, would be back at large, in the God-given open sea, as free as birds, in our own world.

But when our boat had, at last, with tremendous heaves and groans, been shoved into deep water beyond the bridge, the few onlookers remaining had been deathly silent. Then, and only then, we knew that we had won. Then, and only then, I thought about forgiveness, and prayed that I might find it in me.

For your sakes, I will try not, after the bridge of Ban Na Non, to mention those matters of derision, indifference, or disdain again, but they should be always borne in mind. It could not add to our bitterness; a cripple's cup is already full, but by God it added to our pride, to have done it all ourselves, and in that way those people may have unwittingly done us great favors.

The whole day long, as we worked and sweated under the bridge at Ban Na Non, a desultory badinage went on between our crew and the small crowd of merry people on the bridge. I remarked to Thomas that though we'd been given plenty of advice, not a soul had offered any physical help.

"We must look poor, eh?" he suggested.

I did not reply. It was better to be silent at the thought that if we had offered them money, they certainly would have helped us. We both knew that was true, but we also both knew we were poor. After buying the longtail engine to replace the outboard motor, we had no more than $360. That I had to conserve in case of a sudden emergency. If one of our lads needed medical treatment, we had to have a reserve to pay for it. If heavy rains fell, we would need every penny we had to muster help to drag the boat up a high bank and out of harm's way. There was no time in this race against the monsoon to get to a safe place, to go to Phuket to see if money had arrived from the West. Now we saw how Mr. Patping's smiling intransigence at the Thai frontier had put a spanner in the works. Now we saw how the "chaos principle" operates.

In victory we can afford to be magnanimous. As I collapsed to sleep that early morning, I thought more kindly of our audience; that perhaps after all they didn't feel we needed any assistance because we looked, in their eyes, strong and competent, and knowledgeable about what we were doing.

That night, or early morning, as I changed my bloody, filthy foot bandage, and squeezed more pus out of the sore on my instep, I winced and told myself that it was perhaps as well that none of the locals had tried to help. They were simple peasants, more used to the rice paddies and their hoes than to chain hoists and calculating centers of gravity. They had never seen our two little lads at their normal work on the sea. The skill and knowledge and pure love of the sea that was contained in those two small bodies would be beyond their comprehension.

As I fell into slumber, I thought of the hard lives those peasants lived, of the eternal heat and humidity, the droughts and the floods, of the women's ceaseless toil in the rice fields, of their feudallike systems of allegiance, of their family feuds over centuries, of their incessant guard, at every turn, against cheating, of their humility at the plantation store, of their lack of any easy comfort, and their beliefs in karma and spirits, of the underlying, carefully hidden, violence of their natures, of their immense self-control and the strain of it, and I understood and forgave them for everything except for their making me angry. That I didn't need to forgive, for my anger had fueled my determination to beat that bloody bridge blockage.

When I heard their laughter, which seemed so mocking, I would have dismantled their damned bridge bit by bit, rivet by rivet, brick by brick, if need be, and handed the pieces to them, one by one, just to show them what stout seamen's hearts with a world to gain might do.

Then I remembered: There was good, deep water ahead of

us, and only another thirty miles or so, as the crow flies, to the watershed of the Kra.

I was aware, as sleep overtook me, that there could now be no going back. It had not rained now for a week. On the lower side of the bridge we'd had hardly any water under our keel. In two days' time there would not be enough water below the bridge to float our boat. Now we were committed. We could not go back because of the lack of water in the river lower down; we could hardly go sideways because of the continuous high banks on both sides of the river. We could go only forward, for better or for worse.

If we became irretrievably stuck higher upstream, I would have to send our lads and Thomas back to our shelter in Phuket. If there was no more rain, our boat would sit in the stinking heat of the dry River Trang and rot. I could not abandon her, or her cargo of dreams. If she and her dreams were to die, I would die with them. Without them there would be no reason for me to live, for I would have broken my word with myself, and for that there could be no forgiveness, and forgiveness is everything.

29

Hard Going

During the night Meow somehow found us. On our motorbike he had wandered around for miles the previous day searching for us. Some policemen on the highway close by had stopped and questioned him. Meow had told them about the boat, and the policemen, he said, first said they disbelieved him, then had directed him to Ban Tha Pradhu, much further north on the river and about twenty miles away by road. If those patrolmen knew about the blockage under the bridge at Ban Na Non, they must have been teasing Meow, and for some reason, or perhaps for none, purposely sent him astray. Very little that was at all unusual happened in rural South Thailand that did not reach the ears of the police. Everywhere on the Kra rivers, everyone we encountered who lived anywhere within miles of the river had known about our approach days before we eventually arrived. It was highly improbable that those policemen did not know we were at Ban Na Non. As it was, Meow had slept rough, with the motorbike locking strop around his leg, under the bridge at Ban Tha Pradhu, in case we should turn up there.

We were so pleased to see Meow that we did not stop to concern ourselves about why he had taken so long to find us. Now that our boat was in deeper water, we could joyfully load the bike on board. Now, in the long, winding stretches between bridges, we were no longer so cut off from facilities or help should we be desperate enough to call for it. Now we could get to some shop, too far to walk to, and replenish our supplies of fresh food. Without its sidecar I couldn't ride it alone, of course, but that was not important. I was far too busy watching our boat and our boys to want to go far ashore. The motorbike was a cumbrous object to have sitting in one of the two gangways in the boat, and made the trip from forward to aft an obstacle course, but that was a small price to pay for the mobility it gave us ashore.

While the motorbike was on board, Meow could travel with us, and help us. But on the few miles up from Ban Na Non, where there was enough water for us to carry the bike, we needed Meow's help only when we came to a couple of bamboo bridges across the river. These we part dismantled, enough for the boat to pass, then rebuilt in after us.

On this stretch of twenty miles or so the river twisted and turned every which way, and from my compass we seemed to be going south and west as much as north or east. But it was a fairly easy stretch. There were a few fallen trees in the river, but they were no more than ten feet in diameter, and comparatively easy to shift using the chain hoist or our saws.

Meow was a real nature boy. He seemed to be part of the terrain. On one occasion, when he was returning to our boat from fixing a bridge behind us, I saw him hesitate, and, looking down at the ground, appear to be talking to himself. Anant, arriving back at the boat ahead of Meow, told me that Meow was talking to a snake, telling it not to hurt him, and to go away. Then, as I watched, I saw that it was true: a blue-gray snake, about five feet long, slithered down the bank, and took off downstream along the shallows. Meow had an affinity with birds and animals. Wherever he went, they seemed to flock toward him, a sort of Oriental Saint Francis.

That evening the sky was overcast with thick gray clouds. I decided to moor our boat under a wide-spreading tree in case of rain. With our leaky roof it would keep us reasonably dry. But it didn't rain. We thought it did, for all night long there was a steady plop-plop on the roof. As I dropped off to sleep, I dreamed joyfully of a raised river level, no matter how slight, the next day. But in the morning we found that our whole boat was covered in bird droppings, inches thick, which, when the sun rose high, stank to high heaven, so that we hurried, even in the noon heat, to scrape them off. In the jungle as in life, nothing comes free.

We could already see, from the top of the riverbank, the five hundred-foot limestone outcrop that marked Ban Tha Pradhu. It stuck out of the mists where the flat plain met the mountains, like a raised thumb. Again, it was like something out of a Chinese scroll picture. It seemed to be no more than a couple of miles away. In fact, it must have been, by the bends and turns of the river, well over ten miles, for we reached the base of it, in shallowing water, and after two portages over gravel banks, in the late afternoon of June 28.

The limestone outcrop of Ban Tha Pradhu now loomed over us like a cliff. It rose straight up out of the riverbed. At the foot of the thumb lay a flat, gravelly, rocky plain, about as wide as a football field, and through that, rushing round the corner of the thumb in a narrow, shallow channel, with rocky outcrops everywhere, was our River Trang.

I have explained before the problem of running a longtail engine at low speed: For the cooling system to be effective the boat must be traveling forward at more than three knots, otherwise the engine overheats. At low speeds someone other than the helmsman had to pour water from a bucket directly into the engine cooling-water intake. With two men on the tiny stern, this made for very awkward steering, and demanded all the skill and agility that the helmsman and the cooling had. One false move, one sudden push to one side, and the cooling man might go over the side, and risk being chewed up by our huge, thrashing propeller.

The Mae Nam Trang was no place for faint hearts. At Ban Tha Pradhu Nok was steering. He was our most agile body. Meow was the cooling man. Thomas, our strongest adult, with Anant as helper, was forward with a pole shoving us off rocks. Som brought up the rear in our dinghy. I couldn't let him go ahead in case he got caught between two rocks and we, at full speed, collided with him. Even though there were only three inches of water under the keel, I chose for us to head at full speed for the narrow channel and round the bend, trusting Nok to dodge the rocks as we did so.

We belted for the channel, turned this way and that by a hundred jagged limestone rocks, rounded a gradual bend, and sighted, ahead of us, a bridge. The way through the bridge seemed clear. Nok kept up speed, but immediately on the upstream side of the bridge the river made a sudden right-angle turn. We whizzed around the turn, straight into the white water rushing through a jumble of rocky rapids.

Greathearted Nok held his speed, rammed the boat around five or six rocks, and then a faster current hit our boat and she was caught, flung sideways, and jammed right across the channel between two huge limestone outcrops.

In seconds we were all, except me, out of the boat, and somehow, God only knows how, we had two anchors out from the bow, the engine swung inboard, and the lads were pushing and heaving the bow for all they were worth, while I, inside the boat, heaved mightily on both anchor lines. In that way we got her headed upstream again.

Nok, shaken but seamanlike, restarted the engine, and at full speed we flung ourselves again at the current, gathered up our anchors like madmen, and at last, after another fifty yards or so, we were in calmer water. There was no damage except a couple of nicks on the propeller where it had hit one of the rocks.

We headed upstream, in the shadow of the last mountain on the central spur of the Kra range, for about an hour, before we hit a submerged tree at full speed. With a terrible, jarring shock, our boat's hull was shoved about ten feet onto the tree. It took us hours to get her off again, by levering her with long, heavy branches we cut from nearby jetsam, then pulling her the rest of the way across.

In the rest of that day we covered about another ten miles, all the way to Sapan Bang Di (Bridge of the Good Village). The river was one sharp bend after another. In that ten miles it must have made a hundred right-angle bends. It was like following a maze. Nowhere was there not a fallen tree in sight, either lying across the river or along it. Almost every few feet there were great balks of timber sticking out of the sandy river. There were lines of stakes set upright, close apart, right across the river for fishing. At each bend there was either a fish trap or a bamboo footbridge. Each one we carefully dismantled and rebuilt after we had passed through. In many places the actual watercourse was narrow, and the rest of the riverbed high and dry. In my service days in the navy I had seen troop-training obstacle courses that had looked, compared to the riverbed of the Trang, like golfing greens. And all the while it was hotter than hell and stank like a midden.

I can honestly say that if I had been on that riverbank, visiting from afar, and anyone had told me that a sea boat, no matter how shallow her draft, could get along some of those stretches of river, I would have wondered at his sanity.

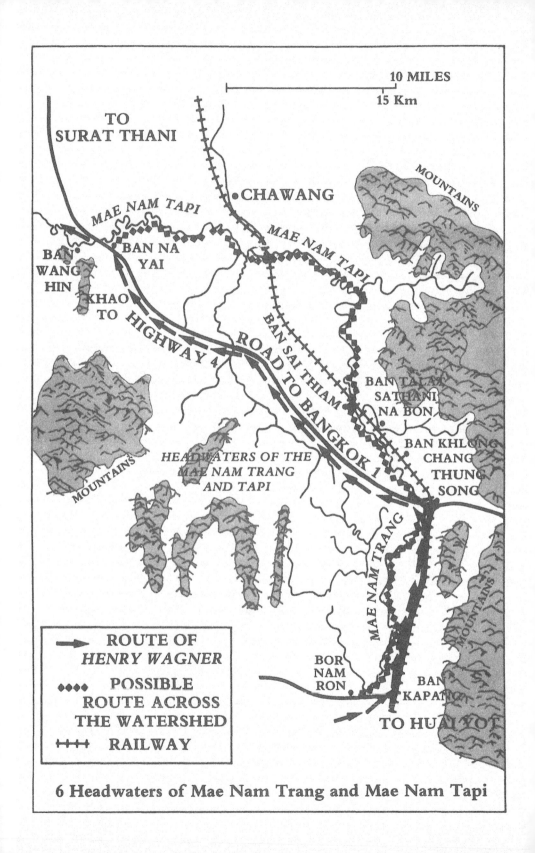

6 Headwaters of Mae Nam Trang and Mae Nam Tapi

30

First Drumbeat

At Sapan Bang Di it was quite obvious that somehow word was out about our coming. About one hundred people lined the bridge to watch our passing. A little upstream of the bridge, stakes had been driven into the riverbed to hold back debris from piling against the bridge itself as it had done at Ban Na Non. The stakes were about four feet apart, and *Henry Wagner*, at water level, is about five feet wide.

In a current as swift as that under the bridge at Bang Di, there was no time to consult anyone, not even myself. I signaled to Thomas to head straight between two stakes in the deepest part of the stream. *That'll clean the bloody barnacles off!* The crowd above leaned over the bridge rail to watch us, probably thinking we were crazy. They didn't know sea boats, of course, or seamen. Straight at the stakes we roared. There was a slight shudder, a scrape, a slight slowing, and then we were through, and our way was clear to the next bridge, barring a few minor obstacles.

The next bridge was only a couple of miles upstream, at Sapan Ban Duan Poon, where we triumphantly tied up for the night. That day we had covered fifty-five miles. That day we had overcome fifteen fallen trees, three rapids, twenty-two bamboo bridges, and thirty-eight fish traps. That day our boys had all become men.

For the second time the police visited us. They were quiet and polite, more curious than anything else. They told us they had heard over the telephone from the Huay Yot police that we were on our way, and that their officer had told them to drop by, and see if we were all right.

Through Som, I thanked the policemen and told them we were fine. They advised us to be careful further upstream. There were, they said, still a few remnants of guerrilla bands roaming around. The Thai Army had been informed of our course, and their patrols, they said, would keep an eye on us, and help us, and get the word around that we were on our way.

When the police left our boat, I told Nok and Anant to come out of hiding. They were terrified of policemen. They had no identity cards. They were under sixteen and away from home (in Thailand, officially "illegal") No one had ever bothered to register a couple of crippled kids. Why should they? They would never need to go anywhere. Officially they did not exist. They were, in everyone's eyes but ours, *nonpersons*.

I made up my mind to change that, and to change it soon. And here at the gateway to the watershed valley of the Kra, further upstream than any seacraft on record had ever reached before, was the place to start.

Now it was the time to bring public relations into action and to use it, as a tool, just as surely as we were using the saws and axes and sledges and levers and the chain hoist—and to the same purpose: to help shift us and our boat to the other side of the Kra.

On the way upstream it had struck me how very remarkable our endeavor was. It was picturesque, there was no doubt, and it was real. It was surely worth some attention from the press or television companies in Thailand? Any kind of public exposure would help our aim: to inspire the disabled to shift for themselves. But tactically, getting the media involved might gently coerce local officials into shifting themselves to help us if we needed it. Many officials the world over loved to preen themselves in front of cameras. It helped them, they probably thought, to justify their otherwise leechlike existences. If they thought they were under public scrutiny, or in the limelight, some of them even tried to become human.

Human nature was not so different, the world over. Even in some remote parts of this world where television had reached, like the Kra, for many people what they saw on TV, whatever it was, was becoming the *reality*. This could be looked on, given the quality of much on TV, as tragic, but nevertheless it was true. The people astern of us, further downstream, until now had not known of our coming. To them we were not reality because they *had not seen us on TV*. There was only one way to change that. We would get the TV to come to us. Then, when we had been on screen in all the coffee shops in Thailand, people would know that we really did exist, and perhaps show a mite more interest. Then our lads would be famous.

But, immodest as ever a Welshman was, I warned them: "If fame had brought me as much money as it has would-be friends, by now I'd be a millionaire!"

The images of us and our boat would be converted into electronic impulses, sent through the ether by some miraculous means, and displayed in living rooms and verandahs. To many viewers it wouldn't matter a jot what we said on TV, or what we would be seen to be doing, or where we were, or how we got there. All that would matter would be that we had *Been On TV*. Having *Been On TV* would put us, in their minds, along with the good, the beautiful, the clever, the powerful, the fit, and the strong. And that's not a bad place to be in anybody's book.

I would play on the average Thai's well-hidden feelings about many *farang* visitors in their country, the many *farangs* who flew in to seek only their own self-gratification. The ones who never bothered to even try to look beneath the gilded surface of things and see the Thais and Thailand as they really are. The ones that the average Thai called *kee-nok*. We would demonstrate that there were *farangs* who did care about a couple or three other things. We would show them three of their own discards, salvaged, aware, renewed, proud of themselves and their actions, and in effect we would silently say, *If we can do this, why cannot you?* We'd stir 'em up. We'd make 'em think!

Now, as we approached the middle of the Kra, the Great Divide, was the time to tell as many media people in Thailand as I could where we were, what we were up to, and where we were heading. Now was "bandwagon" time—not from a studio, but from the gate of hell itself.

It must have been a strange sight for the watchers on the bridge at Bang Di: a sea boat drawn up to the riverbank below the bridge, crewed by one-armed and one-legged youngsters, and a squinting young *farang* almost covered with bloody rags—and then to see an old farang, his one leg glowing with wounds and sores, sitting on deck punching away at a portable computer, its green screen glowing in the evening. And then to see a printing machine, powered by the boat's electric generator, churning out letter after letter. They couldn't know that the old man was telling Bangkok to come to the Kra at Thung Song and see a sight they'd never seen before. They couldn't hear, as he could, the sound of the first drumbeats of a roll that still reverberates around the world: that we pray will never stop, that we beg you to *never let stop*.

Early the next morning we all hefted our motorbike up the steep bank, and Thomas took off, with Meow on the pillion, for the post office at Huay Yot. With him he took letters for, among fifty others, the *Bangkok Post*, the British Broadcasting Corporation, the *Guardian*, Reuters, *High Class* magazine, and two TV stations.

I watched him go, past an old wooden Chinese house with moss drooping from its roof. He stopped on the far side of the bridge for a herd of water buffalo to shuffle past, then he was off. We were in media land once more.

Painfully, with Nok's help, I lowered myself down the bank, and rolled over *Henry Wagner*'s gunwale. I landed on my mattress and stared at my foot. It was swollen to almost twice its normal thickness. Now the swelling was not only scarlet and gold, but emerald green and Tyrian purple, too. It burned like fire, so I knew gangrene had not yet set in. But if that leg was to be saved, we would have to reach the area of the divide and Thung Song within a few days. Either that or I would have to leave the boat to get attention.

I knew that if I did that, our Thais would think an evil spirit had reached into me and made me lose face; they would lose heart and flee the scene. If that happened, Atlantis would have met with defeat.

Better, even at the cost of this burning fire in my only foot, to wait until either I got off our boat at the divide, or until I collapsed. If I collapsed, the medico would have to come to me. That would not frighten off the Thais; by not retreating, I would not lose face. I dared not leave the boat, not even for an hour. I was a prisoner of my own foolish dreams. I had almost committed the cardinal sin of any venturer: *I had almost let my dream become my master. . . .*

31

Some Visitors

My foot now pained me so badly, and heat, humidity, and age had slowed me down so much, that I could no longer jot down lucid notes. So here are some extracts from Thomas Ettenhuber's diary, with my own comments, added later, in parentheses.

June 30, 1987: Leave [Ban Bang Di] early in the morning. Navigation still very difficult, river forever winding all over the place. Steering with Yanmar not too difficult, but need plenty of strength for lifting the propeller out of the water and dropping it at a 90-degree angle from the boat each time we come to a very sharp bend. Then the boat swings 90 degrees on the spot. We have to do this at speed over five knots. Many sharp bends with river current at 3–4 knots. Wish my sight better. About eight miles from Bang Di, we reach a recently fallen big tree, 6 feet across, dropped right across the river, from bank to bank. We stop to inspect it and figure out how to shift or cut through it. Some old men and girls come down. They smile but say nothing.

We [i.e., Thomas, Som, Nok, and Anant—Meow went in to Thung Song to see if there were any replies from the Bangkok media] start to cut tree through with handsaws. They stare at us for half an hour, then the old men disappear and return with two big saws and come down to help us. Four old men help us cut through the tree, and shift the cut section, but will not go away when boat passes through gap. They sat on the boat's side and weigh her down so that she could not pass over shallow banks, until Tristan paid them money. [200 baht, $10.] By then late afternoon.

They think we are tourists [I doubt that] and don't realize the difficulties we have overcome. Nobody knows the river more than 600 yards from their area, or they say they don't know. Pass through bamboo bridge 100 yards upstream from tree. River blocked further upstream by rocks and big old fallen log. Stop below bridge for the night, ready to take it apart, then rebuild it tomorrow, then shift log with chain hoist. Rice and [dried] fish for supper. [I had ordered our canned food to be carefully hoarded for future strenuous days.]

July 1, 1987: Started cutting through big old log at dawn, got through by 4:00 P.M. Then dragged boat through narrow gap between rocks, by hand. Current through rocks about eight knots. Tristan sent me to get the four old saw men to cut through a tree astern to us, to drop it purposely into the river, so as to dam it, to raise the water level ahead of us. They agree to cut down the tree, payment beforehand, but will not listen to how it should fall. The tree falls not across the river but at an angle, so only its twigs and leaves are in the river course, and it makes no difference at all to the level.

Tristan and Som walked over the rocks ahead, to find out how far they went, and what depth on other side. The rocks go for 100 yards and the water further upstream is just enough for *Henry Wagner* to float. Tristan says we'll drag her over the rock shelf tomorrow. By then it was dark. Fish and rice for supper.

July 2, 1987: At dawn we unload the boat and start to drag over the shallow rocks ahead of us. Luckily they are fairly smooth. By noon we have shifted 50 yards around a bend.

Later five soldiers and an officer come on board. Tristan thinks they have been sent to help us. The boys are frightened of them and will not talk to them. We know there is a private dam [illegal] two miles upstream which blocks the river, and beyond it there is three-foot depth of water. I want to take soldiers upstream to the dam owner, to talk to him, to get him to release some water through. Tristan says okay. [Although I was wary of being left with the soldiers. They had that mean and hungry look.]

I want to walk to the dam as risky trying to get to it with the dinghy as only six inches of water over the cascades. The soldiers are lazy and do not want to walk. They insist on piling into the dinghy, and will not be convinced that it will be impossible for the dinghy to float in six inches of water with all their weight on board, until we are caught in the middle of a rapids only yards from the boat, and have to jump out into the river, so they all get wet boots, and leave the dinghy tied to a tree. We set out for the dam. The officer walked along in the shallow river. One soldier, the local headman, and I walked on the bank. The headman carried the officer's gun [automatic rifle]. Walking through rubber plantation, over a deep trench, soldier falls off a fallen tree trunk he was climbing over, onto his rifle. The rifle barrel bends. He wants me to pay for a new rifle. I refuse. He pointed the rifle at me. I looked at the bent barrel and broke out laughing. Then he realized the barrel was bent, and went away, back toward *Henry Wagner*. The headman and I and the officer walked on to the dam, but the owner was away, the people said, in Bangkok. [They said.] The officer went with the headman to get a lift on a motorcycle somewhere. I walked back to the dinghy and towed it back to *Henry Wagner*. The soldiers who had stayed on board, and the one who had returned with the bent rifle, had eaten all food on board, Tristan said, and disappeared into the jungle. As no rice, no fish, eight tiny mussels between us for supper. Rubbery and bitter.

It was true. But Thomas's words are sparse. First the soldiers had burst out from behind a clump of thick bushes on the river's edge, six of them: one officer, four privates, and a sergeant. The sergeant had been a great bruiser of a man; he and the privates had frightened the living daylights out of everybody, with their automatic rifles pointed at us. Then they had clambered aboard in their big, muddy boots. They had dumped their rifles with a clatter onto our duckboards. One of them had grabbed Anant's radio and turned it up as loud as he could to a pop station. They had looked around them, disdainful when they saw our crew. "No women," they commented. "Where do we find *farang* women?" they asked. That much I understood of their Central Thai accents.

Thomas, the officer, one soldier, and the headman had taken off to walk to the dam. Som, Anant, Nok, and I (almost in a state of faint) pushed and shoved at *Henry Wagner* to scrape her along the rockbed, inch by inch.

The four soldiers left on board coolly plonked their weights amidships, under our sun shelter, and dug out all our rice and four remaining cans of food and cooked and ate the whole lot before our sweat-blinded, hungry eyes. I had no strength to protest.

The fifth soldier, when he returned with his bent rifle, grumbled because not much food was left for him. He demanded 98800 baht ($40) from me for a new rifle barrel. I pretended not to understand him. I was an old man, so he would not threaten me, as he had Thomas.

And all the while we pushed and heaved and groaned and grunted as we inched the weight of *Henry Wagner* and the five soldiers over the rock ledge.

And as we shoved, and as the soldiers, replete, swung over the side to disappear into the cool of the late afternoon, we knew that ahead of us, after this rock barrier, were more.

Here is Thomas again:

July 3, 1987: Up before dawn. Last night we had to collect tiny mussels off riverside leaves and some plants that Meow knew, to eat, because the soldiers left us nothing. It was too dark and dangerous to try to walk to the local store, about three and a half miles upstream. Som and I went ahead to scout. Between us and the dam we found eight rocky reefs ahead, cascades, like waterfalls, six inches high. We fought all day. Very hot. Break rocks with lever and sledge. Make passage, then push, pull our way through. [Nok and Anant found three birds' eggs in a nest. We shared them.]

We dismantled five small footbridges and rebuilt them, cut seven logs and reached the dam just before dusk with only half an inch of water under our keel. Tristan's foot very bad.

We had no help at all, all day. Dam was already opened at a three-foot gap in the middle, over which water poured at thirty knots down a one yard drop. People want 1,300 baht ($62) to let us through. Tristan says they can "get stuffed because the dam is illegal."

He says all Thai rivers are crown property. No one is allowed to build from or on the banks without government permission, and the officer yesterday told us [let it slip would be a better term] that there was no permission for this dam. Of the 1,300 baht, 150 is for them to chain-saw down a tree astern of us, to dam the river, and 1,150 to build a proper lock when the water has risen around us enough, so we can pass through. Tristan says he'll sleep on it. Which means he's not going to pay. This is going to be interesting.

July 4, 1987: Tristan says he'll pay for the chain saw to cut down the tree, but not for a lock to be built. He says if they cut the tree down properly, so it dams the river well downstream, they won't need a lock. We can just widen the existing gap. The people have no reply.

Once they were paid, they cut down the tree. Same story as on July 2. They would not listen to us on how to bring it down so it would fall accurately. It fell slanting, and there was no difference to water level. So they've wasted another living tree for nothing. Tristan tells us to widen the gap in the dam anyhow. Anant was too small. He would get washed away. Nok, Meow, and I had to be careful as hell working in that rush of water, but we widened the gap to just seven feet—wide enough for *HW* to scrape through. Meanwhile Tristan and Som—one arm, one leg—carried the dinghy over the dam, then set out two anchors in the deep, still water behind it. It was all or nothing then.

We speeded the engine up to full, rammed the boat's bows into the gap [there was still a six-inch rise], and with Tristan hauling on the anchor lines, and everyone else pushing the sides, we rammed the boat through the dam, and got through. It seems incredible. We actually shoved the boat up six to eight inches, and she weighs over a ton! By that time it was near dusk, so we tied to the riverbank, collected mussels, and stayed the night. Tristan is pleased at having saved the 1,150 baht. He says we will need it later on for sure, to get across the divide. The mussels were chewy but tasty. Better than nothing.

July 5, 1987: Up at dawn and leave. Send Meow on ahead to bridges with motorbike. Way clear for three miles to next bridge, then 200 yards beyond, a fishing line with hooks hanging across river. The second time it has happened to him, lifting the line, Tristan gets hook deep into the flesh of his finger. Som managed to stop the boat only just in time to prevent Tristan being dragged by the hook off the boat. I in panic with first-aid box.

On bank fifty Thais stare at us passively smiling. Much pain for TJ. He insists that we carry on to next bridge and "not waste our time frigging around in the bloody sticks." We get within 200 yards of the bridge and the engine chain-drive broke. The teeth of the gear wheel are stripped right off.

We cannot use engine, so we go over the side and walk-push the boat up to the bridge.

At the bridge Som took off to get a nurse. She returned with him on our motorbike, and cut Tristan's finger open with a pair of ordinary scissors. It might be a good thing, because she also cleaned up Tristan's foot, which was leaking pus everywhere. When I told him that, he said, "Yes, to keep the decks clean, otherwise they might get slippy."

32

High and Dry

July 6, 1987: Set off early, to get a replacement gear wheel. Som and I on the motorbike for Nakhon Sri Thamarrat, [a city about fifty miles away, near the east coast].

First we went in to Thung Song [local district capital] but everybody we spoke to thought we were crazy, looking for a boat spare. They said the nearest boat was sixty miles away. Great ride over the mountains. Wish I could see better. Found a shop with gear wheels in stock, and back on board by noon. Nakhon So Thamarrat busy city. Seems a thousand miles and a million years from where the boat is.

Tristan recovering from yesterday and resting his foot. He has it all bandaged and sticking out over the gunwale. He says that's the way British colonels in the Indian Army traveled because they all drank too much port and had gout. He seems to be recovering, but is suffering with the high humidity. [I could barely breathe.]

After we fixed the engine gear wheel, Som and I went upstream in the dinghy to scout. Very shallow. We cannot go upstream more than two and a quarter miles unless it rains tonight. Tristan wants to get the boat to the bridge at Bor Nam Ron, because it's the only place where we can be sure the riverbanks are not too steep to drag the boat out. [We had seen it on our Kra reconnoiter the previous year.] He says this is vital, because if we are in the river when the heavy monsoons break in a week's time, the boat will be in danger of being swept away and smashed. It's obvious, he says, from all the derelict trees and logs in the fields, that when the river floods, the water wall sweeps all before it. But another reason he wants to get to Bor Nam Ron is that if it rains while we're there, there's a chance we might be able to float the boat across the watershed plain, and so get that way into the River Tapi, which runs down to the Gulf of Thailand.

The locals here are friendly. I think the nurse told them what we are doing. They say that the river here last year was eight feet higher than this year. They say they have never known a season as dry as this one. When I told Tristan that, he said, "My old man used to say that in his day the seas were rougher." Whatever he means by that. [I had been rambling.] Tristan says that it's pointless for us to stay here at this bridge. The banks are forty feet high on either side of the river. They slope up at an almost vertical angle. The only way we could get the boat up on the bridge would be with a crane, and that would have a job getting its jib anywhere near us because of the overhanging trees. Even if there was a crane available nearby. But we all realize that his main objection to the boat leaving the river here is that we would lose the chance of getting right across the Kra by water.

I found out later that the nurse who had treated me, a kind, gentle soul, and intelligent, went on her pedal-cycle all the way to Thung Song that same day and informed the town authorities that we were fifteen miles below the bridge at Bor Nam Ron (Hot Water Well).

Not knowing this, early next morning, July 7, we set off in *Henry Wagner* to get as far as we could up the river, and as near as we could to the low bank at the bridge of Bor Nam Ron. When we started, we had no more than an inch of water under the keel. Yet we still drove the boat, mostly by hand-pushing, three miles upstream, until she was a mere twelve miles below Bor Nam Ron and safety.

We had reached about thirty-five miles, as the crow flies, from Kantang and the Andaman Sea. As the river wound and twisted and wended its way all over the country, we had voyaged up it *eighty-two* miles. And sixty-two of those had been over rapids, clutter, and an almost dry riverbed. Now we were a mere twelve miles short of our goal: the bridge at Bor Nam Ron, which marked the start of the Kra watershed. On the other side of that bridge, we knew, were streams running north. My mind's eye was fixed unswervingly on that bridge. It had become for us a talisman.

On my one wounded foot, I made my way along the riverbed through the shallow water ahead. I slithered and stumbled, winced and groaned, over three miles ahead. When I was convinced that we could go no further, when I knew there was insufficient water to float the boat for at least three miles ahead, we slogged back to the boat and settled down to wait for rain or . . . something.

The banks were still high and steep. The tracks along the tops of them were narrow and rough. There was no chance of a crane getting anywhere near where we were. The riverbed was one jumble of jagged logs and rocks sticking out of the gravel bottom. No tractor, no truck, nothing on wheels would ever be able to get anywhere near us.

Fortunately the boat was stranded under the shade of a big old overhanging boa tree, so at least we were fractionally cooler than we would have been under the glaring sun. All that afternoon we had one visitor after another. First we had the area headman. He, like most of the other headmen who had called on us, was more curious about our belongings than anything else. I had always made a point of telling them, further downstream, that we had three Muslims among us, and so we did not drink alcohol. They usually lost interest in us after that. Our crippled boys drew no sign of surprise, admiration, or any sign of feeling from them. The only way they ever expressed curiosity at our disablements was when they saw my false leg. Even then the fact of my sailing halfway round the world and arriving in their area by boat on one leg did not seem to be remarkable to them. It was the leg, and the way that it was jointed at the knee, and its cost ($3,000) that always excited their interest.

Then, that day at the Head of Navigation (as we sailors call it when we can get no further up a river), we had scores of people come to the boat. We could hardly avoid it, for the river where we were stuck was only inches deep, and they could easily walk out to us, even the youngest children. There were old people— some in their eighties, it seemed—and young, men and women, mothers carrying their babes in arms, all dressed in colorful sarongs and saris. All bathing discreetly around the boat. We were stuck well and truly right in the middle of the local bathing area. That wouldn't have been at all bad, but when they had finished bathing, they didn't go away. They all stood, silently, around the boat, staring at us, smiling. That was embarrassing. We couldn't tell them to hop it; it was their river, their bathing place. All we could do was sit and grin and bear it.

For three hours the Thais stood in the river and watched us silently. I felt like a monkey in a zoo. Toward late afternoon I hit on an idea. I had along with us a few tapes of classical music. There weren't many; the tropical climate had got at most of my old tapes and ruined them. But we had one of Mussorgsky's *Night on Bald Mountain*. I got Thomas to put it on the player, and sure enough, after three minutes of that, at top volume, our Thai crew had all winced and stuffed their ears, and the local people had all started to wander off along the riverbed and up the banks.

Even as the music roared and banged and rolled over the riverbanks, figures appeared on the top of them, far above our heads. One of them waved at us violently. We shut off the music.

I heard the first words in English that I'd heard from anyone except Thomas and Som since we had left Phuket almost three weeks before: "Hello there! *Henry Wagner!* This is the mayor of Thung Song!" He was accompanied by four large men in civilian clothes. One was armed with a machine pistol. Only one of them accompanied the mayor on board. The others stayed on the top of the bank, on the high ground, and looked about them.

Thomas and Som sprang over the boat's side to climb the bank to greet the new arrivals. I was still recuperating from my recent surgery, and as the visitors clambered on board, my foot, bandaged, was still propped up on a shelf.

I could not imagine what the visitors thought of us. Thomas was in filthy, bloody rags, to keep insects from his scratches and wounds. We had between us not one dry or clean article of clothing. To our nattily dressed visitors, we must have looked like a boatload of shipwreck survivors.

The mayor was about ten years younger than I, compact and very fit, and he spoke good, clear English. The first thing he did

when he reached the bow where I was lying was thrust a copy of
The Times (London) in my hands.

"Something to read," he said. It was two weeks old, but
silently I blessed him. My *Oxford Book of English Verse* was falling
to soggy bits in the humidity. My *Admiralty Pilot for the Malacca
Strait* was by then becoming soggy and green with mildew.

The mayor also gave to Thomas a package of canned and
dried food from the Thung Song supermarket. It turned out that
he had lived in England for years, been educated there, and was
married to an Englishwoman. He was the owner of a local plantation (which I presumed meant rubber), and he had heard of the
presence of a mysterious boat on the River Trang, with two *farangs*
on board. What was the situation?

I told the mayor briefly what we were about. I said that
unfortunately before leaving Phuket, I had not had the opportunity
to inform in advance the local authorities of the areas we would
pass through on our trip, but I had been able to inform the Bangkok media, and they would probably be coming to Thung Song
in the next few days looking for us. "And the TV people are
sure to film the boat," I added, just to make sure he got the
message.

The mayor looked around him. He was a good, kind gentleman. He also was no dummy. He knew full well what we had
been through to get here. To anyone with a penny's worth of
common sense who had ever been more than a few miles from
his patch of earth, it was perfectly obvious.

"What can we do for you?" he asked me.

"Help us get our boat to Bor Nam Ron."

"What will you do there?"

"Haul her over the divide to the Mae Nam Tapi, and head
for the Gulf of Thailand. I want my boys to be the first ever to
get a sea boat across the Kra."

The mayor stared around him again. "How the blazes did
you ever get this far? But for now that doesn't matter. How can
you ever get her any further up the river? There's not enough
water. No tractor can get here. No car, no truck." He gazed up
above his head at the branches of the overhanging trees. "It's not
even possible for a helicopter to get to you, even if there was one
around that could lift the boat. . . ."

"I know how I can do it. I know where the solution is.

All I need is your assistance in getting to it, and getting it to
the boat."

"Tell me, what is your 'solution,' Mr. Jones?"

"It's not mine, it's God's. . . ."

The mayor's smile widened as he listened. Soon it was the Thai
smile that meant, *"You crafty old blighter!"*

33

Fluttering Banner

Tong Chai (Fluttering Banner) appeared early the next morning, as the more frugal of us licked the last sticky breakfast rice from our fingers.

All the previous evening, replete with the mayor's gifts of food, we had lain on board, gazing at the fitful starlight gleaming through the monsoon haze above the jungle. To music and song from our radio, we had anticipated with jokes and laughter the arrival of a full-size working elephant to rescue *Henry Wagner* from her predicament. But nothing had prepared us for the sight itself.

Long before the elephant train came into view, we knew it was coming. The riverbed wound twice around two right-angle bends only a short distance upstream. Across the intervening jungle and swamp, we could clearly hear, faint at first, then louder and more raucous, the bellows of Tong Chai.

As his bellows became louder, as Tong Chai's train came closer, children ran along the dry shoals of the riverbed yelling and screaming, and soon every foot of the riverbanks, on both sides, was occupied by excited, staring peasants, many unsmiling now, for manners were forgotten. Tong Chai was coming, and was Tong Chai not the only remaining working elephant in Central South Thailand, and was his strength and ferocity not renowned throughout the Kra, from Songhkla to Ranong? When his great dark gray bulk finally rounded the bend ahead of us and peremptorily kicked a log aside, didn't he just look as if he well knew it?

Tong Chai was massive. His height, from the pads of his feet, which were all of four feet in girth, to his shoulders, was a good ten feet. From the tip of his waving trunk to the end of his stubby tail over his great fat, waddling behind, was all of fourteen feet.

On his shoulders Tong Chai carried his mahout, a thin, dark man in thick clothes and a turban, who sat cross-legged and swayed and chanted a song as he guided his elephant by tapping its great head this way and that with a stick. By the elephant's forefeet marched a boy with a small drum, who banged it in time to Tong Chai's mighty steps. As he thumped along, Tong Chai dragged behind him a long chain. The bight of the chain was lifted over protruding obstacles by men bringing up the rear.

Alongside Tong Chai traipsed ten men wearing gaudy sarongs, all barefoot, and each supporting themselves on the rough riverbed with a long stick.

Tong Chai stopped about twenty feet from the boat. His mahout stayed with him, but the rest of the men gathered around us. We knew that, by their lights, it was party time—*share-out time*. We handed out a filled pot of cooked rice and two cans of corned beef. Silently, with smiles and bows, they squatted on the gunwales of *Henry Wagner* and, after they had scooped up their rice and swallowed it, as was the custom, inspected us, our boat, and everything in it with a dissecting scrutiny.

Meanwhile Tong Chai was taken to the side of the river, and consumed, with much grunting and sighing, about a quarter of a ton of green leaves and grass.

Nothing could be done with urgency in the Kra. A thousand centuries have passed by without our attendance. A few more hours would not matter one whit. Silently, patiently, we waited for the mahout to call the men to work.

Thomas and I recalled how, on our motorcycle exploration of the rivers of the Kra the previous year, we had caught a glimpse of a working elephant. He had been rolling a tree trunk along with his foot and trunk. It had been near the town of Thung Song.

We had slowed down for a minute or two, to watch the elephant at work, and afterward had thought no more of it. It was the first elephant we had seen since we had been in Sri Lanka. That, we thought then, was the only remarkable thing about the sight. We thought that elephants were many in Thailand. One would be no exception. We may even have stopped, but I didn't think so. Subsequently, when we reached the upper Trang River in *Henry Wagner*, we had asked many people about the possibility of hiring a working elephant to clear the riverbed. We had been laughed at. There were, we had been told each time, no working elephants in South Thailand. They were all in the north. Every Thai schoolchild knew that.

But the mayor of Thung Song not only had known of the elephant, and where it worked, but he also had known of its owner. Thomas had gone to him and fixed a price; $48 a day, from dawn to dusk, with time off for meals. Three men, to accompany the elephant, were to be paid $10 each for each day.

By Western elephant-hiring standards, I imagined, this was cheap, but by the standards at that time of South Thailand, where the minimum laborer's daily wage was around $3, this was good pay indeed for the mahout and the two escorts. We also knew the going rate for the hire of an elephant in rural Thailand. It was $20 a day. Tong Chai's owner was having a field day.

I did a quick mental calculation. We had departed from Phuket seventeen days before, with 15,000 baht ($688). Our replacement dinghy engine had cost $322. Our food and fuel, so far, had set us back another $92. That left $274. Three days of elephant work at $27 a day plus three men at $30 for each of three days would be $144. Plus a week's food at Bor Nam Ron, say $36, would leave us $94 to take us from the watershed to the Gulf of Thailand, a total of over 180 miles by river. We could count on the trip down the River Tapi taking at least a week. A week's food and fuel would be at least $60. That would leave a margin of $34 when we arrived at Surat Thani on the Gulf. It wasn't a wide margin, but more had been done with less. I had once sailed across the Atlantic Ocean, from England to the West Indies, on a $10 margin, but that had been for a $20 bet.

Besides, there might be another advance arrived on the book I'd finished the previous year. It was due to be published very shortly in Britain. Thomas could travel back to Phuket when we reached the town of Thung Song, to check on the mail. There and back was only 360 or so miles. A change would do him good. Meow could go with him as his eyes. $10 should get him enough gas; $5 could keep our remaining three for three days . . . Such is the reality of "adventure."

Tong Chai gently moved his massive bulk closer to *Henry Wagner*'s bow. While he inspected this strange creature, his trunk wandered all over the bow, inside and out, and his pink snout sniffed and chuffed at each object it encountered. He felt the boat with his snout like a farmer feeling a horse. His snout almost seemed to have a life of its own, like some strange creature from another world. To me it looked as if there were a remarkable intelligence behind that inspection. Certainly I've seen prospective boat buyers who seemed to know less about a hull's construction than that elephant's snout did when it had done feeling around *Henry Wagner*.

The temptation was irresistible. Within a minute or two I had some of the mayor's biscuits in my hand, and was feeding them to Tong Chai's snout. He curled up his trunk and gently placed the biscuits, one by one, in his mouth, and blinked at me with his huge eyelids, and sighed. "*This old* farang *and I are going to get along fine*," he seemed to be thinking.

"Price fixed." I told the mahout, when he finally got around to talking.

"No problem," he replied. "*Khun To-mass* [Thomas] talk with *chao-kong* [owner]. *Chao-kong* say okay. Okay."

"Why did you bring ten men beside yourself?" I asked. "The *chao-kong* said he would send only three, the mahout and two men to fix the chain around our boat."

The mahout smiled even wider, with the Thai smile that meant "What business is that of yours?" but he said, "No problem. These men are my relatives and family of the other two. They only come along to keep us company."

"I can't pay them. Only you and the two others."

"No problem. They don't want pay. Only food okay."

"How long, here to Bor Nam Ron?" That was a mistake. I should never have asked anything beyond the immediate here and now. It would lose me some face, because I was admitting I did not know something.

The escort were fixing Tong Chai's long chain around *Henry Wagner*. The eight hangers–on watched idly.

The mahout's smile changed. It was the Thai smile that said, "I have something that you don't have." He replied, "Two days, maybe three. Have many trees and rocks in riverbed."

"When can we start?" That was another mistake. It indicated

that he was in control of the process. The chain was now tightened around the boat. I changed my question to a statement: "We go now."

The mahout smiled the smile that said, "I said that," and swung up lithely onto Tong Chai's shoulders. Then he gestured for Nok to go over to him. He leaned down and murmured something to Nok. Nok came to the boat, scrabbled around for our hammer, and handed it up to the mahout. Grinning, the mahout threw away his stick and tapped Tong Chai, not lightly, on the dome of his skull with the hammer.

I was in the bow. I was fascinated. I stared and stared at the stern end of that elephant and his swaying, six-foot beam. Tong Chai first dug his great hind legs into the gravel our boat was sitting in; then, with an ear-shattering bellow and a mighty strain forward, he threw all his weight, his whole massive, heavy body, onto his forelegs. I thought, for a second, that he would drag off the whole of the topsides of *Henry Wagner*. But the chain was securely strapped around our own massive sternpost, down where it joined our keel, so all the boat's structure took the strain. With a jarring shock, and a scrunching, crunching roar from the gravel below the hull, the whole boat, and us, and all the gear onboard and the dinghy, trailed astern, the whole shooting match, started to move.

When I say "move," I don't mean merely creep forward; not with Tong Chai pulling us. Over that gravel bank we must have accelerated, within seconds, to four or five knots.

As the elephant moved, so moved all his escort, although the drummer boy had been dismissed because the elephant's steps would be too irregular. When Tong Chai hesitated, so did the escort. When he plunged forward, they did likewise. No one spoke. The only noises near the boat were the grunts and groans of the elephant as he strained, the snapping of branches as he broke them with his massive head, the dull thump as a kicked tree trunk flew to one side, and the rumblings from the bottom of our boat's hull. It was like a huge, ponderously moving ballet. But in the distance, the sounds were different: As Tong Chai, bellowing and grunting, moved forward, so the people at the sides of the river fell back and ran up the banks, small boys pelted ahead, to warn the waiting throng, old men hurried away and little children yelled in terror and clutched their wide-eyed mothers, and babies cried at the transmitted fear and panic. Then it was easy to reflect that old Siam was where criminals (and probably innocents too) were executed by being stepped on by an elephant.

But Tong Chai amazed us all. That animal was ten thousand times more efficient and useful, in those circumstances, than any machine made by man could possibly have been. When he came to a tree trunk, he would hesitate and inspect it with his trunk. He would feel it all over, its texture, its shape, its protuberances, and test for its center of gravity. Once he'd found it, he would wrap his trunk around it and lift. Nine times out of ten the tree trunk would be flung aside. If he couldn't lift it, he would lower himself onto his knees, rest his head against that tree, and shove. If that didn't do the trick, he would simply wait, and do nothing until his chain had been taken off our boat and secured around the tree. Then he pulled it, bellowing mightily, and sooner or later that tree either moved or broke in half. There was nothing an ocean sailor could teach Tong Chai. I began to love that elephant.

34

Strike!

But Tong Chai took his time in between bustling rushes. He would work for only about fifteen minutes at a stretch, and then he'd stop, and the whole circus with him, to rest. When he stopped, he would lie down in the river and squirt water all over himself, so that his immense body would seem to turn into yet another gleaming black rock in the riverbed.

At other times he would stop at the side of the river, under an overhanging tree, and eat about a half-ton of leaves, stripping the branches bare with his trunk.

Often we would come to a place where there was only bare rock with an inch of water flowing over it. Tong Chai would drag the boat bodily onto the rock, and Nok and I, understanding the terrific strains *Henry Wagner* was undergoing, feeling them in our nerves and in our hearts, would, as we were jerked along, gaze gloomily at the ribs inside the boat, waiting for one of them to give way and take half the boat's side flying with it, into the edge of the jungle.

We had nothing below our keel, nothing to protect the hull; no cradle, no rollers, nothing but the boat herself. We had neither the time nor the money to afford such things. But *Henry Wagner* was built by seamen for seamen, as truehearted as anything that ever set out for the horizons, and she held as tight as a drum.

Sometimes there were stretches where the river deepened so much that Tong Chai was swimming, but he never hesitated; he plunged on and on. Once, when he had been swimming with us in tow, at the end of the deep section there was a completely dry gravel bank. We did not stop for one second, we came straight onto the bank and "sailed" across it at about four knots for one hundred yards. It was like being in a cross between a tank and a hovercraft.

That day, by elephant power alone, we covered about six miles. That was almost halfway to the bridge at Bor Nam Ron. At 4:00 P.M. the mahout and the escort simply stopped.

I wanted to go on, but as we had done so well that day, I said nothing. But I did get them to take our boat under an over-hanging tree, in case of rain, or a flash flood. We tied the boat's mooring lines firmly to the tree's upper branches and hoped that if a flood did come its swiftness would not break our lines.

Tong Chai was put to graze in a patch of long grass, and tethered with his chain to a tree, well clear of the boat and of us.

The mahout and his escort had brought with them no food supplies. They gathered round *Henry Wagner* and were fed out of our rice pot and common compassion. This consumed almost all the food we had on board. They seemed to have little thought of the morrow. Only the present mattered. They were soon tucked up under rocks and bushes, to sleep. Our boat was already jammed and crowded.

I let them get on with it. More expeditions have failed because of neurotic leaders worrying their guts out about relatively un-important details than for any other reason. *When in Rome . . .* I have always eaten little in any case, and was accustomed to fasting for a day or two. Thomas, I knew, could also live on his gristle for a spell, if he needed to. All I cared about was that the elephant had enough to eat, so he could pull the boat as well in the morning. I'd made sure that some scraps of food had been surreptitiously hidden away for our own Thai boys the following day. I was damned if I would worry about eight extra fit, healthy grown men, whose presence had not been requested anyway. It was only six miles to the bridge, and then we could send someone from our crew into Thung Song for supplies. I had already paid the mahout money for two days' hire of Tong Chai.

In that mood, first checking our samurai sword under my mattress, I set the boat guard among our crew for the night, cocked my burning foot up, with its filthy bandage, and tried to sleep.

As usual, we were all up and about at dawn next morning. We needn't have bothered. It took a good hour and a half for the elephant train to get in motion, and then, except for Tong Chai, sulkily. There had been no breakfast for the mahout, or for the two-man escort and the eight hangers-on. The mahout muttered to Som that if they did not eat, they would not move the boat.

I sent Nok ahead, with some money, and told him to buy rice and meat, enough for one meal each—man, boy, and hangers-on—at the nearest shop he could find, and to return to the river three miles from where we were starting from, and to wait for us there. This solved the first labor crisis that day; as soon as they knew that food would be waiting for them three miles upstream, the whole train again started to move forward.

All the forenoon things went much the same as they had on the previous day. Pull, drag, shove, haul. Tong Chai stopped every fifteen minutes or so, showered himself or ate, and then returned to the boat and resumed his valiant toil. Whenever the elephant stopped, so did the men, and they stood, as still as storks, all the time they waited for Tong Chai to rest or refresh himself.

The riverbed was cluttered with obstacles all the way. It was like trying to get the boat over a bomb site. Sometimes, when Tong Chai was absolutely stumped, we cripples had to cut the tree for him to kick or drag it apart. Then the escort and their hangers-on stood and patiently watched us, smiling the while.

It was just after such an occasion that I underwent an experience I'd never had in almost fifty years at sea. As he dragged *Henry Wagner* along a fairly clear stretch, suddenly the boat stopped dead. It was by no means the first time this had happened. It was usually a lumpy rock or a log end-on, over which the bow of the boat refused to slide. This time, the shock of the boat stopping strained Tong Chai's chain so much that it almost pulled him backward, but he recovered in time. I was up on the bow of our boat, and strained over to see what the obstacle was that we had hit.

Even as he regained his balance, Tong Chai, with a tremendous fart, relieved himself of about a quarter of a ton of digested vegetation all over me and our bow. His feces were a dull green, a good eighteen inches round and a couple of feet long. As they hit me and the boat, they shattered into a million shards of surprisingly dry dung.

I rolled over quickly, the green shrapnel all over my upper

body, and threw myself down into the boat. I dropped heavily on my sore-covered foot, and I cursed, by God I cursed. I cursed the Kra, the elephant, the mahout, our boat, the river, our crew, the escort, the hangers-on, the day, the hour, and the minute. I just let rip. It must have done me good, because I was in much less tense humor after that.

At first our boys had winced, and looked aghast at the sight of their captain, covered in elephant dung, falling into the boat. Then they had broken into laughter so loud and deep that I thought they would burst. When I recovered myself and stared around me, little Anant, crutch cast aside, hugging his tiny leg, was rolled up in the bottom of our boat. Nok was in real tears, laughing so much. Thomas, being a German and so always ready to laugh at shit, followed suit. Som, a bit of a puritan in his own way, ran forward in the boat and tried to dust me down, apologetically. But all I could do was lie back, stare at the tree branches above me (we were on the move again), and laugh and laugh and wonder what in the name of God, I, who should by rights be in a neat little cottage somewhere on the British coast, writing my mem-oirs, was doing in a thirty-eight-foot sea-boat in the middle of the Thai jungle with elephant dung all over me. When I stopped laughing, I tried to imagine what people would say if, in an English pub, for example, I were to tell them this story. I decided I never would; it was too farfetched. And I never have, until now, when I remember that the truth can bear laughter as well as tears.

All the late forenoon Tong Chai and the escort and their eight hangers-on trudged and clambered and sloshed on, until around noon we came in view of a shady tree. Under it sat Nok, holding close to his body a sack of rice and some plastic bags of buffalo meat. We stopped and cooked the food, while Tong Chai ate his fill from nearby vegetation on the riverbank. We were miles from the nearest house, right in the jungle, but only three miles by the riverbed from Bor Nam Ron and relief.

After everyone had eaten, in the full heat of the noon sun we all rested in whatever shade we could find.

Two o'clock came around. It was the kind of day when even God must have been gasping. The heat was intense and muggy, with not a breath of breeze. The sun moved further over to the west behind the tree, and lengthened its merciful shadow. Two-thirty. No sign of movement. Three o'clock, still no sign, except that the escort and the mahout and the hangers-on were in a huddle. There were no smiles among them. Clearly something was in the air.

It took another twenty minutes for Som to sidle up to me and say, "They want more money for the elephant. They say if they don't get it, they won't go on. They say they leave now."

I looked over at the mahout. His face was sour and grim. No smiles now. The escort men all avoided my gaze.

"How much do they want now?"

"They say $96 a day . . ."

"But that's a hundred percent increase! We're already paying twice the going rate for a working elephant, and we're feeding an extra eight men!"

Som returned to the mahout and talked with him. Soon he was back at the boat. "They say they go now. They want more money."

"But we're stuck on an almost dry riverbed in the middle of nowhere! We can't go back, and we can't move without the elephant!"

"These men are bad. They do not care. They will go home now. They have money to buy Mekong whiskey. They do not care."

"But they've eaten all the food. . . ." (We had only $32 to spare!)

"*Mai pen rai* . . . it doesn't matter. They go now."

Even as Som spoke, the escort started to gather the chains away from around our boat, and the mahout made to clamber onto Tong Chai's shoulders. The eight hangers-on were already strolling away along the riverbed.

In my mind's eye I saw that river the whole way back to the Andaman Sea. All the bloody terrible Calvary that we had been through. In that minute I felt every burn of my foot, every ache in my stump, every thorn scratch, every mosquito bite, every weary push of a saw, every nerve-racking strain along the whole sodding way. I saw every tree, every rock, every bank, every fish trap, every fishhook line, the whole distance, all *ninety miles of it*.

I imploded inside, with one of those inverted bangs that we Celts like to think only we know. I doubt if it's true, but we like to think so. It's an anger that doesn't rise from within, but that comes from the outside somewhere and drives right deep down into our souls. It shouts inside: BUGGER THE CONSEQUENCES! It cries *HAVOC*!

I stopped even trying to speak any Thai. All thought of *chai yen*, losing face, and conflict avoidance and not disturbing the spirits was gone with the wind. I swung over our boat's side and balanced myself so that most of my weight was on my false leg, to ease the pain in my burning foot. I spoke, in my captain's voice now, not quietly anymore, to Thomas and to him alone.

"Thomas, you do exactly as I say, no more and no less. When I tell you to do something, you tell that bloody beturbaned mahout exactly what I've told you to do. Got it?"

"Got it!"

"Right. Now you and the kids get your best bibs and tuck-ers. . ." I remembered Thomas was German, ". . . your best clothes on, whatever is clean enough. Do that now. And take the radios and the computer out of the boat!"

Thomas told the mahout what they were doing even as they did it. Changing into clean clothes didn't take long. They had next to none.

Through the blood in my eyes I caught a glimpse of the eight hangers-on. They had halted in their tracks and were staring at me, goggle-eyed.

"Now take all the gasoline out of the boat, and bring it here to me."

The mahout and the escort and the hangers-on stared at our crew doing as they were bid. They gazed fascinated, silent, un-smiling, puzzled.

There wasn't much gasoline on board *Henry Wagner*. About four gallons in two red jerricans. Nok brought one to me, Som the other.

"Thomas, get the motorbike up the bank. Take Anant with you. Tell Nok and Som to pour this gasoline all around the boat, and splash the sides well, and don't be afraid to pour it good, right around."

In a couple of minutes the jerricans were empty.

"Now tell Nok and Som to join you up the bank, and get ready to go into Thung Song town and tell the mayor and the chief of police what I have done and why!"

Thomas again repeated, in Thai, what I had told him to do.

The mahout and escort and hangers-on all looked as if they could not believe their eyes.

Now we'd see, by God, who really believed in karma! I took

a box of matches out of my shirt pocket, and extracted a single match. I held it up, ready to strike the box.

"Now, Thomas,"—I gestured at the mahout—"you ask that squatting greedy bastard, is he going to get that bloody elephant moving my boat, or do I *strike this sodding match?*"

35

The Bridge at Bor Nam Ron

They moved all right.

I don't know how long I stood there, in dead silence, in the sweaty heat, stinking petrol fumes all around me, staring into that mahout's fathomless black eyes. To me it seemed like a year, but Som told me later it had been no more than two minutes.

As Thomas tried to watch from the top of the bank, Anant and Nok, not doubting for one second my determination, had crawled away into a safe place beyond the bank, kneeled down, placed their hands over their hands, and awaited the explosion. Som, not being able to place two hands together, had pressed his stump to his hand, and prayed to Buddha. Meow had stood and grinned. The throng of onlookers, from all the villages around, had backed off the bank, as if by a signal, and now peeped from bushes and behind trees far away.

The mahout was first to blink. He dropped his gaze and muttered, "*Chang kin torng* . . . The elephant must eat. . . ." He dug his heels into Tong Chai viciously and steered him to a nearby tree. The tension dissipated so sharply, so suddenly, it was as if the temperature had dropped by five degrees in as many seconds.

Then, as the elephant ate, the mahout shouted sharply at his two helpers. They, as if electrified, sprang suddenly into life and frenetic activity, refixing the chains on our boat, bowing and smiling every time I glanced at them. The eight hangers-on, as if by magic, had disappeared. No one saw them go. One minute eight bellies, full of our food, were there, incensing us by their very presence, the next they were all gone.

As the crowds of locals returned to their vantage points on the banks close to the boat, Thomas and the crew silently returned to the boat. Without a word, Anant, Nok, and Som gathered up river water and sloshed the gasoline from *Henry Wagner*'s sides. I had no concern about anyone smoking near the boat. None of us had possessed a cigarette for days, and the mahout's two helpers, who both smoked like chimneys, were only too anxious to get as far away from me as they decently might.

"*Napnnm nemp ma ma!*" shouted Nok when the tension and the gasoline fumes had dissipated.

Anant said, "*Nok phut Kaptan keng-keng maak ma . . .* Nok said Captain is very, very *keng*, very much so."

He meant I was "big", strong, clever, rich, virtuous, that I was the tops, the bee's knees, the Wrath of Jehovah, you name it.

Thomas was quiet, except to mutter to me, "Lean and mean and full of protein, huh?"

It was an in-joke with us, ever since two years before and more, when we had lightened *Outward Leg* of everything that didn't help her to float, before we left Ingoldstadt, on the Upper Danube, to fling her into the rushing torrents of the South Bavarian gorges, headed to crack the Iron Curtain.

I was back in *Henry Wagner* now, my burning foot propped up on our treasure-chest, our samurai sword by my side, in case of any sudden drastic changes of opinion about me or moving our boat. I was shaking like an alarm clock's striker. The elephant had been backed up to the boat now, and the chains tightened, ready for the off.

"Tell him you're not so bad yourselves," I told Anant, then to Thomas, "But cut out the landlubber's crap and get this boat to the bridge. Tell the mahout if anyone stops before we get there, I'll cut his balls off and feed them to the elephant!"

I was half-joking, of course, but after Thomas had patiently interpreted for me, little Anant, now even more obedient and obliging than usual, smiled at me, then crabbed a run on his crutch to Tong Chai's forefeet, and called up to the mahout my message. Tong Chai flapped his immense ears. He wriggled his immense stern. The mahout turned, his smile as wide as the Gulf of Thailand, bowed, thwacked Tong Chai with our hammer, and with an almighty jerk *Henry Wagner* lurched forward, which flung my foot off its resting place, making me yelp with pain, and we were off again.

I had sent Meow ahead with the motorbike, to let the town officials know we were on our way, and that we should arrive at the bridge the same day. I reckoned they would presume that the media would probably turn up there, too.

The rest of that day's haul was a repeat performance of the earlier elephant treks, except that now there were far fewer halts for rests and elephant showers. Now, without the eight hangers-on, we really were much more "lean and mean and full of protein." Now it seemed that nothing could stop us reaching the watershed.

Tong Chai (who gave me the impression that he, at least, liked me) kicked boulders and logs out of our way and dragged *Henry Wagner* over one gravel bank or rocky ledge after another. The whole way the mahout leaned around and smiled and bowed. His two escorts, marching now with more eager pace, bowed almost low enough to touch their foreheads on the riverbed every time I glanced at them. When the elephant stopped to rest, they ran now, like Olympic sprinters, to release his chains, and when Tong Chai decided to resume his labors, they sang to him and cosseted him to give him heart and make him feel appreciated. Now, even while he strained and bellowed, the helpers scooped river water with their hands, and threw it, in silver sprays, across his mighty back, to cool him, and to let him know that we were with him, and admired him, lived in the same world, and loved him.

A thousand broken tree branches after the showdown, in the late afternoon, the bridge at Bor Nam Ron, our talisman, hove into view, golden in the sun, surrounded by tree shadows. Seeing it bathed in sunlight, I felt as though we were emerging from some nightmarishly long, clammy, dark tunnel. Beside the bridge, running down to the river, was the promised land; a gently sloping track that ran right down to the water's edge. Here was relief, and safety. If the rains tumbled down now, if flash floods threatened to kill our boat, and me with her, we could, even unaided, in pelting monsoon rain, drag her up the slope and onto high ground.

It was the first gentle slope in very close to one hundred miles of river, all the way from Ban Meow, near Trang.

A party is it? We'll give 'em one!

"Give us the pipes, Thomas!" I called.

Thomas dived for our box of music tapes. In a minute the strains of the Donald McPherson's bagpipes playing "The Campbells Are Coming" rent the jungle air, to let everyone know that we few cripples, for all the world's disabled kids, had brought the first sea boat ever to the watershed of the Kra.

Surprisingly, or perhaps not, Tong Chai liked the bagpipe music and waved his trunk at us as he was unchained, then chained again. Our boys winced. It was the first time we had played the pipes on board *Henry Wagner*. They would soon smile whenever they heard them, when they had realized what it meant: another step on the road to victory.

As we drew, bit by bit, ever closer to the bridge, the scene was almost out of this world. I raised myself painfully above the gunwale, took one look ahead, gazed to each side of our elephant's hindquarters as he waddled and we jerked along, and told Thomas, "Hoist the flags, mate!"

All across the bridge, all two hundred feet of it, cars, jeeps, and trucks, even buses, were lined up, their windows reflecting the sunlight. In front of the cars a thousand people waited. On the sloping ramp to the east of the bridge, a few hundred school-children, all drawn up in their uniforms, all carrying little Thai flags, waited patiently with their teachers in the sunlight. In the temple grounds, in the western side of the riverbed, another thousand monks and peasants stared at us silently from the shade of the great boa trees. Half the populations for miles around were gathered around the bridge at Bor Nam Ron.

In a flurry of activity on board *Henry Wagner*, as Tong Chai dragged her for the last hundred feet, six long bamboo poles, each with a flag tied on its end, were raised and jammed into the stringers of our boat, three to a side, to add to the tattered Thai ensign that was always worn at our stern.

Up went the flag of the World Trade Centre, London. (They had given us the outboard we had lost at Kantang.) Up went the bright blue flag of the United Nations (gift of the UN contingent in Cyprus, worn because we worked for the disabled in every land). Aloft went the British Red Ensign (for we had come from the ocean, and this was an ocean flag). Up went the pennant of Bavaria (for Thomas, the Rhine, and the Danube). Up went the flag of Saudi Arabia (one of our "courtesy flags," from *Outward Leg*, worn for our two Muslims. They didn't know the country it hailed from, but they knew, by its emerald-green color and gorgeous Arabic script, that it symbolized their faith, and were very proud of it). And up, up went my big *Draigh a Goch*, the old Red Dragon flag of Wales.

"You good man, big man!" The mahout, pausing from his bewildered survey of the scene at the bridge, called to me from his perch atop Tong Chai, as he waited to waddle off up the slope. "You will not tell the people? I am a small man, I have a big family. . . ." he whined.

I could not address him. "Som, tell him to go in peace, and to be back here with the elephant tomorrow morning at the crack of dawn. And tell him that tomorrow, the TV are coming . . . oh, never mind!"

Som spoke to the mahout quickly, then turned to me and said, "He say you good friend. You have many sons. You live many years. You make him very happy. Tomorrow he come and elephant work free. Four hours!"

We had found our first Thai donor.

So, after almost one hundred miles of strain and struggle, we came to the Great Divide of the Kra, at the bridge at Bor Nam Ron, near the town of Thung Song. Our friend the mayor of Thung Song, we were told, had been called to the capital on business. In his place he had sent to welcome us two or three minor town officials . . . and an ambulance!

It stood there, clean and cream and gleaming in the sun, its white-uniformed attendants all now wading, knee-deep, in brown river water, come to fetch me.

As politely as I could, I waved them away. There was no disdain or false pride, no bravado in my gesture. More, there was sorrow and certainly pain, for my foot was afire. It was swollen to twice its normal size and was aflame with red and green blotches, out of which oozed a continual trickle of bright yellow pus. There was no way I could go off in an ambulance and not lose face with my crew. I might even lose them altogether. They might be little fisherboys, but they knew very well what ambulances were, and that when they had come to Ao Chalong, as they had very infrequently, they had taken away old sick people who had never been seen again.

"If they'd only kept the ambulance out of sight!" I moaned, as Thomas and Meow (returned from Thung Song), their hands entwined under my stern end, carried me up the slope.

36

The Field of the Cloth of Gold

Note: This was the site in France of an historical treaty between the English and their traditional enemies, the French, in the English King Henry VIII's time. It is also the meaning of Patong, incidentally.

A Thai gentleman, who turned out to be a town official, greeted us as we made our way to the road track at the top of the slope. Around his neck was slung a camera case. He bowed slightly and "*weh*ed" me, smiling hugely. "Where are the TV people?" he demanded. "We have arranged the schoolchildren, and everybody has waited for three hours, . . ."

They propped me up on our motorbike, while Meow handed me letters and cables from Bangkok. The media people, all of them, couldn't make it to Thung Song today. They would be along tomorrow. One of the cables, from an international TV film company, was worded: "*If you reach the bridge today, can you go back down the river a little way and reenact your arrival tomorrow please?*"

The official, unaccustomed to being out in the sun, was, very unusual for the Thais we knew, perspiring. I told him, "Sorry, they're coming tomorrow." The official's face dropped. He waved at the schoolteachers. The children, looking downcast, glanced over their shoulders at *Henry Wagner* and the grazing elephant, and wended their dejected way back to the main road and the strange modern world that was so swiftly overtaking them and that would soon overwhelm them.

Thomas started the bike, and we hared off for Thung Song, with me feeling faint and almost done for. I hardly remember the road or the town; only being laid on a clean bed in a cool room and being locally anesthetized in my good lower limb, then dropping off into a doze.

When I came to an hour or so later, with a clean-bandaged foot, despite the staff's protestations and dire forecasts of complications, I insisted on returning to our boat. It was not that I did not trust Thomas to be able to handle anything that was needed on board. It was far more personal than that. I'd taken our boat into the Mae Nam Trang. It was up to me to get her out of it, safe.

My concern at our crew's catching despair at my absence and "fleeing the scene" never ceased. I was their captain, true, but this was Thailand. I was also their father, their confessor, their mainstay. I didn't fool myself on that; when we returned to our boat, we were greeted with real tears of joy and relief. While we'd been away, Nok had catapulted two small but unlucky birds "for my supper," and Anant had collected a plastic bag full of nuts, two tiny fish from the stream, and a grubby little bunch of flowers. Meow had collected medicine herbs from the riverbanks. Those small gifts were the only rewards I ever appreciated or kept for myself from our Kra venture; they said more than words could ever say.

But first Thomas and I went to the town's telecommunications office and phoned Bangkok. A cable awaited us there saying that TV teams were on their way.

The scene, next day, around the bridge at Bor Nam Ron, was of continuous frenetic activity. First our sun-rain shelter was unshipped and set up on its frame on the bank, at the top of the track slope. Then our flags were set up all around it. A seat was made for me, and like a proper invalid I was carried up and set down under the shelter. Our twelve-volt battery and generator were soon buzzing near my shelter, and a little car fan, borrowed from a doctor, was humming away, wafting a hot breeze over me. Anant, clean and hair combed, set up our stove near my tent and self-importantly poured out a continual supply of hot tea. It was all colourful and grand and made me think of the "Field of the Cloth of Gold."

By ten o'clock the journalists and cameramen started to arrive, even as Tong Chai and his mahout, now all rigged out in his best suit, arrived on the scene. Soon the bridge, and the temple grounds, were crowded with onlookers old and young.

Journalists, English and Thai, and even a Singapore Chinese, were crowding me with questions, while I, from my regal perch, tried to direct operations from a distance of a hundred yards. The riverbed at the bottom of the slope was a nightmare of clutter, big and small trees, and soft mud. I wanted no slipup, no breakdowns, no catastrophe, not in front of the cameras. Now we were to open up our long-planned and rightfully earned (God knows!) broadsides on the consciousness of the able-bodied world.

Eventually, as the cameras whirled for practice shots, and with much assistance from eager volunteers old and young, all laughing and smiling broadly at the cameras, the riverbed at the bottom of the slope was cleared.

Tong Chai was chained to *Henry Wagner* and did his stuff, easily, almost imperiously. He was like a bull chewing daisies. Our boat was dragged, in two minutes, from the bottom of the river course to the high ground at the top of the slope. As it moved, almost smoothly, onto dry land, all the Thais, and our new *farang* friends, gave a hearty cheer, and waved at us, the best of friends.

Even as four cameras were aimed at my head, an army officer appeared on the scene. He spoke into the microphones, but his Thai was far too rapid for me to understand.

Som sidled—he always seemed to sidle—up to me. "He says the Thai Fourth Army help you. He say the general order for a truck to come and . . ." Som held out his one arm and swung it around.

"A crane . . . ?"

"Yes. He say they come tomorrow. He say they take boat to Surat Thani. . . ."

Our two small boys were laughing and smiling at the thought of no more rivers.

"Stop him!" I told Som. "We're not going to be hauled to the coast by road! Our boat's meant for water, for Christ's sake! We're going by river! By the Mae Nam Tapi! It's only a few miles from here. . . ."

Som and now Thomas listened, as did all the journalists within earshot while I protested: "Look, we've got here from the Andaman Sea. I know from our altimeter and sextant sights we're two-hundred-ninety-five feet above sea level. That's what we've done. We've lifted our one-and-a-quarter-ton boat and ourselves, mainly by hand, about one hundred twenty feet in just over two weeks. Our engine raised us one-hundred-sixty-five feet . . . the elephant raised us about another ten. You might think that's enough to prove our point, but I don't. I want to find a way across the Isthmus of Thailand by water. I told you that before we left Phuket. This is as far as we can hope to get, without rainfall, with *Henry Wagner*. But there must be a way from this bridge to the River Tapi. I can feel it in my bone marrow. If we had rain, we could even get across the watershed with *Henry Wagner*. But the streams are low. I want Thomas to go and look for that connection in our dinghy. I'm set on us at least trying to find it. This is supposed to be mainly a Thai effort. If Som or Nok wants to go with Thomas and look for a possible waterway, that's fine. If you don't, then stay here, help Meow and Anant guard our boat, and wait for Thomas to return. Agreed?"

Of course, in rudimentary Thai and fractured English, it took about an hour to get this across to our crew, but in the end, considering our lack of money, and that it would be cheaper for Thomas to probe for the mystery route alone, that was agreed.

The army officer, a pleasant-natured young man of about thirty, agreed to delay the arrival of the army truck and crane for one week. Then they would come to pick up *Henry Wagner* and transport her wherever I wished. But that would be our only chance. They would not come twice. It was agreed that I would pay the army's fuel costs and feed those of their men who would be involved in the haul.

That seemed fair enough; in fact very generous of them, we thought. Twenty-two miles wouldn't take long. *Outward Leg*, with a good stiff stern breeze, could sail that distance in two hours, easily. *Henry Wagner*, under her own power in deep water, could make it in three and a bit.

The next morning, having bought some small provisions in Thung Song, and taking with him the awning for a sun-rain shelter, Thomas set off across the watershed in our dinghy, with the jigger driving him at about three knots on average, except where he came to obstructions or shallows.

(Here is Thomas's account of his trip, as I wrote it down on his return):

The river Mae Nam Tapi between the bridge at Bor Nam Ron, and Thung Song town, about 11 miles distance, was eight inches deep. From what I could see through the town it was a sewer. Over two choked bridges in the town, I dragged our dinghy. Above the town a branch of the river to the north-west led to a small village called Ban Khlong Chang. This was on the main north–south railway line through Thailand from Bangkok to Malaysia. I camped there, and a train rumbled by in the wee small hours, heading south. I wondered if there might be on it anyone I knew. There was a hot, damp mist all around. As I fingered cold sardines from a can and swatted mosquitoes, I tried to imagine the passengers in the air-conditioned cars, perhaps ordering cooked food and cold beer from the restaurant car.

Next morning I managed another two to three miles along what was little more than a soggy trickle in a ditch, almost parallel to the railway. I came at last to a complete earth blockage, on the other side of which was a rice paddy. This was near a hamlet called Ban Talat Sathani Na Bon. An ancient wizened man, a field worker, wearing a conical hat and leather sandals, told me that the stream on the other side of the railway ran north to the banks of the River Tapi at a place, he said, called Ban Talat Sathani Khlong Chan Di. He had often, he said, when he was young, punted a boat down there, and even further, all the way to Amphoe Chawang.

I pricked up my ears sharply when Thomas told me the old man's claim. Although our maps were inaccurate, there was no doubt about Chawang town being on the River Tapi.

Thomas continued:

I listened for any trains but heard none. I dragged our dinghy, then, across the hot railway lines. There was no road. I plonked our dinghy in the water. The stream was no more than seven inches deep. I looked at my hand-bearing compass and checked it for the direction of flow of the water. It ran north. Due north. I pushed our dinghy, stumbling alongside it, sometimes floundering when the stream bottom was rough; sometimes, when the water was deeper, I collapsed into our dinghy. Then I came to a cooler stretch, under the shade of trees, and shortly after, to the village of Ban Sai Tiam, which again was back on the railway, but on the western side of it. Here the stream was wider and deeper. It was still running north. I camped again under the railway embankment. Some railway workers, trundling along in a man-carrying trolley, stopped and confirmed to me that the stream did indeed join with the River Tapi at Chawang.

The end of our search for the watercourse across the Kra was anticlimactic. There seemed, There seemed, according to Thomas, to be nothing but two insignificant, ordinary-looking little ditches wandering in a heat haze through rice paddies, separated by a man-made railway embankment.

But we had found that there existed, except for one small rice-paddy dike, and a railway embankment, *a clear water connection right across the Isthmus of Thailand (broader than the actual Kra area), from the Andaman Sea to the Gulf of Thailand.*

I was content; I knew that the search is always more important than the finding. It is the refusal to yield to the whims of fate that matters, not rewards. Defiance for good is the real achievement.

Weary but triumphant, Thomas had returned to *Henry Wagner* and the bridge at Bor Nam Ron the same way he had gone. How he managed with his poor eyesight is beyond my ability to explain. My guess is pure hardheaded German determination.

According to Thomas, even if it had rained, we would not have been able to get right across in *Henry Wagner* entirely by water, because of the high railway embankment. But the natural course of a water connection was there.

Thomas calculated that if *Henry Wagner* had had enough water under her to reach the railway we could have manhandled our boat over it and so into the Tapi watershed. The monsoon clouds' gathering, signifying doom-dodging on a flooded, wild river, heading downstream, dictated against our attempting that. We had to get *Henry Wagner*, as fast as we could, down to the coast again, or be stuck in the Kra for another three or four months. Our dwindling purse forbade that, if it could be at all avoided. Besides, having now achieved one main aim, I could reveal to our

Thai lads another. That was no less than to reach the capital, Bangkok. The third destination—Chiang Rai and the River Mekong—I kept to myself at this stage, not even letting on to Thomas.

The prospect of Bangkok delighted our crew, and fired an eagerness in them that was irresistible. Back under the scoffs of the peasants at the bloody bridge of Ban Na Non, I had sworn to myself that I would make our lads among the most renowned in Thailand. So to the capital they must go.

As it was, to get our boat down to the Tapi, we would have to haul her about twenty-two miles by road, to the nearest place where there was water deep enough for her to float. That was about seven miles downstream from Chawang, at Ban Na Yai, where a bridge across the Tapi River carried Thai Highway 41.

This, then, was the next effort, but not before I had rested and aired my foot in an air-conditioned hotel room for twenty-four hours and written three long articles for magazines, to earn money to pay for the coming voyage 360 miles north up through the Gulf of Thailand to Bangkok.

Then, having paid the hotel, and bought some diesel fuel and gasoline, along with a week's dry food, we had 130 baht left on which to get to the coast at Surat Thani, and quickly, before the coming monsoon rains broke and turned that river into a raging maelstrom. So tiny are the acorns from which tremendous oaks might grow!

The following week, while we were still struggling downstream on the River Tapi, Associated Press distributed around the world a picture of Tong Chai hauling our boat. It appeared, to my certain knowledge, in places as far apart as New Zealand, Canada, and Mexico. The short caption under the picture, in all cases, declared that I was a round-the-world sailor whose boat had gone aground on a mudbank in Thailand, and who had been salvaged by an elephant. There was no mention of our crew or our purpose. We had no sponsors to insist the media publish the truth.

It confirmed my previous suspicions: The cameras and the people behind them often didn't merely record "news"—*they made it*. They had become so enraptured by "show business" that they often were not content just to record the image—they "made the image," so that the "image" became more important than the reality, or the two became confused. And this confusion between what was real and what was not, I was to observe in the following few weeks, seemed all too often to transfer itself, tragically, to the people it was aimed at.

But at least the promise, the threat, of the media presence did help us, at my contrivance, to get *Henry Wagner* across the Kra.

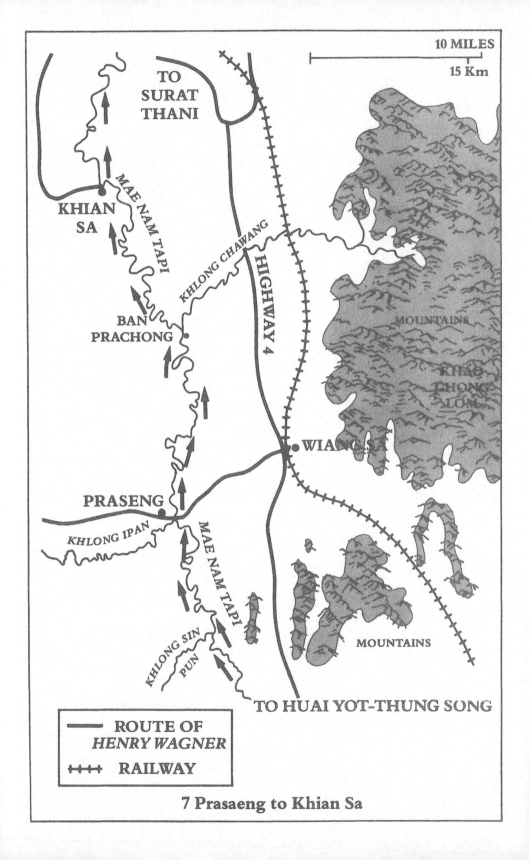

10 MILES
15 Km

TO SURAT THANI

KHIAN SA

MAE NAM TAPI

KHLONG CHAWANG

HIGHWAY 4

BAN PRACHONG

MOUNTAINS

KHAO CHONG LOM

WIANG SA

PRASENG

KHLONG IPAN

MAE NAM TAPI

KHLONG SIN PUN

MOUNTAINS

TO HUAI YOT-THUNG SONG

ROUTE OF
HENRY WAGNER

RAILWAY

7 Prasaeng to Khian Sa

37

Escape

The Thai Fourth Army did us proud. Into what had been a hot but peaceful haven, atop the slope by the bridge at Bor Nam Ron, suddenly, at about eight o'clock on the morning of July 14, rolled what seemed at first to be a full army corps.

First came two pickups, crowded with soldiers, each with an officer beside its driver, stirring dust on the bone-dry track. Behind them lumbered a great fourteen-wheeler tank carrier also crowded with soldiers. Next appeared a huge civilian mobile crane, with a forty-foot jib. The rearguard was taken up by a Thung Song taxi carrying three reporters, one free-lancing for the British newspaper the *Guardian*, one for the Thai *Rath* newspaper, and one for *Asia Weekly*, Hong Kong. We were glad to see the soldiers, of course, but from their numbers and the sizes of their truck and crane, you would have thought they were going to haul the *QE2*.

No sooner had the crane positioned itself to lift our boat (we had worked early to place our lifting strops around her hull) than four food-vending motor tricycles, such as were seen on roads all over Thailand, with plastic bags of rice and assorted accompaniments a-dangling, turned up to feed the troops. Their drivers, all middle-aged, well-fed men in blue shirts, all ominously smiled and made *wehs* at me as though I were the patron saint of every roadside food vendor in South Thailand. This had me, for a time, concerned. It meant I'd be paying.

The officers, one of whom could speak good English, conversed with me for a while. They were courteous, polite, and friendly to Thomas and me. They never addressed a private directly, it was all done through a sergeant, a tough old campaigner. He must have had one medal ribbon for every soldier in his charge.

I'd managed to get a count of the soldiers on our boat convoy. There were, besides two officers and the veteran sergeant (who looked as though he could eat our boat), forty-two. They were mostly, it seemed to me, fairly new recruits, or serving their national call-up time. Someone told me their pay was about $18 a month. They had little in common with the five grizzled guerrilla-hunters who had eaten us out of boat and home back downstream on the River Trang. These were mostly in their late teens or early twenties, and they all looked, as the sayings go, as brown as berries and as fit as fiddles. But by God could they eat!

Within seconds of the first tricycle's arrival, it was bare of food. Lines of privates had already formed up before the other three motor tricycles. They were a clean, smart, cheerful lot, all smiling and joshing each other. But it surprised me to see so many uniformed men talking to each other so gently, and being so intricately polite to one another. One would hand another a bag of food, and the recipient would *weh* and bow. Nothing could be further from what I had been accustomed to in the Royal Navy, in my younger days, than the behavior of those Thai privates. It all seemed so incongruous. It was fascinating.

I was becoming more and more concerned. I knew that the plastic bags of rice and spicy gunk were only 5 baht (5 cents) each, but five bags per private would be 25 baht each (25 cents), and there were forty-two of them. That would make 1050 baht ($50). And that would be merely for breakfast! There would still be their early Thai lunch at the other end, around 11:00 A.M. Mentally I riffled the 250 baht ($12) I had in my pocket—all we had to take us to Surat Thani, 180 miles away.

I must have looked downcast. One of the Asian photographers, of Chinese descent, was insistently shoving his camera right in my face. I was thinking up a suitable revenge for that. The free-lance *Guardian* correspondent, bless England, came up, patted my shoulder, and said, "Cheer up, Tristan! The food and fuel's on me!"

I wondered if that was the first time that the *Guardian* a liberal paper, a favorite of peaceniks, had ever supported for half a day a whole battalion of American-armed soldiers.

"Okay, Nick, as long as they can all have a cold drink, too!"

"Done!" he replied.

"But only Thai cola!" I told him, and all my crew grinned.

By that time, with the soldiers safely out of the way in the food queues, now fondling their cold bottles of cola, our boat was swinging in midair, being lowered onto the tank transporter. Soon, with strops firmly in place around our hull, we were ready for the off. All we had to do now was wait for the soldiers to finish their meals.

The thought of our getting all this scot-free made me grin all the way to the River Tapi. *A whole $12 to reach the coast!*

Our crew traveled in our boat atop the tank transporter, so that they could show off with their flags to girls who smiled at them from the roadside, and glower at the boys. I was on the back of our motorcycle, my bandaged foot stuck out to one side, my false foot continually slipping off the pedal on the other, hanging on for dear life, as Thomas squinted and tried to see the tank transporter ahead and follow it.

Once we were off the rough side tracks and on the main highway, the haul ran smoothly. By then the crane had disappeared, but the soldiers and the journalists were still with us. I looked astern as we flashed along the road. There was a quick view of hazy blue mountains behind vast, sky-blue rice-paddy plains, and there, behind us, were the four food-vendor motor tricycles, now joined by a fifth, chasing our goose and its golden egg. We laughed and admired their determination to squeeze this serendipitous fat lemon to its last drop.

When we came to the bridge at Ban Na Yai, we were in familiar surroundings. Thomas and I had visited it on our motorcycle trip to the Malaysian frontier the previous year. We had admired its situation, between the looming hills of Khao To and Khao Pra, and the blossom trees on the riverbanks. We had even bathed under the bridge then. We knew there was a sloping track running right down to the water's edge. The track sloped at a steep angle, and the truck driver was anxious to go home, so while the soldiers crowded around the food vendors again, the truck driver backed down the slope, our crew let go of the strops, and hey presto, *Henry Wagner* slid off the bed of the truck, bows first, and into the River Mae Nam Tapi.

Then the truck took off, leaving only the soldiers, their gentlemen officers, the sergeant, the journalists, our crew, and the food vendors. These latter were doing a roaring trade and making the most of this *farang* nonsense, so much so that they had to send twice for relief supplies from the nearest coffee shop.

We moored the boat under the bridge, and squared her up. There was a problem. In the rush and flurry of the army's arrival we had neglected to remove our engine from the boat's stern. The pounding and bouncing on the solid road had broken the engine-bearer gimbal on one side.

Normally we would have dismounted the engine and taken the frame ashore to be rewelded. But these were not normal times. For almost a month there had been not one drop of rain over the Kra. It was unheard of in living memory. There was no time or money for repairs. The rain was not falling, the river levels were dropping seriously, and we had to get to deep water.

On top of that was our perennial problem of supplies and money. We had just enough for ten days on the river. If we could get to the coast, we would be safe. If there were any delays in money arriving for us in Thailand, or in our getting it from my bank in Phuket, the sea would feed us. The sea was my mistress and our crew's mother, and she would feed us. Even if the engine was ruined when we got to the coast, we might sail our boat somehow into the offing, anchor off, and catch fish. For sure with salt water around and fishing gear on board, we would not starve.

It was obvious. We must get down that river now, right away, even if we had to drift down, engineless.

I sent Meow, together with his catapult to hunt for food and 100 baht ($4), off on our motorbike with instructions to follow us down the river as best he could by road. I hobbled through the shallow water at the river's edge and clambered on board the boat. As I gazed around at the scenery at Ban Na Yai, I wished Thomas could see it all. I saw mountains gold and blue in the early afternoon light, and the dried-up grass and trees all along the bank, and the water rushing over shallow banks, washing against half-sunken logs and rocks, all the way downstream, as far as my eye could see. I made up my mind.

"Tie the engine down to the frame, Thomas. We're taking off!"

Even as I sang out, the Chinese cameraman (from a "*society*" journal), wet to the waist, had scrambled on board and pushed his camera into my beard.

Right, I thought. "You want a little ride?" I asked him. "Very nice day, breezy on the river, better than the office, eh?"

He smiled the smile that says "Another party!" and settled

down in the boat, clicking away at me. Under the bridge, on the bank, in the cool shade, all the soldiers, now replete, lay down and rested.

Thomas grabbed the starting handle and swung it. As I watched it, wincing, our engine, now tied down with string and wire, danced alarmingly in its frame.

Even as Anant gathered up our anchor line, even as our boat started to drift downstream on the current, the senior army officer shouted for us to wait a moment. Alongside him was a man in his forties perhaps, wearing a suit jacket and khaki trousers. On his head was a baseball cap. He was basking in the attentions of the press photographers ashore. "This is the *kamnan* [the headman of headmen of villages] for the area! He wants to show you the way, make sure you're all right!"

I have often wondered, in places like the Suez Canal or the Panama Canal, why the authorities insist on every vessel, no matter what its size, carrying a pilot "to show the way." When there's only upstream and downstream, it's not as if there's much prospect of the boat going the wrong way, is there? But here, on the River Tapi, with a depth in the channel of only one inch or so more than the draught of our boat, every extra bit of weight on board was crucial. I didn't want the *kamnan* on board. He didn't look the type to hop over the side and push, if it was needed. But I could say nothing. The Thai Army had been very generous and helpful to us, and if they wanted the *kamnan* to accompany us, then so be it.

38

We Beat the Kra!

Somehow, Lord knows how, Thomas, who was steering on our gaily dancing engine, managed to swerve our boat around 180 degrees, and shove our bow past a dozen half-sunken logs and rocks, back up to the bridge. Luck was with us. That was obvious.

The *kamnan* jumped aboard, smiling and nodding. He asked me for a cigarette, and as he settled down under our shelter, we got off our thanks and good-byes to the soldiers and journalists. Thomas, somehow, amid a nightmarish clutter of debris poking up from the riverbed, swung our boat around again, and we were off, bound for the sea, in a five-knot current.

Because of its loose frame, and the current, Thomas had to run the engine at half-speed or less. That meant that Nok had to be "coolie" and pour water into the engine intake. That meant two men on our tiny stern.

You simply could not imagine a more difficult and awkward navigation. In a heavy, thirty eight-foot boat with no rudder, steered only with an engine that threatened to dance away among the hills at any moment, and her propeller, heading downstream in a five-knot current between a maze of obstructions, the absolute need, on the part of the helmsman, for agility, quickness, foresight, guile, strength, and pure skill, was greater than anything that I had ever known the sea or the ocean demand from any human.

I can honestly say that I have crossed whole wide oceans in small craft under sail, beset with storms and gales, with less effort and fewer problems than we exerted and overcame in each of any hundred yards of the upper River Tapi. I can state without any doubt that a voyage all the way round the world in a modern state-of-the-art ocean-sailing craft would be like a stroll around Piccadilly, compared to that.

We got about twenty yards before we hit the first sunken tree, at a speed of about seven knots. The shock almost knocked me off my foot. Our Chinese cameraman, perched on our gunwale to aim his lens at me, fell off and banged into me. He was shaken, and smiling the smile that meant, "Must be careful!"

We had hit the tree at a 90-degree angle, and run our bows right onto it. We were now jammed onto it, and the current was holding us on it.

I wish I could say that our crew all jumped into the water cheerfully to shove *Henry Wagner* off that tree. They didn't. They knew this was to be the first of many. (They didn't, fortunately, know that it would be *hundreds*.) But the sun was hot, and so they merely sighed silently as they slid over the side. Thomas, Anant, and Som started to heave, while little Nok grabbed our sheet anchor and walked upstream with it for a hundred feet, then jammed it into the riverbed. Then he rejoined the rest of our crew at the heaving, while I grunted and huffed, hauling at the anchor line.

I'll give our Chinese cameraman his due, though. No sooner were the crew over the side and pushing than so was he, and he heaved with the best of us, and he did this for the whole of the rest of that afternoon, as we pushed ourselves off another three dozen sunken trees and gravel banks. May his gods and mine bless him!

At the end of our first day on the River Tapi, four miles downstream after ten hours' struggle, that cameraman was our admired friend. He pushed as though he would lever the world for us.

As for our *kamnan*, he had smoked so many of our cigarettes, eaten so much of our rice and biscuits, and drunk so much of our tea, I wondered that he had the strength to bear the weight of it all ashore.

It was late dusk when we hit the last tree that evening. We were all so tired I allowed us to sit on the tree all night, and we slept in the moonlight at an angle, as though we were at sea under sail in calm water but a good wind.

That day had been so full of strain, as we freed our boat time after time, and anguish, as we hit yet another obstacle time after time, that we'd hardly been able to observe the beauty around us.

There was no doubt the prospects from our boat as we struggled down the River Tapi were some of the most entrancing I had ever encountered in a lifetime of roving. Always the far-off hazy blue mountains were with us, the mountains of the central Kra range, rugged and ageless. It never ceased to amaze me, that through those mountains we had found a potential waterway, the highest point of which was only just over one hundred feet above sea level.

How I wished that Thomas could see it all!

All around us were fields and meadows, bright emerald green, and sky-reflecting rice paddies that seemed to mirror heaven, and amid them peasants in conical hats stooped at their labor. Sometimes they straightened their bent backs to watch us, expressionlessly, as we heaved ourselves off another gravel bank, stern first, against the current.

It was a treacherous current, not only because of its speed and eddies, but because it was hourly depriving us of what we most needed in the world at that moment: enough water to float our boat. On the upper Tapi it was obvious how unusual the dry spell in early July was: All along the riverbank, at each place where a road approached the river, people were filling pickup loads of buckets and cans. Some were even loading water buffalo with jerricans. These people, we were told, often came from areas over twelve miles from the river, and sold the water to farmers and householders in remote, now bone-dry areas.

The following day we woke before dawn, and later, between heaving the boat off trees and banks, everyone but Thomas gazed, fascinated, at what must be one of the most beautiful river prospects in the world: the temple at Ban Wang Hin. It was like the stage setting for a fairy tale. It was at the base of a greenery-covered limestone outcrop that seemed to reach into the clouds. The temple roof was scarlet and gold, and all around its grounds in the early-morning silver sunlight, or in the shade of great outspreading boa trees, orange-robed monks strolled or washed themselves in the river below.

There was nothing to disturb the scene, no road traffic, no noise but the crowing of a cock, or the bark of a dog in the distance, and the slam, slam, slam of our sledgehammer as we levered the boat off yet another tree trunk. The noise of our hammer echoed off the vertical outcrop on the far side of the river, so that if we didn't look at the slammer, we thought he was working twice as fast.

That second day on the River Tapi was much like the first, only then we had neither the help of the Chinese cameraman, nor the extra weight of the *kamnan*. The absence of one was balanced by the absence of the other: We moved at about the same rate, six miles in fourteen hours. On that day, in the dawn, we had unloaded all movable weight off *Henry Wagner* and loaded it onto the dinghy. Som towed the dinghy on foot downstream. Sometimes he stayed vertical above the water, often he fell into a sudden deep. That was his day.

Thomas's diary:

> *July 18, 1987*: We push on all day downstream. Very hard going. We are desperate to keep before the dropping water. No time to cook. We eat cold canned food on the move. We try to get down where other river [the Khlong Sin Pun] joins the Tapi. Tristan says bound to be deeper water there because yesterday he saw rain shower on the mountain where the river comes from. When we reach the second stream [Khlong Sin Pun], a little better, but many gravel banks, which we push over with engine.

The smaller streams, as they rushed down from the mountain of Kao Krom, brought with them small pebbles, which they deposited in the River Tapi. To get over these pebble banks, we first sent Som ahead in the loaded dinghy to find them and mark them. Then we made our way back upstream a little if we could. We aimed *Henry Wagner*'s bowstem straight at the bank, accelerated our engine to full speed, and drove at thirteen knots and more, right for the bank. In the shallow river, this raised a huge wake wave astern of us, which tried to catch up with us. A moment before our bow reached the upstream edge of the bank, we raised our propeller out of the water, and our boat slowed right down. The rushing nine-knot wake wave astern of us caught up with us, and then lifted us bodily a foot or so and pushed us a good hundred feet; sometimes far enough to clear the downstream edge of the bank. This we did at least fifty times before we reached the town of Prasaeng. Nok, each time on our helm, loved it.

This surfing over the banks was hair-raising and thrilling, but we were desperate not to be stranded in a wide, shallow, hazard-fraught river winding between high mountains, far from any track or road. In a flash flood it could be a death trap.

On the last bank surf, as we swept around yet one more bend and realized that this was different, that it was deeper and wider, and as we sighted the beautiful teak houses of Prasaeng, with smiling people on their stoops, waving to us from under their television antennas, we knew that the people here knew who we were, even before we landed.

We were all smiling, but silent; not because we were known, but because someone had told us that from here was deep water, all of two feet deep and more, all the way to the sea, and it was time to eat a cooked meal, and perhaps sleep peacefully for a night without feeling trapped.

We knew there was still over a hundred miles to go before we reached the sea, but we knew we had, under God, Buddha, and Allah, and barring foolish catastrophe of our own making, beaten the Kra.

Even as under a shady tree we basked in our own wisdom and happiness, Som, in the dinghy, smacked into an unseen log in the murky brown river and broke the long shaft clean away from his engine.

All we saw was the jigger go flying from the dinghy stern board, more or less straight at Som. We glimpsed him throw himself over the side, and the dinghy stopped dead in the water.

39

Mud!

Despite having only one arm, Som was a good swimmer, and soon he had the dinghy under control. He ignored a line Nok threw him, and swam back, against the strong current, gasping and trying to smile. It was the Thai smile that said, "I'm all right, even if there's chaos all around."

The jigger was all right, too. It had fallen inside the dinghy, and rested on its side. But the longtail shaft was broken about halfway along its length, snapped like a matchstick.

There was no repair shop in the village that could deal with welding. So I made splints out of strips of bamboo, and bound them tightly all the way up the shaft with thin cord ("serving," we sailors call it).

When the crew finished serving the splints, it was around midnight. I was a bit doubtful of the splints holding when the engine turned the shaft fast. Because of the risk involved, I tried it out in the dinghy myself, in the dark. Fortunately it held together tight, and it served our purposes until we reached Surat Thani. Of course, with a dicey shaft and deep water ahead anyway, we would use the jigger as little as possible.

The next morning, July 19, we soon found out that we had been wrong to believe the good people in Prasaeng when they had told us that there were two feet at least of depth further down. I'd been a bit suspicious of the information; the few Chinese-Thais among them had said nothing when I had tried to ask them about depths.

As we came to our first grinding, crashing, slamming, roaring halt on the first of *fifty gravel banks* downstream from Prasaeng, we tried to find excuses for the locals' giving us wrong information. Maybe they had been trying to make us feel better. They did try to be helpful, because they knew us. Or they thought they knew us. They recognized our images would be a better way to put it. We were famous now. *We Had Been On TV*. But they could hardly know what we had done. Our appearances on all channels, it seemed, had been short; shots of Tong Chai the elephant hauling our boat, a quick comment on a funny old cove with one leg, an eccentric rich *farang* paying for Thai boys' boat trips, but that didn't really matter. The locals had seen our reflections on their goggle boxes. Now we were images *made flesh!*

The younger ones had given me the impression that we were, in their minds, up there in the Halls of Fame with People Who Mattered, like Michael Jackson and Madonna and Carabao (a Thai pop singer), or all the others whose *job it is is to be famous*. Now we were perhaps more worthy of helping. Maybe a smidgen of the fame that had rubbed onto us, by our Being On TV, would somehow rub off onto them? Or maybe, just maybe, the people on the River Tapi were friendlier to strangers than the people on the River Trang? I'll never know the answer to that conundrum, so I'll hope for the best and say that they were. Now the smiles did not seem to be so empty, or perhaps we were just more confident, now that at last we were seeing the end of our long tunnel.

But Som said the villagers' misinformation was because they probably didn't know the river. Why should they? Prasaeng was on a road. They used motorcycles and bicycles now, to get to and from the market and the surrounding villages. They didn't know the river.

Som spoke as though the locals thought that anyone who used a boat in the river current, with all the skill that demanded, when he might instead kick a starter pedal and be an instant world champion, was a fool.

It seemed that the villagers' attitude was: Why submit ourselves to nature's whims, why fight it, when we could control it, kill it? What good was nature, anyhow? We hadn't been able to master it for ten thousand years, but now, with technology, we could. Kill it! Construct no more beautifully carved wooden houses; raise slab-sided concrete boxes!

Between Prasaeng and the confluence of the Tapi and the River Chawang at Ban Prachong, a distance by water of about twenty-five miles, we surfed over almost as many gravel banks. Sometimes our stern wave failed to lift us right over; then we dug a channel with our shovels forward of the boat and dragged her into deeper water.

All the time our engine, tied down with wire and string, shuddered and jumped on its frame. With all the speeding and slowing of the engine, the teeth on the longtail gear wheel were worn to mere bumps. By the evening of the nineteenth, because the chain on the gear was slipping so much, our propeller was turning about half as fast as the gear wheel.

All day, the scenery was superb. On the upper Tapi River there were few riverside habitations, and once we left Prasaeng, we were far from roads or even tracks. To the east, the heights of Khao Chong Lom rose to 4,600 feet, to the west, forest land extended, as far as the eyes could see from the top of the bank. Wildlife was prolific. It was like being in some immense nature park. In the cool of the mornings and the late afternoons, birds and butterflies were busy everywhere. Even in the heat of the day, herons and kingfishers were at every bend of the river. Wherever the river's edge was cultivated, old people worked, almost the same color as the earth they tended. Backs bent, they hardly raised themselves as we went by. Most wore long light gray coats and wide-brimmed conical straw hats. We could only see the women's eyes when they stopped, the younger ones, evidently, to watch us. They were well wrapped in layers of clothing not, as in some Muslim lands, to foil men's lust, but merely as protection from the sun's rays, to keep their skins from darkening. Wrapped in their layers of clothing, they reminded me, somehow, of Eskimos. Again I looked at Thomas. He could see only six feet.

We stayed overnight at the confluence with the Chawang River. Nok caught a lizard, a biggish one, about fourteen inches long from snout to tail tip. Him we roasted, using our rock lever as a spit. He probably had a fancy name—there are scores of different kinds of lizards in Thailand—but to us he was a chicken lizard; that's how the meat from his breast and legs tasted. The

head I don't know about. Anant grabbed that, and claimed it was
aroy . . . tasty. Nok had wanted it, but settled, instead, for the
feet and tail.

The next day, July 20, we made our way through what turned
out to be about the most isolated stretch of inland river of all the
ones we were to navigate in Thailand. This was between the
confluence of the Chawang (which deepened the Tapi by three
inches) and the small town of Khian Sa, a distance of about twenty-
five miles. On that stretch there was only one dirt track that
approached the river, and that led to nowhere, deep in the forest
to our west. Now, because of gravel banks being very few and
far between, we were able to enjoy the scenery much more, so
far as the banging and jumping of our engine, and the screeching
of our gear chain would let us. Our nails in our teeth, we bumped
on and on into deeper, even deeper, water.

Now Som, ahead in the dinghy, raised his arm straight up
more and more often, indicating a free way ahead. Now Nok, on
the bow, dipping his dripping, flashing bamboo sounding pole
over and over again in the hot sun, turned his head round and
grinned more and more. The memory of the blinding sight of a
thousand water drops flashing in the sun around Nok's face, once
every ten seconds, hour in, hour out, will never leave me. Now
an inch to spare under the keel, now an inch and a half, then two
inches and no more grave-banks.

Suddenly, a promised gift from the gods. At Nok's first shout
of *"Neeh!"* I fought my way forward to our bow, half-blinded
by my own sweat. Mud! I could hardly believe it. I grabbed the
mucky black bottom of the dipping pole and slid my hand las-
civiously into the murky mass of ooze on its end.

Mud! MUD!

After days and days, hot, sweaty, humid days, and hot,
sweaty humid nights, of sand, gravel, stones, rocks, and half-
sunken petrified tree-tumps, we had *mud!*

The engine was still banging away. Trees, fields, rice paddies,
and peasants slipped past us. Our boat jumped regularly to the
vibrations set up by our slipping chain. I climbed aft outside of
our shelter, all the way aft, and, with my muddy paw, grabbed
Thomas's hand to shake it. He was trying to peer ahead, jerk his
head round to watch our bouncing engine, and at the same time
grin at me. I smeared some of the remaining mud on my hand
over his chest.

"Mud! Mud! Glorious mud!" I sang like a madman, at the top of my voice, over the engine screech, as our Thai boys looked up and grinned widely:

" . . . Nothing quite like it
For cooling the blood,
So follow me, follow,
Down to the hollow,
And there we shall wallow
In glorious mud!"

Clickety-bang, clickety-bang! and as soon as Thomas caught the words and joined in, *clickety-bang wwwzzzzz!* The engine raced and *Henry Wagner* stopped almost dead in the water. The gear wheel sprocket-teeth were almost completely stripped, and the chain, untautened by the engine's jumping, was not gripping the stumps, but merely whizzing round and round.

Quickly Thomas stopped the engine. Golden silence. In a trice we had the dipping poles out over the side, and our flagpoles, and we were punting our boat into the riverbank. It was still hot, and when our bow nudged the bank we hopped over the side and pushed her to the shade of an overhanging tree.

We set to, Thomas and I, to get our engine to work. We were still about a hundred miles, by river, from the coast (although we had no way of knowing the exact distance—our map was a fantasy). We were in the middle of nowhere. The landscape was so primeval that I would not, I think, have been much surprised to see a brontosaurus raise its head over the riverbank, or a pterodactyl settle on a tree branch. I wondered what my mate would say, if only he could see it.

We had only a few baht left; we needed to save that for motorbike fuel for Thomas to go from the coast to Phuket. In any case there were no villages, no roads, nothing but rice paddies and mountains, all around us.

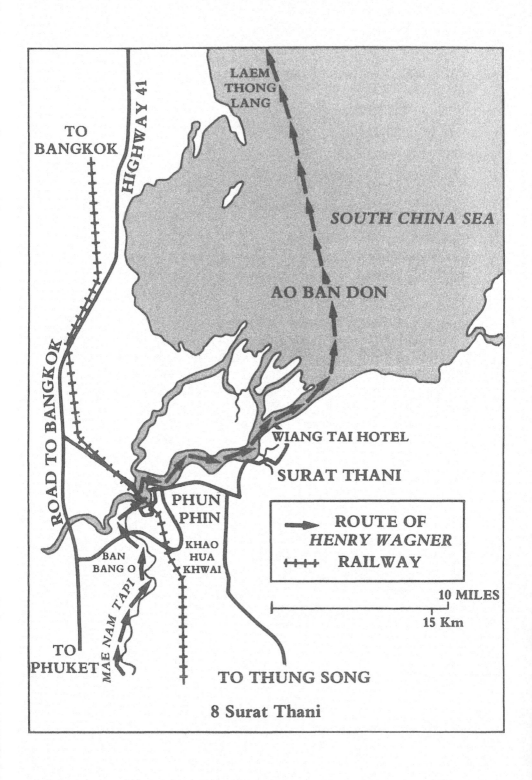

8 Surat Thani

40

Thalassa!

Doctor Sam Johnson said there was nothing like the prospect of his own hanging to concentrate a man's mind (or words to that effect). Isolation and the prospect of hunger or sudden death in a flash flood on a river notorious for its sudden murderous madness can also have much the same result.

A concentrated mind, even a concentrated Welsh mind (if that's possible), means clear reckoning, and fast, if hunger's in the offing. It was obvious that we had no way of rebuilding the teeth on the gear wheel. The only thing to do was tighten the chain so that the mere adhesion of metal to metal would make it spin with the wheel, however much it might slip now and then. We needed a piece of metal flexible enough to shape, yet strong enough to hold the engine down hard and stiff on its frame.

We racked our brains in that heat, to think of a suitable piece of metal worthy of our attentions. We dragged out into view every bit of metal on board. Our rock-breaking chisels, our tools, our shovels and spades, were all too malleable or tough.

I suddenly had an idea, but it took me a while to get used to it. As a solution, it was, after all, a bit drastic. Then I said aloud, "Ah, the hell with it!"

As Thomas and our Thai boys all stared, I grabbed our claw hammer, doffed my false leg, delved inside it with the claw, and ripped out the walking spring. That's the flat spring bit that snaps the lower limb back in line with the upper limb when I stand up or walk. It was stainless steel, springy, and it bent fairly easily. It was ideal. In a few minutes we had a sharp bend at one end of the spring, had clamped it over the engine, wrapped the other end around the frame, and banged it with our sledgehammer into another tight bend, so that the engine was secured firmly to the frame. We tested the engine; the chain, now much tighter, moved round, more or less, with the gear wheel, and we were back in business. It wasn't perfect, but it would be better than drifting engineless down to the sea, which might take ten days or more. With three days' food supply, that would be beyond thought.

And that's how we got from the edge of nowhere to the Gulf of Thailand.

It was dark when we hobbled into Khian Sa. Lights were shining, all different colors, over a riverside restaurant and people in small fishing boats were friendly and greeted us quietly as we drifted in under the moon.

We anchored the boat in a side stream that joined the Tapi River within the small town. Silently, in the relief of the sudden respite from the clatter and bang of the engine, I inspected the bottom of the riverbank. I suspected something, but I wasn't sure. And then I saw it, in the wan moonlight. The merest discoloration of the mud on the water's edge. Dark, thin, it would tell a landsman nothing. To me that little line of damp mud all along the water's edge under the moon sang of universal forces beyond our knowing, of assurance, of life, of all the narrow seas and the wide oceans of the world. It sang of freedom. It sang of love that flows for ever. To me, it sang of the presence of God.

I stared and stared, and stared again, until my eyes were wet with the strain. There was no doubt about it. I'd know it anywhere.

It was a tide line.

It was like seeing my own dead mother's handwriting on a letter long forgotten and tucked away. It was holy and very, very private.

But that could not be; it was far too great a thing for anyone alone.

Quietly I took Nok's shoulder with my right hand and pointed to the line. He stared, but then looked nonplussed at me.

"*Tha seh nam* . . . tidewater!" I whispered.

His eyes widened. He stared down at the dark riverbank line again. *"Naa na eeh?"* he murmured. He was trying to say, *"Nam thaleh?"*—"Sea-tide?" It was like the note of a song.

"Thaleh! . . . Sea!" I confirmed. *"All things bright and beautiful."*

I'd heard and read the phrase "jumped for joy" a thousand times, but I'd never consciously seen anyone do it until I saw Nok do it that night under the moon at Khian Sa. He almost jumped off our boat. Then he scrambled forward, rousting Anant, who was sleepily pumping our bilge. *"Taa-ehh! Taa-ehh!"* He shouted at the top of his voice.

"What's he shouting?" Thomas asked sleepily from his perch aft.

"Thaleh . . . sea," I replied. "We've reached bloody tide-water, Thomas! We've crossed from sea to sea!"

We were quiet for a moment. I knew Thomas was remembering when we had sighted the Black Sea in Constanza, Romania, after our long voyage down the Danube two years before. It was I who had done the shouting then.

Sure enough, he turned to me. "What was it you shouted back in Constanza?"

"Thalassa!" It was what the remnants of Homer's Greek ten thousand had shouted when they, too, had sighted that same sea. "The sea!"

I knew we were thinking in lines practically parallel, Thomas and I. Almost together, we both said,*"Thaleh? Thalassa?"*

So are ancient verbal links between men the world over serendipitously uncovered, even by roving ocean-wanderers.

To celebrate our reaching tidewater and clearing the Kra, I handed our Thai boys ten baht each (40 cents). "Less has been rewarded for more," I pontificated to Thomas, when he protested at the small amount. But I couldn't think of the occasion.

I couldn't be expected to go ashore. My false leg was out of commission. The boys donned clean shirts and trousers and wandered off up a steep wooden ramp between old Chinese-style houses. It was July 20, exactly one month to the day since we had left our beach in Phuket. Good God, I thought, in *Outward Leg* we could have crossed a whole ocean in a month!

Meow, with our motorcycle, was waiting at the jetty in Khian Sa. He had run out of gasoline halfway from Chawang, and having no money left (whiskey was seventy baht a bottle), had spent the whole of the previous day pushing the bike along Highway 41, until a truck driver had taken pity on him and given him and the bike a lift to a place called Ban Na. Then Meow had pushed the bike from there, about five miles, across tracks through sun-dried swampland, to Khian Sa.

Meow (ever the hunter) had with him half a dozen tiny birds that he had shot and killed by catapult that day. I was so hungry, and we were so short of protein, that I forgot for once my revulsion at the eating of small birds. Roasted, they tasted like capons, but there was very little meat on the tiny bones. Our boys, who returned flushed from being recognized ashore, thought the little skinny birds were a feast; there was much oohing and aahing and licking of fingers that night in Khian Sa. This time Nok got the heads, for having steered well.

Next dawn we woke early and took off before breakfast, to try to reach the coast by dusk. We had deep enough water before us, we knew, all the way to the sea. If the river became shallow, we could await a tide, a tide that the sea, knowing we were trying our damnedest to return to her, would send us, and stretching out her helping, loving arms, bring us to her.

Now, with a tide, we would be returning to our old rhythms of life, to our own customs, our own timetables. We were seamen, the tide was in our bloodstreams, all of us. From now on it would be our turn to gaze, puzzled, at the landsmen and their strange ways, and their odd fixations on clocks and their seeming igno-rance of surges and backwashes, flows and ebbs, neaps and springs. We felt them in our very bones, every minute of our lives, awake or asleep, wherever we might be.

By river, it was a long, twisty way from Khian Sa to the coast; all of about eighty-five miles. We rushed down the river, which was deepening and widening all the time. We could make five or six knots with the engine, and the current, on the outgoing tide further downstream, gave us another five or six.

Gradually the riverside scenery became more and more "civ-ilized." There were fewer wooden houses now, and more concrete ones, and more roads near the river, more motorbikes and cars. More and more houses had television antennas poking up high above their roofs, and more and more people gathered on the banks to smile, real smiles, not vacant now but knowing, and wave and even call out to us, and cheer us on our way. I described it all to Thomas.

There had been no bridges at all across the River Tapi from where we had joined it, all the way to Ban Bang O, four miles above the confluence of the Tapi with the Khlong Duang, a mighty main river.

That last day in the Kra we didn't stop anywhere. We didn't even cook rice, though Anant kept our teapot filled. We were too busy searching the river ahead for hazards, or relieving the helm or the "coolie," or up on the bows looking for underwater obstructions. We were still alert, still Kra-minded, always on the lookout for some danger or obstacle.

About four o'clock in the afternoon we shot out of the mouth of the Mae Nam Tapi, like a cork out of a bottle, at all of fifteen knots on our engine and on the swift outgoing tide. hardly looking around, we headed for the last bridge before the sea, at Phun Phin, where the main roads and the railway crossed the river.

Then we broke out all six of our flags, and with all the élan we could muster (for this was *Henry Wagner*, now known the length and breadth of Thailand), bravely, triumphantly, we rushed at the fastest speed we could manage for the bridge. And as we passed under it, and as all our boys stared up at the mighty structure, I gave a prayer of thanks to the gods of the seas, for our safe arrival back in their sweet, sweet salt water.

There was no feeling of anticlimax as we passed the bridge, but neither did we rant or rave. We were all too well aware of what we'd achieved, and of what we might have achieved even better if the monsoon rains had not failed us. We had taken a sea boat, for the first time ever in recorded history, to the headwaters of two notoriously dangerous rivers, and we had found a potential waterway across the Kra. Already, although little or nothing was ever said about it, our Thai boys had started to get the hang of what we were about; that we were doing all these "impossible" things, in heat, humidity, sometimes hard hunger, always discomfort, for people whom we might never see, to tell them that we knew they were there, wherever they were, and that we knew how they felt, and that we understood and that we recognized and loved them, all, *crippled or not*.

The river was a mile or more wide, from the bridge ten miles to Surat Thani, and fathomless to our ten-foot poles. Every craft, large and small, that we passed, waved and cheered us. Every ferry blew its horn in greeting. All the people of the river, and of the coast, knew immediately, even from afar, that *Henry Wagner* was not of the east coast of Thailand. Every graceful curve of her hull, the sheer of her massive bow, told them that here indeed was an Andaman Sea boat, so different to a seaman's eye from their chubbier, chunkier Gulf boats. A thousand people waved to us, and it seemed as if the whole world knew of our return to our life-giving seas.

At the time we may have felt a bit like conquering heroes, but now we know that we really looked like burned, ragged, scarred scarecrows. Coming into a busy, strange port from the sea was confusing enough; coming to it from the rivers and the jungle was even more so.

Surat Thani's waterfront was like Kantang's, only there was much more of it, and the harbor was ten times busier. It was all confusing. We were tired. The engine was beginning to smoke with overheating. The tide was strong.

Suddenly a ferryboat roared alongside at speed, then stopped. Her skipper bellowed in Thai and in English, "Hey, where you go?"

On the stern deck of the ferry there were three policemen, in uniform, the big silver badges on their caps flashing in the sun. One of them spoke to the ferry skipper. He shouted to me, "You go to that big place over there! Up the side river!"

I stared at where he was pointing. It was a great white box of a place. Then, with a loud roar, the ferry shot off.

Thomas stared at me, puzzled, then turned to work the engine again. Both our smaller boys had burrowed down into the bilges, to hide themselves. Their fear of police had never left them.

"Head up that side river, Nok!" I shouted, wearily. There was no point in letting Thomas steer us to it. The stream was busy.

Som sidled up to me. "Captain," he said, "I think we're in trouble. I think they say we go police station. They think we're refugees from Cambodia!"

PART THREE

... AND THE OTHER

"A man's a man for a' that."
Robert Burns, "For a' that
and a' that"

41

One Reception

On board *Henry Wagner*, and all about her, all was confusion. Surat Thani's crowded harbor, the sight of the sea, our lack of any map or chart, the nervousness of our crew, our engine almost coming off its perch at every stroke, our disablements, the running sores all over us, our filthy clothes, our half-starved state, our battered boat, our tattered flags—no wonder! For me there was also the memory of a thousand facedowns with authorities (most of them corrupt) from Manila to Mexico, Durban to Bratislava.

The ferryboat, with its policemen, seemed to be trailing, watching us, but then, as we pushed our way up round the bend its skipper had indicated, suddenly it was out of sight.

Now we were in a quieter stream, but working against a more rapid current. Our engine, pushing hard, was doing the Charleston by now. To make for the big white building, we turned in to a backwater. About a hundred yards up the backwater was a large pontoon at the foot of a high bank, right below the edifice that the policemen had pointed out to us.

There were no crowds, no bands, no waiting office wallahs, no men in uniforms, guns at hips. There was a large pontoon, and, to my intense relief, no one on it. The pontoon was huge, by our standards, with a roof and a platform as big as a tennis court. Across it a slight breeze moved from the river. There were, I could see as we pulled alongside, a few old, dusty chairs and tables.

* * *

Once we had tied up, our boys, excited, searched around as only boys can. Being fisherboys, they scanned first the river. There were fish! Food! Security! Cock-a-hoop and whooping, they ran around the pontoon and found ~ther treasures: an abandoned kitchen and bar, with a running freshwater tap in it, and a small sit-down toilet. This was better than home from home!

On the last leg downstream on the Tapi River my main preoccupation about our arrival had been how I was to get about once we arrived in Surat Thani. We'd better not dismount my leg spring off the engine frame; we might need power to shift the boat swiftly if we were scared off. I had set to and made some bamboo splints for my leg. That done, I could wear the prosthesis, but not bend its knee. For the able-bodied: That was a bit like trying to walk around with your whole left leg encased in plaster with large lead weights set in it. It was far worse than mere discomfort: It was torture.

Aching with pain, weariness, and anticlimactical relief, I let Thomas help me over the high rail of the pontoon, and sit me down in one of its dusty chairs. A voice called down the pontoon ramp. Som replied in rapid Thai. There was a sharp interchange for about ten minutes. This is it, I thought. We're being thrown off . . . It's too good to last.

Som, still under a cloud for raising gloom and despondency out in the harbor, sidled up to me. "He say if we keep the boat here, we must get permission from the hotel. . . ."

"Hotel?" This was a surprise to me. To my weary eyes, from the harbor, it had seemed that the big building was in a rundown neighborhood. Between it and the river had been the rusty iron roofs of a couple of hundred old tenements and godowns. It had seemed to be the right location for a police building.

"Yes. Big hotel. Biggest in Surat Thani. *Wiang Tai* [Royal South]. In the season many *farang* tourists come here."

I was still gathering my wits. "Hotel? They have air-conditioning?"

Som smiled his "Are you kidding?" smile. "Yes, have."

"Thomas, send Anant up with a clean shirt and a bucket. I'm going to clean up!"

"You don't need a bucket, there's a sink here, in this old kitchen," Thomas pointed out.

It shows how confused and weary we were. Or dirty. A

hundred feet from one of the biggest hotels in South Thailand, I dragged my splinted leg into a semi-abandoned pontoon scullery to try to wash. My body was almost one huge, open, running sore from soft-scabbed scratches, unable to harden in the high humidity. All around the top of my stump, around my groin, where my leg had chafed, was like raw meat on the point of rotting. My foot was still alive with pus. I stank like a midden. Disgusted with myself, and sick at heart, I dusted myself off with a wet flannel. I remembered bitterly the times I could have danced around that damned pontoon, and then taken off for a three-day drunk, and then gone back up the bloody Tapi. *Bitter is the limping wolf in winter!*

Accompanied by Thomas and Som, Nok and Anant—their bodies all cleaned up, hair brushed and combed—and helped a dozen times to regain my balance or to rest; it took me about an hour to climb the ramp and clomp up the path and into the hotel lobby. Inside was the first dry, cool air for us since Thung Song, eight days before. The lobby was enormous. Smart-uniformed staff were everywhere. We were ten thousand miles away from the Kra and the Tapi and the Trang, their heat and humidity and daily struggle of life. There were notices in the English language. There was the foreign-currency exchange rate. For the first time since Ko Phiphidon, a month before, we were back, and momentarily at least thankful for it, in "Farangistan," Tourist Thailand.

Anant and Nok, overwhelmed by a magnificence they could hardly imagine, stood humbly just inside the lobby door. They would budge no further. Nervously Som assisted me by lending me his shoulder as I half hopped toward an immense hotel desk.

A male desk clerk studied our appearances, as if we really were "refugees from Cambodia" (or perhaps the *kamoys* who preyed on them). We could hardly blame him for that; we were in a bad way after rushing 180 miles downstream on the wild Tapi in seven days. He was about twenty-eight or so. His English was good, but, like my Thai, restricted to his job and stilted. His pronunciation was fair. Like many Orientals, his *L*s and *R*s were interchanged freely: "room" was "loom" and "leave passport as security" was "reave passpo' as secu'ri'y." Those two examples just about sum up his response when I told him I needed a room for two days, but could not pay until Thomas returned from Phuket with some money. We knew it would take a week or more to get it transferred from my Phuket bank to Surat Thani, unless we knew someone locally, and we didn't. I had to listen intently when the clerk spoke, but I could hardly help smiling at him almost as much as he was smiling at me.

"But," I told him, "leaving my passport anywhere is simply not on. For one thing it is not my property. It belongs to the British government. It was given into my safekeeping on trust. No one can legally demand it from me unless I have committed an offense against local laws." I'd had this argument in a score of countries, with right-wing bullies and left-wing armed bureaucrats, from Argentina to Romania. And in over thirty-five years of crossing frontiers and landing on distant shores, I'd never yet left my passport anywhere! In a couple of cases I'd even departed from safe haven and faced raging gales, rather than cave in to an illegal demand. "But I can leave my boat as security. . . ." I offered.

The clerk's Thai smile, the one that said, "I don't understand, but it sounds interesting" faded. His eyebrows screwed up. His mouth dropped open. I never knew what the word "flummoxed" really meant until that clerk showed me. By now half a dozen young women, all petite and pretty, all smiling, had crowded around, and were inspecting us.

"Boa'?"

"Yes, boat . . . er, *lua* . . . *lua tok pla* . . . fishing boat . . . she's down at your pontoon. We just got in from Khian Sa on the River Mae Nam Tapi. . . ." I felt like I was telling him we had a spacecraft outside and we'd just landed from Mars.

The clerk smiled widely now. It was the one that meant, "I have the answer to that one and it's still no!" "Canno' accep' boa' for secu'ri'y. Managemen' no' arrow, no' in ho'err rurres. Car yes! Boa' no!"

I was almost falling over with pain from my stump and my sores. I expostulated, "But our boat is worth at least four thousand dollars, with all the gear in her! It's only for two days. You can keep a guard on board, if you like, to make sure we don't leave, and I'll pay his wages!"

To cut a long tale sideways, our clerk bowed and disappeared into an inner sanctum. Five minutes later he came out bowing and nodding, smiling widely. Through Som he told me that I could have a double room if I paid for the guard the hotel would place on board *Henry Wagner*, but our boys would have to stay quietly on the boat and not walk through the hotel grounds. *The guests might not like it.*

I exploded. I forgot I was in Thailand. I forgot all about *chai yen*. The hotel lobby disappeared, and everyone in it. Before my eyes there was only blood. The *Draig a Goch*, the old angry Red Dragon, battered and bruised from the Arctic to the Horn, Dover to Rorke's Drift, clawed inside my head as Som told me what the clerk meant.

"Guests? *Guests*. . . ?" I stammered loudly. I was choking.

Som cringed as I shouted at him. I thrust my stick toward Nok and Anant, as they tried to hide themselves behind a potted palm. "What in the name of hellfire does he think those kids are? And you, Som? You're all my bloody guests for life! You tell this smarmed-down bloody jack-in-the-box, you tell him, Som, you're the lads who conquered the bloody Kra! I'll not lay my bleeding head down anywhere that you blokes can't move as freely as anyone else! I'd rather croak it here and now! You tell him that anyone who's fit to suffer and strain with me is fit to go any bloody where that I go, and if they're not welcome, then by the living eyes of Jesus Christ, neither am I! I'll lie right down and die before I'll allow that! You tell him that if my crew can't use his bloody hotel grounds, that's exactly what I'm going to do! I'll lie down by their godamned swimming pool and . . ."

The blood before me cleared for a spasm. Som, halfway ready to burst into tears, looked as if he was facing, hypnotized, a striking tiger. I got no further.

Everything happened far quicker than I can write it over a year later. There was a sudden commotion in the hall. Out of the corner of my eye I saw a flurry of police uniforms approaching. Wearily I awaited arrest. *On my ground I'll stand! I don't give a damn! My crew is my crew, come hell, high water, or a year in a festering jail!*"

42

Another Reception

There was much shouting. I was trembling with anger. I understood not one word. I recognized a policeman in the group as one who had been on board the ferryboat that had directed us to the hotel. He made a *weh!* He knew us: We Had Been On TV!

Quickly, astonished at the policeman's machine-gun rattle of words, the clerk bowed and made a *weh* to me, then to Thomas. And then, to my utter amazement, he made a *weh* to Som! But then, a *weh* right across the lobby toward Nok and Anant! Those two looked almost as shocked as I felt.

A young lady, beautiful, in a long dress, introduced herself as the hotel "public relations officer." She gazed into my eyes and made me wish I'd been working on Madison Avenue instead of slogging across the Kra. There was canned music, soft and sugary, in the background. Her voice was sweet and low, and I had to strain to hear her.

" . . . and you may stay as long as you wish at a fifty percent discount, and please tell your boys to behave, to clean themselves well for tonight. . . ."

I must have knitted my brows. What did she think they'd done already?

"What do the boys like to eat?" the PR lady asked.

I gathered that she already knew, somehow, that Nok and Anant were probably Muslim. She was fishing for confirmation.

It was always a mystery to me how the average Thai always very soon knew they were Muslim.

"Ice cream," I said jocularly. "But no pork," I added.

She nodded, jotted something down, and went on, "The governor and his party will be here for your official reception at seven o'clock. The mayor of Surat Thani and the head of the Surat Thani office of the TAT [Tourism Authority of Thailand] and of their organization in Ko Samui Island, too, they will all be coming. And there will be two TV stations. . . ."

It was already six-thirty. There was hardly time for us to clean up anymore.

We were told that the governor, and his whole entourage, had been down to the hotel pontoon, to see the boat. They wouldn't have stayed long. *Henry Wagner* looked a mess. So would any boat that had been where she had.

Before the reception started, the TV cameras rolled. I excused myself from the interviewers' insistent attempts to center on me, saying I had bronchitis (it was very close to the truth). The artful media people kept trying to get Thomas and me more involved, to "expose" us more.

Conscious of this tendency, I slyly pushed our Thai lads forward into the remorseless blank stares of the cameras, and turned to them and consulted them, to make them seem to matter. It was a job.

All three of our lads were stiff and rigid with shyness and, I suspect, some fright, but I wouldn't let them, for one second, be left in the background. It was their voyage. They had crossed the Kra. I had been along only for the ride, as a passenger. Oh, now and then I had advised them, but they, and they alone, had done it. They were the first-recorded conquerors of the Kra, from sea to sea! *Me?* Oh, all I wanted to do was get back to sea. Didn't like being ashore. (Blunder!) *Not even in Thailand?* Oh no, no! Thailand was different. Yes, I liked being ashore in Thailand, especially working with our Thai crew. *Beautiful country?* Yes, very beautiful; our boys had been much impressed with the beauty inland, too. *Good people?* Yes, very good, especially our three crew members. *Good welcomes everywhere?* Incredibly so, always; my boys had welcomed me with little presents every time I returned to our boat. *Thai people always smiling?* Yes, our boys smiled all the while. *Helpful?* (Careful!) There had never been, not once, all the way across the Kra, one word of discouragement or objection from anyone; remarkable! *Thomas?* Thomas was my interpreter. He took photographs on our trips. It was his job, but the boys did all the heavy boat work. *What good had it done Thomas and me?* Oh, that was irrelevant. It had done Thailand and the Thai disabled, especially kids, a world of good. Now Thailand had three more young heroes whom she could be proud of, like her boxers and her longboat-rowers, and their names would be part of the history of this wonderful, beautiful land with all its smiling, helpful, welcoming people, and other disabled kids in Thailand, and all the world, would know their names, *Nok, Anant and Som*, and they would be legend, for ever, for as long as there were people in the Kra, their names would never die. . . . Oh, not at all, pleasure to be here!

Then the arc lights dimmed and went out, and we returned to the "real" world of the luxurious hotel lobby. Before we could catch our breaths, we were led into a brilliantly lit dining room. Along it ran a long table, set for about thirty places, groaning with food. Dewy wine bottles rested in frosted chromium buckets on stands by every few seats. The governor of Surat Thani Province was at the head of the table. Uniforms glittered.

By the side of the room was an alcove. In it was a small table. On that small table was a heap, two feet high, of about ten different kinds of ice cream. Nok and Anant had been relegated, but with high honor. Relegation or not, when they sighted that ice cream, their faces looked as they had done when, after we had been left half-starved by the army patrol, they had discovered tiny eggs in a bird's nest.

The meal started off stiffly and formally, but by the end of it, verbal wheels, well lubricated, rolled. After the meal, over coffee, the governor asked me what I thought of the planned canal across the Kra. Som was with me, at my request, as my interpreter.

I'd studied the problem and developments for some years. The vast tonnage of the world's cargo is carried by ships, airplanes carry an infinitesimal amount by comparison. For ships bound to and from Europe and Japan or China a ship canal across the Kra, from the Andaman Sea (the Indian Ocean) to the Gulf of Thailand (the South China Sea), would save a wasteful thousand mile traipse around Singapore.

Several schemes had been mooted over the previous two decades. One particularly mad plot (although promoted seriously at the time) was by Japanese entrepreneurs. They had wanted to cut a canal across the narrowest part of the Kra, where the Burmese border reaches its southernmost point. There the isthmus was only forty miles or so wide. Their problem was that the narrowest part was also the most rugged, with the highest mountains. Their proposed solution had been to blow a passage at sea level through the mountains, using atomic devices! God only knows what damage this would have done, with radioactive alien fish swarming from sea to sea.

Science and sense had prevailed; the Japanese atomic plot had been quietly shelved. Two favorite schemes remained on the Thai government's drafting boards.

One was to cut through the same way, across the narrowest part of the Kra, widening and dredging the existing rivers for ten miles or so, and then carving vast chasms through the mountains. A series of locks would then be constructed to lift ships up and down. There were two snags to this first scheme: The expense of such an enterprise would be horrendous, and the canal would have to be treated by all as an international waterway. It would have to be built with foreign money, and foreigners would have, to some degree at least, control over it. It would physically cut a good chunk of South Thailand off from the rest of the country. Politically this was difficult for the Thais to accept. Only now were the four decades of communist insurgency in the extreme south coming to a slow end. But now Muslim fundamentalists, with separatist aims, were beginning to agitate for more autonomy in local affairs, if not outright independence.

The second plan was to drive a cutting right through the southernmost districts of Thailand, through Songkla and Satun. This canal would start at Songkla port, head through the great saltwater lake north of the town, across eighteen miles of fairly flat lands, to the central mountains of the Kra. There a system of locks would lift ships around 490 feet. The canal would run on through the western coastal flatlands, to end somewhere between Satun and Thung Wa. From the Andaman Sea exit a deep channel through the shallow seabed would have to be dredged, and maintained, far out to sea.

This second, southern, scheme the Thais favored because it would separate the least part of the country from the main, and because it would bring much-needed income into a relatively poor area of the country. But not poorer than Trang, Thung Song, and Surat Thani.

"What do you think of the proposed canal, Mr. Jones?" asked the governor or one of his companions. I can't recall exactly.

"I don't think a ship canal is what you need at all," I replied.

The governor was a short, stocky man, perhaps a couple of years younger than I, but unlike me, of a handsome, quiet, studious, reposed dignity. He leaned forward, the better to understand me, although he had an official interpreter with him. He was smiling, but quizzically.

I went on, "A ship canal has too many drawbacks."

Now the interpreter screwed his face.

"Disadvantages," I explained. "It will lead to political wrangling by other powers who will seek to control access to it. It will alienate Singapore, because it will reduce the shipping calling there a great deal. The building and maintenance will be very heavy. They will add much to the cost of goods transshipped."

"What would you do?" asked the governor.

"I think the results—getting cargo from A to B—could be gained much more cheaply by building cargo-transfer depots in Surat Thani and Kantang. That would provide much more work for Thai cargo-handlers. Then build a canal for container barges along the route which our boat has just passed, using the rivers Tapi and Trang. The divide between them is only one-hundred-nineteen feet above sea level. You won't need to widen the rivers, certainly not the Tapi. You can install six or seven locks on the Trang to maintain water level, and about seven simple barriers and locks on the Tapi, and dig a ditch between the two rivers on the watershed plain. A few ditchdiggers would be enough—it's mainly clay or gravel." I didn't have to remember how the ground was: My good foot had felt every pebble.

"What about in the dry season?" asked the governor. He knew his stuff. He meant water evaporation from the heat of the sun.

"You dig out a couple of reservoirs in the clay on the watershed. You let the streams from the mountains flow into them. You plant wide-spreading trees on little islets all across the reservoir, and there you are. Good for wildlife, too. Then, when your canal-water level drops a touch, you open sluices and feed more water in. The farmers will love it, too. Half the ones we saw hadn't had rain for the past month! As for the inshore fishermen on both coasts of Thailand, they would love it, too, because when the monsoon wind blows from either southwest or north-east, and things are too rough to work, they could simply transfer their boats from one sea to the other, and work in safe waters all year round."

I think the governor was touched by my enthusiasm for a more natural waterway across the Kra. All the while his companion had taken notes. I don't know where he stowed them.

It was getting late. Our boys, dozy and bored and full of ice cream to their gunwales, had taken off back to our boat, to sleep.

The Ko Samui tourist-office manager invited us to his island. I thought only of getting to a doctor. My chest was wheezing, my whole body on fire.

"Come and visit us in Ko Samui, so you can write about our beautiful island," he said.

"We'd like to, but we're off to Bangkok in a couple of days," I replied.

"Really?" His smile widened. It was the one that said, "Business?" "Perhaps I can arrange for your tickets to be sent to the hotel?"

"No . . . no, thanks all the same. We're going in our boat."

The tourist official's eyes opened wide, his mouth opened, and he lost his smile for a fraction of a second.

"Not in that boat you brought here?" He recovered his composure. "There are big ferries that go to Bangkok," he said, "from Ko Samui. I can arrange tickets. . . ."

"Our boat's a good sea boat," I told him.

"But . . . but the Gulf of Thailand is . . . it might be a little risky. . . ."

"Any sea trip is," I said. "So is crossing the road."

"But there might be bad people. . . ."

I was tired, bone-tired.

Impatiently I replied, "Well, if there aren't now, there will be when we get out there!"

In my cool, dry, air-conditioned room I dozed fitfully all night. The wheezing of my lungs, the itching and burning of all my sores, from my head to my feet, would not let me sleep.

In the morning, desperate for relief, I borrowed 100 baht ($5) from the beautiful PR lady and told Som and Thomas to get me to a hospital. Our two small crew insisted on coming along. They knew I was in a bad way. It was as though they thought their presence might bolster my courage. I let them come: They would not "flee the scene."

Our first job was to fix the spring back inside my leg. That took most of the morning. We knocked it off the engine frame and battered it straight. We were lucky that Anant's hands were so small he could reach right down inside my leg and hook the spring back on. Then we all piled into a cheap chug-chug, though I had to crouch outside the car, clinging to Thomas and Som: I could not sit down without pain.

The hospital was government-run. The outpatients' department was as big, busy, and crowded as a city railway station. I was half-lifted into a large room, with ceiling fans to stir the warm air, and laid down on a high leather couch under a thin white sheet. My outer clothes had been removed. The nurses (two women and a man) let our crew stand by the couch.

I tried to cheer our lads as I waited to be anesthetized. "It'll all be over in a few minutes," I told them. "I go to sleep, and wake up feeling like Rambo. . . ."

The kids all laughed. They all knew what I thought of Rambo. Back in Phuket I'd even bestowed the name on a stray dog, who had adopted us for a few weeks, and had been afraid of flies.

They were still laughing when, as the two female nurses grabbed me and pinned me down, out of the corner of my eye I caught a glimpse of the male nurse, a cutthroat razor in his hand, place it on the huge soft scab on my good foot, and, without more ado, scrape my good leg, from toe to thigh.

I had gritted my teeth. I was sure I was going to hit the fan ten feet above me. I couldn't murmur. I was the captain. I couldn't lose face before my crew.

My mate, Thomas, a real hard nut if ever there was one, unable to drag his eyes away from the razor, fell to the floor in a dead faint.

Our three brave Thai lads, silent, all smiled widely. It was the Thai way. It was the smile that said, "I *chai yen*."

43

Time to Leave

Thomas, when he came round, took off, along with Meow, to ride on our motorbike, the 360 miles to Phuket and back.

I, with brand-new clean bandages and sticking plaster all over me, returned to the Wiang Tai Hotel, and rested for the day. That is, I set up my laptop computer and wrote a dozen letters and a magazine article for *Cruising Helmsman* in Australia.

I was still wheezing, but in cool air-conditioning writing was no hardship at all. Compared to trying to write in my confined corner of the bow in *Henry Wagner* in the Kra, with the temperature at 100-plus, it was a pleasure.

On the second day in Surat Thani I managed to make my way, with Nok's help, down to the hotel pontoon, and for an hour or two, in the morning breeze, sit near our boat.

Our boys had done well. They had cleaned her up topsides and below. Six flags and an ensign, lazily wafting, seemed to echo our feeling of relief and anticipation in heading back into the open sea.

Many curious strollers wandered down through the hotel grounds to stare at *Henry Wagner*. There were hotel staff, of course, and some of the few Thai guests, but none of the dozen or so *farang* guests knew of us, or if they did, bothered to go. From what I saw and heard of them in the hotel lobby, they had seemed to be mostly Swiss. Probably, seeing her from their hotel windows, they had imagined she was some kind of local tour boat.

One of our Thai visitors turned out to be a High Personage. His bodyguard, a well-armed gorilla (rare among Thais), showed how high. His master, at a very advanced age, had traveled down by air from Pattaya, especially to see *Henry Wagner*. He had been educated in England between the wars; his inflections were perfect Oxford. He said he had heard about foreign "yachtsmen" having crossed the Kra, and had come down expecting to see some "super-duper, whizz-bang, Styrofoam venturers in the latest style, their boat covered with advertisements for cigarettes or perfumes." At first he had been disappointed, he said, to see an old Thai wooden longboat, but then, seeing our crew, he realized what we were achieving. He was interested in the film business in some way. He told me the crossing of the Kra would make a fine adventure film, but it couldn't be made with a crippled crew depicted.

"Why not?" I demanded. "A crippled crew did it."

"Wouldn't sell," he replied. "Public wouldn't go for it. They don't mind . . . er . . ." he groped for an "inoffensive" word.

"Handicapped?"

"Yes, handicapped. They don't mind someone handicapped with a bit part, walking . . . coming on now and again, or someone in a wheelchair, but they're not going to sit and watch . . ." Again he groped for a suitable word.

"Stumps? Amputated limbs?"

"That's it. They wouldn't sit and watch them for an hour or two."

"Why not? *We* have to!"

"Oh, I love the way you yachtsmen are so honest and blunt and straightforward," reflected our High Personage. "That's what attracted me to yachting in the first place, sixty years ago. It was such a relief from all the pretense, all the dissemblance ashore. . . ."

"You mean in England?" I asked, testing him. I tried to imagine him as a young man, in Oxford bags, wearing a cricket blazer. Somehow it fitted.

"Oh, no, no! It wasn't at all like that there. I mean in Thailand, old chap!"

The next day Som arranged for us a cheap chug-chug to take us into the town market. Central Surat Thani was less Chinese than Kantang had been. There was more road traffic, more signs of garish modernity. From the chug-chug I could see shops full of boat gear, fishing nets, lines, and cordage. Outside one of these we stopped for Som to check the price of some two-inch nylon line. We might buy some when Thomas arrived back from Phuket with money. Our own mooring lines were frayed to frazzles.

Our chug-chug must have been a strange sight, with leg and arm stumps poking out everywhere. It was far too hot for our boys to have worn long trousers or longsleeved shirts even if they'd had any. They had little self-consciousness about their appearance. It was part of their nature to know that no matter how well they dressed, or how much they covered their stumps, how much Nok tried to hide his lower face, they would still be the objects of idle curiosity, laughter, or scorn.

We waited for Som to return from inside the shop, and . . . *we were mobbed.* Someone had run out of the shop with a copy of that day's *Rath* newspaper. Unknown to us, our boys were slap-bang on its front page! All over it!

Within half a minute half the marketplace was crowded around our chug-chug. Half a dozen plastic bags of cooked food were thrust into our boys' hands. A bottle of cola, dripping cold, was shoved at my beard. There was suddenly an even greater commotion at the back of the crowd. It was bedlam let loose.

Before I could do anything, a whole reel of two-inch nylon line was thrust onto my knees, all of five hundred feet, as it turned out. I almost shot up through the roof of the chug-chug as the reel banged onto particularly sensitive sores. "Free! FREE!" they shouted, in English. "You! You! *Pu-yai!* (Big man!)"

Then our boys were practically dragged out of the chug-chug. They were envied by a hundred other boys, smiled at by fifty girls, given *wehs* by a score of cordage sellers, patted on the shoulder by ten fishermen, and mothered by half a dozen chubby market women.

A passing businessman in a suit quickly bought an ornamental wooden elephant from the dozens that were on sale, and gave it to Som. It was about a foot high and a foot long. We took it back on board with us, triumphantly, and fixed it with four huge screws to the sawed-off stump of our bowstem. It is still there, as I write, to remind us, and everyone, of Tong Chai and how he helped us across the Kra, and of the good people of Surat Thani.

I was thankful for all the noise and fuss over our lads, for I was forgotten and left in peace. I was a bit concerned about sudden fame turning the boys' heads. There was no patronizing concern about this. I had yet many days to spend with them in the cramped confines of a small boat.

I needn't have worried. It was all far too sudden. Before they knew it, more by instinct than design, I had them back on board *Henry Wagner* getting the boat ready for sea.

The sea and her needs soon cure all shoreside foolishness, like believing in your own legend. The sea very quickly sobers up the intoxication of excessive praise. She can be a hard mistress. You don't head out for the widow-maker with your head in the clouds. Before you go, you open your eyes, stop dreaming, check your gear, and dive into the oily bilge. Or else.

In desperation, Thomas managed to get back the next day alone. (Meow was seasickness-prone and took off again for Phuket.) He had some good news and an outboard engine borrowed from friends in Phuket. My advance on the book *Somewheres East of Suez* had been paid into my account. We weren't rich, but we were not, now, in penury.

On the fourth day in Surat Thani, July 25, we had the engine off the boat by 6:00 A.M., and we had a whole new cradle made by eight. By nine our engine was back on board, and its cradle was painted. By nine-thirty we had unshipped our yellow awning and stowed it in the bottom of our boat. No sense in having top hamper aloft in a seaway, even if rain was forecast. We let go of the mooring lines and set off for Bangkok, about four-hundred miles to the north by my plot (made on a tourist brochure).

Before we set off from the hotel pontoon, I telephoned the Thai Navy antipiracy patrol headquarters in Songkla.

A personable-sounding lieutenant answered me in good, clear English: "Heading up the coast to Hua Hin? No problem! No, not sure how many miles. Yes, will have navy patrol boats warned by radio. Yes, they'll watch out. Thank you for giving full description of your boat! Oh good—you have VHF radio! Keep open your radio—channel 16 shipping frequency. Oh, no trouble! Pleasure! Yes, thank you, good-bye!"

We felt safer then, as if technology could protect us from the terror that we all knew stalked small craft of distant origin in the Gulf of Thailand.

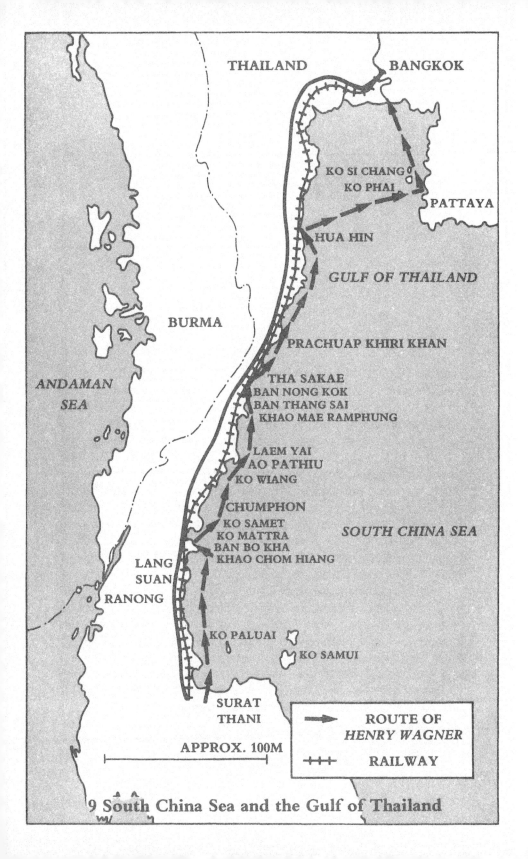

THAILAND   BANGKOK

KO SI CHANG
KO PHAI

PATTAYA

HUA HIN

GULF OF THAILAND

BURMA

PRACHUAP KHIRI KHAN

*ANDAMAN
SEA*

THA SAKAE
BAN NONG KOK
BAN THANG SAI
KHAO MAE RAMPHUNG

LAEM YAI
AO PATHIU
KO WIANG

CHUMPHON
KO SAMET
KO MATTRA
BAN BO KHA
KHAO CHOM HIANG

SOUTH CHINA SEA

LANG
SUAN
RANONG

KO PALUAI

KO SAMUI

SURAT
THANI

ROUTE OF
HENRY WAGNER

+++ RAILWAY

APPROX. 100M

9 South China Sea and the Gulf of Thailand

44

Into the Gulf

Back in Phuket I'd had neither the spare money nor the time to look for charts of the Gulf of Thailand. Besides, there had been no knowing if we would manage to reach the Gulf. The odds on it I had reckoned at 5 percent. In Surat Thani we could find none, and we had no time to wait for them to arrive from the capital.

But in a good sea boat, able to beach on shores even in a steepish swell, sea charts were not so vital. We would follow the coast, once we had cleared the mess of shallows north of Surat. There we would have to stand out to seaward about forty miles. We found two land-survey maps, showing the coastal areas between Surat and Khiri Khan, and the hotel presented me with a tourist brochure, on which was a tiny map of Thailand, and on those we set out to navigate to Bangkok.

Our departure from Surat Thani took us right along the whole town waterfront. No one except the hotel staff, so far as we knew, was aware that we were leaving. Yet as we passed down the harbor, a couple of thousand people on board craft of all sizes, from tiny dugouts to huge ocean trawlers, sang out and cheered and waved as *Henry Wagner*, bagpipes tape playing at full volume ("Lament for the Old Sword"), all our flags bravely streaming, steered out to sea at full speed, thirteen knots.

All along the waterfront, outside all the huge, dark godowns, men and women paused in their work to watch us pass by and to frenziedly wave and throw huge smiles in our direction. Half-loaded fish trucks waited, ponderous cranes hesitated, as we passed.

Our send-off from Surat Thani was, it seemed, spontaneous, and all the better received for that. There was nothing phonier, to my mind, than meticulously organized receptions and departures. All it needed, at those times, was for one button to be missing, one flag to be upside down, and the whole thing, to me, collapsed into ridiculousness. As I told Thomas, as we cleared for the offing, "No wonder so many military and show-business people are neurotic, worrying about buttons!"

The main ten-mile-long channel outside of Surat Thani, into the Gulf of Thailand, was busy with fishing craft rushing in and out. It was narrow, between shallow mudbanks, but fairly well marked. To keep out of the way of the fishing trawlers steaming at twenty knots, we stuck to the north edge of the channel, and felt our way round the mudbanks, until we were heading northeast.

All the fishing trawlers were crowded. Some of them were headed out for weeks. With fifty or sixty men all packed into their small space, we wondered at the living conditions on board them. Silently I reflected that if I lived as did those fishermen for weeks, on fish and rice, in crowded squalor the likes of which had not been seen in Western craft for a hundred years, I might not be so averse to a bit of piracy myself now and again.

But out in the offing for the first time in the Gulf, I didn't think much about piracy. I was all too pleased to be out at sea again, with a very lovable assembly of old hardwood, a firm engine cradle, some rice and canned food, fishing gear and good companions. What more could anyone wish for?

I supposed that many a landsman, seeing *Henry Wagner* crashing at speed over the swells, might have thought it a mite unsafe. Not I. Even hearing, below the engine noise, all the ominous creakings and groanings of timbers that had been subjected, as ours had, to such stresses and strains for so long, even when I considered the potential weakening of stringers, timbers, floors, and fastenings, I felt comfort. I remembered the old days, all the deep-keeled wooden yachts I'd sailed in, some of them bigger and longer than train engines, and constructed like cathedrals. I also remembered the desperate hopelessness that I had felt, often, when those yachts had sprung leaks; water mounting up through inaccessible seams down in the cramped darkness of their flooded bilges, deep below the waterlines, so that it was impossible to find out where it was coming from. Not for me. A small, open wooden boat was much safer.

As we crept up on the outer buoy of the channel, with wide horizons all to the north, east, and south of us, *Henry Wagner*'s elephant figurehead would dip, spear a big sea, toss a lather of spray over us all, and then jump high and aim for the next biggie. With no roof to our shelter frame, it was wet going. Then Anant, down in the bilge, would increase his pumping rhythm, to get rid of another gallon of salt water or rain.

Ko Samui (the island to which we had been invited at the reception) loomed on the horizon in the northeast, faint but beautiful, over a flat, calm gray morning sea. Over it, and all along the horizon to the east, dark rain clouds hovered.

"Shouldn't affect us," I told Thomas. "Not in the southwest monsoon. Those clouds should move away from us. Pity."

"They'll get rain in Cambodia and Vietnam, then, today," Thomas reflected.

I was silent. Thomas had unwittingly alluded to my main, but forgotten, concern. *Henry Wagner* might very well be mistaken, from a distance, for a refugee boat from either one of those countries. But once that distance was closed, what was to guarantee that the would-be pirate, once he had potential victims and loot in his sight, would not carry out an attack anyway?

I had talked about it with our boys back in Surat Thani. We had sharpened our axes, and had made more arrows for our hunting bow. Thomas had concocted four Molotov cocktails ("Don't use Coke bottles—they're too thick to break easily on impact!"). But apart from that, our samurai sword, and a signal gun with two flares, we had no means of defending ourselves against assault and possible death, except the sensible sailors' way: hide ourselves, even as we moved.

That was why I regretted the prospect of the rain clouds moving away from us. We could hide in rainstorms. Fortunately I was wrong about the rain clouds. They didn't move away. The heat of the land under the sun caused the hot air to rise. That attracted the nearest cool air to replace it. That was over the sea, so the wind direction was from *southeast*.

By early afternoon the wind had sprung up. It soon rose to a Force Seven gale and it *pissed* down. It was our first rain in a month! At first we joyfully let it run over us, and drank it, but then it became familiar, then a nuisance, and we settled down to suffer it.

Soon the sea rose with the wind, and then we were thrown around, and spray blew high over us and rain whipped us. With no roof, no protection, we were always soaked through to the skin, and I was uncomfortable in the extreme, but we were much safer, we imagined, from possible piracy. At thirteen knots we might head for any thick rain we saw, and be inside its cover in minutes, safe from ever-watching, merciless eyes. The writ of Buddha, the four rules of the *brahmaviharas*, did not, I knew full well, run far out to seaward in the Gulf of Thailand. Many, many of the fishermen were Muslims, in any case, and did not the Holy Koran state quite clearly that to rid the world of an infidel was by no means an unworthy act?

Our two Muslim boys made sure the flag of Saudi Arabia was worn apeak, the highest of the high; what Muslim would dare to attack a flag of True Believers?

And that, *mainly*, was the story each day and night at sea in the Gulf of Thailand.

Out in the huge Ao Ban Don, navigation was not easy. Because of the overcast sky it had to be dead reckoning on my hand-bearing compass. Not too difficult with a proper sea chart, but a bit more so with a land-survey map.

Once we had worked our way around breakers off the immense shoals of the bay, my aim was to try to make a landfall on the flat, low headland of Laem Thong Lang, about fifteen miles due north of the port of Surat Thani. Once past our landfall we would keep the coast in sight, but not too close, and work our way up it to Chumphon, a city about fifty miles by land from Surat Thani. There I planned we would spend the night.

We eased down our speed to around five knots because of the high seas. On a beam sea our boat was thrown about violently. About ten miles due west of Ko Paluai Island, we turned off the wind to head northwest for the low coast, to sight our landfall.

For another two hours, dashed by sharp, sudden rainstorms, and tossing, and about like a mad thing, *Henry Wagner* ploughed on. In heavy seas like these Thomas and the boys relieved each other after fifteen minutes each on our shuddering engine-helm. That was as much as anyone could take, balanced on our tiny stern poop, rolling like crazy and swooping up and down, ten feet at a time, once every five seconds or so.

As we emerged from one of those heavy, wind–driven rainstorms, we sighted, gray and dim, away to the east, about three miles from us, a boat. Through our binoculars I inspected her; not an easy thing to do with our boat rolling thirty degrees both ways. Her hull was shaped like a longboat's, but chubbier, and she had a small wheelhouse, and no longtail engine. That meant she had an inboard engine, and so more draught below the waterline. As she closed with us, I saw she had been painted gray. That was suspicious in itself. In the Gulf of Thailand, paranoia is the surest pilot.

I increased our speed, even despite the heavily rolling seas coming from our starboard quarter. I can't say exactly why I did that. I don't know what it was about her. Maybe it was the way she turned toward us so suddenly as we came out of the rain drives, maybe it was something intangibly sinister about her. In the Gulf of Thailand a skipper just doesn't debate with himself, or discuss any suspicion with anyone else: He shifts, fast. Or he might soon be very dead indeed.

I gave up all ambition of making a classic landfall on Laem Thong Lang. As the gray boat made in our direction at speed, throwing water off her bow, all I wanted was to get more speed, and drive our boat as fast as I could, yet on a safe course. That meant putting the heavy roller seas almost astern. That meant heading in to the coast further north than Laem Thong Lang.

It had to be Thomas on the helm now, half–blind or not. We couldn't chance our lighter-weight boys being thrown off our stern with the violent movement as we were heaved off one sea and then plunged into another. I crawled on one hip over the soaring, plunging deck, to tie a safety line around our mate's waist. With one eye I saw that the gray boat was heading the same way as we. There was no reason for her to do this. There was no fishing port, that I knew of, anywhere near the line where our heading met the coast. He must be chasing us!

We headed into a nearby rainsquall, and I glued my eyes to our compass, to make certain of our course through it, so we did not inadvertently give any ground to our pursuer. Then we were out in the gray day again, streaming wet.

I hung on for dear life to our shelter rail and peered astern. The gray boat had emerged from the squall, still on our tail, still at high speed. Slowly but surely he was gaining on us.

Nok, scared, had seen our chaser's slight gain. He clambered onto our tiny poop, and held down the engine's throttle lever. He grimaced at me as he flew up in the sky and then down into the troughs, along with Thomas.

I glared back at him. I spoke to Som. Quickly our one-armed lad delved into the bilge and brought out a wooden wedge and our hammer (the same one that the mahout had used to steer the elephant) and handed them to Nok.

In went the wedge, between the throttle lever and the engine casing. Bang went the hammer, and the engine belched black smoke that trailed all the way back to the gray boat.

Now the low coast was in sight. Before, it had been below the horizon, although the massive mountain range, far inland, had been in plain view, stark and beautiful. I peered astern.

Even despite our increased speed, our pursuer was gaining on us. Even though we were bucketing along at at least fourteen knots, she was slowly closing the gap between us. I looked at the low coast, with a small headland, which as we neared turned out to be in fact a low island. By dead reckoning on our survey map, I worked this out to be Ko Pithack. Our survey map showed some rocks around the island, but no depths. It also showed, behind the island, to its northwest, away from the weather, an extensive drying bank, which would probably have a couple of feet of water over it.

This was the kind of moment that captains are there for. Should we continue on our course up the coast, hoping to outrun our pursuer, at least until we came to somewhere that looked like a safe haven, and risk his overtaking us? Should we turn in toward the coast at a sharper angle and aim to get behind the island and into shallow water, hoping that our pursuer's deeper draught would stop him from following us in too close to the beach? And if we made it to shallow water, in that swell, with those breakers, would we risk overturning our boat?

"Turn her in, Thomas!" I held my arm in the direction of the breakers on the near side of the island, only a thousand yards away now. Better drown than a bullet or a knife, I thought.

Thomas with no hesitation obeyed. Our two small boys dropped into the bottom of the boat. Som smiled, but it was the Thai smile that said, "I'm scared out of my wits."

"What are you hiding for?" I shouted at our two tots. "You've taken longboats into beaches before!"

Som couldn't sidle up to me. He was thrown up against me as the boat pitched. "They very bad men here!" he shouted.

"I know! That's why we're racing them! We're going to beach her round the other side of that island!"

"No, not just the men on the boat. All the men. Over there!"

Even as Som waved his stump at the fast-approaching coastline, only three-hundred yards away now, our engine suddenly stopped dead. Our boat slowed down, then stopped. Thomas bent over our engine. He grabbed the wedge, heaved it out, and threw it down into the boat. He looked about ready to cry.

"Sorry, Tristan, I forgot to top up the fuel. . . ." We were about two-hundred yards from the outermost breakers.

The breakers seemed, from seaward, enormous. They rose from the shallow seabed, mounted up and up, and crashed on that rocky island shore. There'd be no way, without power, that we could get our boat in around the northern tip of the island, without her broaching and capsizing! I turned around and stared to seaward, at our pursuer.

"*Suffering Christ!*" I murmured to myself.

45

Back at Sea

Out of the corner of my eye, as the boys flung themselves at the engine and the bilge, to drag out fuel, I saw that our pursuer was slowed down, almost hove to, about a hundred yards from us. There were six people on his deck, standing as if they were staring at us. It was too far away for us to see their faces.

Thomas screwed up his eyes in the effort to see further than six feet.

I scrabbled below in the midship's section and laid my hand on a broom handle we kept there—one of those inexplicable bits and pieces that collect in a boat. I dragged myself painfully back to the stern, and stood holding it in front of me, as though it were a rifle. It might be mistaken for one, at that distance, if they had no binoculars.

I never saw three men or boys move as fast as Nok, Som, and Anant did. Nok had the duckboard up in a second, and was down in the watery bilge. Som (one hand!) already had the engine fuel-tank cap off and our funnel in place. Even before Nok had lugged a heavy fuel jerrican out of the bilge, Anant had its cap unscrewed. In no more than thirty seconds our fuel tank was half-full and Thomas had restarted the engine.

The wind and tide drifted us toward the island. By now *Henry Wagner* was no more than thirty yards off the rocks. Nok didn't even wait to replace the duckboard. He hared up forward, grabbed our sounding pole, and tested for depth. We had no more than two feet depth in the troughs.

"We'll keep to the shoals!" I shouted to Thomas. "Get the dinghy over the side! Som! Into the dinghy! Drive ahead as long as that other boat's with us! I'll con our boat! Nok and Anant will sound! Thomas, you steer on me!"

To get our boat around that island, and into the shoals behind it, would have been a miracle for a crew of big, able-bodied men. How we did it, as we were, must have been with the strength of fright and despair. As the seas threw us again and again toward the jagged fangs around the island, we crawled and scraped our way past the rocky northern tip.

Som, unquestioning, jumped into the violently heaving dinghy, and with Nok's help somehow clamped its longtail into place. Then, with only one arm, he bashed and crashed ahead of us, and steered the tiny craft as close as he could to the rocks, in between them, and showed me a safe passage. I bit my heart in my dry mouth, and directed Thomas after Som's course, along the very edge of a fine line between life and a watery death.

After an agonizingly long, slow push against the tide, we finally crawled around the point and found a large bay of calm water behind the island. Then we made for the mainland shore, and crept north, as close as we could to it, only twenty feet from the beach, until we saw that our pursuer had given up the chase, and headed out into the offing. But we stuck to the coast, close inshore, for the rest of that day. Anant and Nok, in the bow, sounded their way, dipping their poles alternately, just as they had learned up the rivers, once every ten seconds, for another two hours, until there was no sign of our erstwhile pursuer, and we were alone by the sea-beaten shore. Then we took Som and the dinghy back on board and speeded up.

We came to another headland, a high one, called Khao Chom Hiang, and just to the north of it, on our survey map, was shown a small village, Ban Bo Kha, where a rare road led to the coast. On the chance that there might be police where there was a road, we made our way there and, weary but relieved, anchored our boat in the gathering darkness. There were a few small vessels, mere shadows, lying to their anchors so still they seemed to sleep profoundly.

Before the dusk descended, we caught glimpses of the land behind the coast. It was beautiful. The late-afternoon sun shining behind the high mountains threw rays of gold into a sky scattered with clouds, so it looked as if a flock of golden-fleeced lambs were skittering from one horizon to the other.

Quietly we had supper, rice and canned fish, and turned in, setting the watch for the night. I always, on this passage through the Gulf of Thailand, kept the middle watch, from midnight until 4:00 A.M., so that our crew could have as much sleep as possible. No one should pass sleepy-eyed through the Gulf.

On July 25 we were all up and about even before the sun rose above the eastern horizon. We took off into a calm sea, with no breeze. It was ideal for getting north up the coast before the afternoon wind set in and turned the seas over the shoals into violent, moving hills.

We steered direct for the islands of Ko Mattra, then Ko Samet, perfect emerald pimples covered with palms. By breakfast time we were off the bay of Chumphon, and saw commercial ships riding at anchor, all agleam in the early-morning sun. The sea was silver under scattered clouds, and the mountains aglow with silver and gold.

All that forenoon we kept up our pace, and *Henry Wagner* shoved the seas out of her path with a quivering sort of joy. But the best fun was when Nok and Anant held the helm together, and they shifted their weight about and rolled the boat and she cuddled her gunwale down to the blue, and kept a little homemade rainbow arching over the wooden elephant on her bowstem.

The boys stopped that at a glower from me (*old spoilsport*), and shaped themselves up, so that they and our boat became two separate entities, yet working together; they full of mischief, she a live being impelled by strange wiles and impulses. A spirit of contagious joy, irresistible, was soon affecting everyone on board, and then we all laughed and sang, without wondering why.

By noon we had covered thirty miles, and the wind was rousting up the sea. A dead lee shore was no place to be in a small open boat in a gale, if it could be avoided. Ahead of us reared the small, high island of Ko Wiang. Behind it, according to our survey map, there was a bay and shelter from the high afternoon wind. It was obvious that the best shelter would be at the northern end of the bay, furthest away from the direction of the wind. The closer we came to Ko Wiang, the steeper the seas. By the time we reached its southwest tip, we were rising and falling at least twenty feet up onto the crests and down into the troughs.

No sooner had we slid into the southern entrance to the bay, behind the island, and into flat water, than *brrumpp!* there was that old Kra feeling, and we glided aground, but softly, on mud. It all happened so suddenly that there was nothing we could do about it. One minute we were in deep water, the next we were on a mudbank. When our boat stopped, her stern was only a couple of yards from where great rollers were deflected past us, clear onto the far mainland.

This was just up our street. Over the side went our lads, and before a half hour was up, they'd shoved our boat another hundred yards into the bay and further into the shelter of the island. Then we waited for the tide to rise a mite and do our work for us.

In the early afternoon the crew slept, while I kept an eye out and looked around. There was no doubt about it, Ko Wiang Bay was one of the most beautiful places I had ever seen. Close to us, the island rose steeply, all bedecked in gleaming greenery. Along the shore there was a sandy beach in between rocky outcrops. A few huts made up a hamlet. On the mainland side of the bay mudbanks extended out almost as far as the island. The coastline was so low that even at two miles' distance I could not see it. But beyond the unseen shore the vast mountains reached far into the sky, like the descant of a soaring hymn of praise. I wondered to myself if this was the kind of thing old Beethoven, deaf as a post, had envisioned when he wrote his Ninth Symphony.

On the island there were very few people around. An old man sat and nodded on a hut porch; by his side two young women stared at our boat. All was peace.

Thomas went ashore in the late afternoon for supplies. He found that the village store had little but locally produced food: rice, fruit, dried fish. It had no electricity, no radios, no television. What would heaven want to view?

The early start the next day led first past the foot of a headland with very high cliffs, Laem Yai. One wreck after the other on its rock-toothed sea fringe told the story of trawlers seeking shelter on stormy, moonless nights, and missing the entrance by a matter of feet or yards.

When we passed the headland, the coast fell away to the west, all bright and freshly laundered in the early sun. The far peaks we gazed at were in Burma. Thomas was even more astonished than I at this fact. I showed him our survey map. Further up the coast, near Prachuap Khiri Khan, the Burmese-Thai frontier was only about seven miles from the coast.

Neither Anant nor Nok could get it into their heads that the Phuket islands, their home turfs, were not in the sea that we were in. Ever since we had left Surat Thani and headed out into the Gulf, they had not been able to grasp that they were on the other side of Thailand. Many times I had shown them our maps, and tried to explain that this was a different sea, that Phuket was on the west side of Thailand. They would nod, and then look around them and shake their heads and say it could not be, the sea was the same. At each far headland we sighted, they would gaze longingly and ask, "Phuket?" And I, feeling a cheating schemer, would nod and reply, "Further!" But that's part of a skipper's job, after all.

By now, two days out from Surat Thani, they had become accustomed to the thought that perhaps Phuket was on the other side of Bangkok. Then, Anant explained to Nok, it was simple: if we came to Bangkok, we would be well on our way to Phuket.

They could not grasp the fact that a headland, jutting out from the coast so that it looked like an island, was not, in fact, an island. To have proved it, we would have had to round close to each headland, and seek the coast, to show them that it was joined to the main. It made me realize, again, just how patiently the first navigators, in ancient times, had learned their trade. It also showed us how very terrifying it must have been for man to become accustomed to the sea. Each and every time we argued with Nok and Anant, and patiently tried to explain our knowledge of geography (so easy!), it drove home to me what courage must have been in the hearts of the first people to set out to cross a sea to an unseen, unknown shore. It made me think how blasé we all are nowadays about our knowledge of the world, and how easy it is for us to forget that every time we travel any distance at all, by sea, land, or air, we tread on the blood, sweat and pain-racked bodies of the generations who have gone that way before us.

46

Running the Gauntlet

Now, back at sea again, I was slowly but steadily recovering from the effects of the rivers and jungle: their heat and humidity, and the ceaseless need for me to will our boat forward inch by inch. Now I had only two main concerns: weather and piracy. Good weather might help pirates.

We had rain almost every hour. But we could dry ourselves between showers in the breeze of our forward speed. Now I could find a spot in our cluttered, crowded boat and make myself a little spray shelter, and let the early sun dry my sores. I had cast off all my bandages as we had cast off the trammels of Surat Thani. The sea breeze and salt air did me more good than all the cutthroat razors and sticking plasters in existence.

Even though *Henry Wagner* was cluttered and crowded, if we looked closely at her, we would find that she had retained her essential air of almost puritanical simplicity. There was nothing about her, nothing in her, that did not aid our existence and her voyage. There was no one item of luxury in her from stem to stern, except perhaps for our elephant figurehead, and that ornament we felt she'd earned and, anyway, it was a continual reminder of what we were about.

Our boat had been superbly built. The Kra had proved that.

She was faithful and true. Sometimes she maddened us by rolling a mite too far, or by plunging when she should have been rising, but these were her tricks, to remind us what we owed her.

We roared toward the offing of Khao Mae Ramphung, a high headland, and our eastern and southern horizons being clear of everything except trawlers, we made out into the open sea.

In midforenoon we sighted, about a mile away, a Thai navy patrol boat at anchor and tried to rouse her crew on our radio. Channel 16: We'd remembered our instructions from the navy headquarters. There was no reply. I broke out my binoculars. There was no one in her wheelhouse or on her decks. Down aft, shirts and underpants were suspended on a line and swung with her every roll. I told our boys to keep their eyes sharp and to watch for anything that moved anywhere near us, or in our direction. I told Thomas, "We're going to have to be our own bloody navy!"

Soon there was nothing but sea and the headland ahead of us, and the blue-gold peaks of Burma to the west. Then we felt more strongly, as we did every time we left the confines of the shore, our own cherishing friendship with our boat. We knew every plank, every seam, in her, and we loved her, too. She was a good boat, and out in the offing she was like a desert horse that knows it must go on if it is to get to the other side. Then the shore lost its importance, and my compass took its place as the focus of my attentions.

Our boat seemed to know our intentions. Even as our helmsmen relieved each other, she would not change her pace. When the Gulf wind got ready to kick our teeth in as the sea arose, she was magnificent. With her six inches of freeboard above her waterline, she took each sea as though she belonged to it. And so she went, riding in high-bred fashion, worthy of all praise, and praise she silently received from me as she took each comber, one after the other. I gave her perpetual silent encouragement: No boat will do her best unless she is sufficiently flattered.

With such thoughts in my head I had half-dreamed in my corner, until the fact of where we were came back to me. I jerked my head up and gazed astern.

There were two boats following us, two miles astern.

Forgetful of Thai sensitivities about pointing, I wagged my forefinger at Som and chucked my beard in the direction of the strangers. He turned, stared for a moment, and nodded, unsmiling now.

Nok had seen my gesture; within a minute his throttle jammer—the wooden wedge—was knocked again into place. This time we remembered the fuel level. With our engine roaring full tilt, Thomas and Nok balanced precariously, somehow, around Som, moving as did he, and refilled the tank. Much spilled diesel oil sprayed aft in a golden shower.

There was no uncalled-for fear, no unjustified wariness about our reactions to these strangers out in the offing of the Gulf of Thailand. There was no need for them. Everything was done in deadly seriousness. We knew there might be danger of even death very close to us unless we did what we must do, and did it as fast as we could. I checked our radio transmitter and spoke into it: "*Henry Wagner* calling Thai Navy . . ."

Silence but for loud interference from our engine.

Now, being a cynic myself to some degree, I know there are others who will say that I am exaggerating the dangers we faced. Some travelers might say that they have been out on boat tours around the tourist centers of Thailand and that all I am writing here is nonsense. Take no notice of anyone unless they have been in a small open boat, of a strange origin and build, obviously not engaged in fishing, voyaging up the coast of the Gulf of Thailand well off the beaten tourist track.

The boats following us astern might have been innocent fishing craft on their way to or from their working grounds. But they had changed their original courses, and turned toward us, and now they were both on the same course as *Henry Wagner*. We could take no chances: This was the Gulf of Thailand. *We ran.*

We headed, at first, straight for Khao Mae Ramphung headland, on the chance that we might, as we had done the previous day, get close to it, inside the shallows, safe from deep-keeled marauders.

We opened up our midships treasure chest and dragged out our bow and arrows. Again we lined up our Molotov cocktails behind the stringers. Again I wished we carried half a dozen sticks of dynamite. Now both Thomas and Nok had the helm, to hold it steadier, so we could carry a course as dead straight as could be amid the mounting seas, and give away no distance to the strangers following us.

We steered to close the coast again: The chasers changed also to our new course. I thought of all the traffic heading north and south through that narrow strip of Thailand between the sea and the Burmese mountains; all the cars and trucks, all the tourists in air-conditioned buses, all the backpackers on the trains that went that way. I wondered if, when they turned their heads away from the sights of mountains, smiling peasants, and golden temples, and caught a glimpse of distant blue sea, they had any inkling, any idea at all, of the terror that stalked the Gulf. They were blameless, of course, those tourists, but I wondered if they ever gave a moment's thought to what it must be like to cross the Gulf of Thailand in a small boat from Cambodia or Vietnam? I wondered if, as they rushed from one touted fleshpot to the next, they related that sparkling sea they glimpsed to the horrific tales of robbery, murder, and rape that had reached the West? I wondered if they wanted to.

For sure the tour operators would not breathe a word about what was happening every day, every night. Not much about it appeared in the press, unless one could read between the lines. Like the presence of Anant, Nok, and Som on the lawn of the hotel Wiang Tai, it might "disturb the guests."

I looked astern and saw that the two followers were barely keeping up with us, but they were still on our tail. Now we had closed right up with Khao Mae Ramphung headland, and were rushing past it, butting the tidal current in fine spray that flew right aft.

Wordlessly our boys were all at their work: Thomas and Som on the helm, Anant in the bilge, pumping like mad. Nok was busy digging out another can of fuel from the bilge aft. I, in a rare spare moment, was reaching under our dinghy, where it lay forward in our bow, to drag out my samurai sword. If anyone tried to take me, I'd take him along. That must be the small-craft voyager's rule.

We were about six miles north of Khao Mae Ramphung. It was about 1:00 P.M. The wind had risen as the sun crossed our meridian. There was a line of white breakers all along the shore. We were doing well. We were right on the edge of the shallows, close enough to the beach to see the line of telegraph poles that marched along the railway close to it.

We had even gained ground on our pursuers, and now we were driving north as fast as we could, so as to get to Prachuap Khiri Khan, and perhaps safety, before dusk. I told Nok to take our helm and steer out to seaward gradually. We should be all right, as we were slightly faster than the two followers. We headed out at a slight angle. We got out perhaps a hundred yards, just off the shoals, and suddenly there was a noise even over the roar of the engine: *wwhhhrrn!* The engine itself seemed to want to take off into the air.

Swiftly, Nok knocked the wedge away from the throttle lever and stopped the engine. He leaned over it, then turned. His mauled face looked as if he would burst into tears.

"*Nah nah nah nah!*"

Thomas sprang up, stared over the engine, and shouted, "The longtail shaft's busted! It's split . . . *broken!* Just below where the shaft joins the gear wheel! Cut clean in two!"

I glared around. The two boats were pointed straight at us, and making for the shoals. I thought fast. "*Right*, Thomas, keep the engine longtail in the water for a bit of steerage! Everybody else help me grab the shelter cover! Hold it up, as much as we can. We'll catch the wind. We'll sail her in over the combers!"

And that's what we did.

But we couldn't sail her into the beach at right angles. The beach there was deserted, and I was wary of our pursuers sending men ashore to attack us. There would be no way for Anant and me to get away from the boat fast enough to avoid them.

The wind was strong, in the southeast. Further along the shore, about a mile away, our survey map showed a coral island, and north of it a village, Ban Nong Kok. There might be police there. With the wind dead astern of us, we would *sail* our boat very close up the shore, and get into the narrow strait between the coral outcrop and the beach.

Thomas, half-blind, steered somehow. The rest of us dragged our heavy yellow shelter awning out of the bottom of the boat, and stretched ourselves up as high as we could, and held one end of it up, to catch the wind, and made ourselves into human masts. As we closed up to the village, at about half a knot, probably less, we reached the shoals. We all, me included, hopped over the side, and pushed our boat along the beach, through the three-foot combers, until we had the coral rock between us and the weather.

Seeing our intentions, and the impossibility of following us, the two boats in the offing turned out into the open sea, and before long were lost over the horizon.

The whole time this had been happening, our boys had been

shaking with apprehension over the thought of what our reception at the village might be. The stories of wildness and mayhem in the Gulf of Thailand and all around its shores were part of their heritage. They had been terrified. We arrived in the early afternoon, when no one was about, but at four o'clock, as everywhere else in Thailand, the whole scene would spring to life. And it was four o'clock now!

"They're bad people here," muttered one of them. "Everybody in Phuket say. They know how bad these people are. . . ."

I rested against the side of our boat. I was panting in the heat. I would have to take my leg off to drain the water out. Stone the crows! What a Life! I was thinking.

I looked up. To seaward, over the low coral shelf behind which we sheltered, huge green combers approached one after the other and broke, roaring, on the rock, and smashed themselves into steamlike spray that vaporized into lovely rainbows.

Far along the beach a line of small longtail boats was drawn up bows forward on the beach, in the shade of high palm trees. Beyond the palms there was a rise. Beyond the rise a quick flash of dim color caught my eye. I stared more intently. It was surprising how a two-day cruise in the Gulf of Thailand had sharpened even my eyesight.

A gang of people—mostly men—were marching through the shadows below the trees, toward the beach and toward us.

"Here we go!" I muttered to Thomas.

47

On the Beach

Anyone who has seen a Thai boxing match (and it was within living memory that big fights had been fought to the death) would know that a vicious streak of violence can be contained even in a people so outwardly gentle and well-mannered. Watching a Thai fight, it seemed to the innocent spectator anything was allowed. Feet, knees, heels, elbows, heads, and fists, all were used in sudden flurries of wicked brutality. Only a recently arrived *farang*, a fool, a masochist, or a first-class Judo black belt purposely insulted or harmed a Thai man or youth unknown to him.

As the gang approached us, along the shore, we saw, by their black baggy trousers, that they were fishermen. They were mostly shirtless. Their faces were set, unsmiling. They did not talk among themselves. They must have ranged from twenty to fifty. They were mostly spare and lean, and their muscles, hard as rocks, glistened as they moved. A couple of them, in their early thirties, likely, were built like prize-fighters. Two of these had their sun-browned torsos almost covered in dark blue tattoos. These, we knew, were Khmer tattoos, probably (but not necessarily) applied in Cambodia. Their inscriptions were Buddhist prayers, meant to keep away evil spirits.

Three of them toted small bottles of cheap Mekong whiskey. One or two of them had the sleepy, almost dead eyes of regular ganja smokers. We knew, from Kantang and Surat Thani, that many, many Thai fishermen smoked the ganja weed to dull their heavy labor, or to while away their waiting hours in crowded vessels where conditions were worse than in the worst slums.

These were small-boat fishermen. The weed, we knew, was popular among those also. Golden beaches and waving palms were not the be-all and end-all of men whose living depended on sitting for hours in a half-gale or a night storm throwing and hauling lines. For Muslim fishermen, mainly further south, or scattered in small groups around the northern bight of the Gulf of Thailand, there was not even the solace of alcohol.

These men, most of them anyway, were clearly not Muslims.

Our lads had somehow moved silently behind me.

I made a *weh* to the fishermen, as they neared, and tried to smile.

Suddenly all the tenseness in the air dissipated. The fishermen crowded round us, bowing and smiling and chattering in gentle, low voices. They spoke too low for me to be able to understand very much of what they said. Even Som had some difficulty in making out their speech. They called me *Aharn*, Teacher. It was their innocent form of compliment.

We were finding, as we passed further north in Thailand, that the difference in dialects between districts was becoming an increasing problem. It was as though there were several distinct languages.

Then Som sidled up to me, smiling the Thai smile that said, "I don't think these people are bad." "They say they know us," he said. "They saw us on TV!"

Anyone who might by now have gained the impression that I am against the transmission of images by means of electronic impulses per se should have known the relief I felt when Som told me that. It's not TV I'm against. It's the churning out of so much chaff day and night. God only knows what any intelligent beings that might be out among the stars of some distant galaxy will think of us when some of our present tide of waffle reaches their signal-detectors millions of years hence. But with the signals go my apologies.

On the beach, in a few moments everyone was friends in the Thai way. Our Muslim boys, naturally, gave slight smiles and looked at the men from below their brows. I got them busy. They tied a long bowline to the nearest palm tree, then set to dragging our three anchors out of our boat, and walking them out into deep water. They did that eagerly; anxious to show these strangers that they knew their stuff.

"They say," Som explained to me, "that we can move our boat down with theirs, if we like, further down the beach."

"Tell them thanks, but no. We'll stay here."

"They say the sea come here heavy when the tide rise."

"Tell them I don't like sleeping in a still boat."

It was unusual for me to attempt to make excuses, even jocular ones. I had long before given up trying to explain my wishes or my actions in everyday matters in Thailand. I had found that (on our level, remember) no one ever showed objection to this, or wanted an explanation. A simple "yes" or "no" worked much better, and the Thais seemed to appreciate knowing where they stood.

I may have been right or wrong, but I had found, mainly by instinct, that, for example, if I wished someone to leave me, it was much better simply to say "Please go now" than to make any kind of attempt at drawn-out real excuses, or, in the Western way of politeness, to invent white lies. It was better to be blunt, simple, and honest, even if at times, to a Western onlooker, I might have seemed discourteous, overbearing, impolite, or brutal. (As the *Guardian* newspaper had, though marginally more kindly, reported me.) The Thais understood it, and respected me for it; that's what mattered in our situation.

But the main reason I had refused the fishermen's offer was simply that I could not afford to take the chance of trusting them. They were friendly enough in broad daylight, but what might happen when their evident euphoria at meeting strangers who Had Been On TV wore off? When they realized we were only human?

We explained our immediate problem to them: the broken longtail shaft. No problem, they said, we could take it into the closest town, Tha Sakae. There were longtail-engine agents there, and workshops. The most-tattooed fisherman offered to go into town on his motorbike for twenty baht ($1) and fetch a chug-chug to carry the shaft the six miles or so into Tha Sakae.

Very soon we got our longtail shaft ashore and had our boat sitting out to her three anchors, in deeper water, close to the coral shelf for some shelter, but she reared in the heavy seas like a wounded bullock.

Thomas and Som, trailed by the gang of fishermen, took off

along the beach with our longtail shaft. I hopped into our bouncing dinghy, and Nok pushed me over to *Henry Wagner.*

Over the Burmese mountain peaks black rain clouds clung. The monsoon wind was blowing hard up there, from the southwest. Soon dark tendrils tore themselves from their mother clouds and started toward the sea. The first patters of rain hit me as I rolled myself over our heaving gunwales and dropped down into the bottom of our plunging boat.

Breathing wheezily in the hot, wet air, I crawled to my damp mattress, all laid out ready for me by little Anant, and threw a damp sheet over me. I removed my false leg and my trousers. As carefully as I could in our tossing, pitching boat, I took rainwater to wash the encrusted salt from a hundred scabs and the leaking ooze from the red, raw ring around my left thigh.

As I tended myself, scrunched up in our forepeak, Nok and Anant dragged the heavy awning over our shelter frame and tied it down. They were quiet now, and kept themselves busy. In some unspoken, inexplicable way they seemed to be much closer to me now. I was no longer, it seemed, merely "*Captan.*"

They knew me. We were terribly vulnerable, out at anchor off an open beach; vulnerable from both the sea and the land. They knew that, too. Now I was their defender against all terrors. Now I was their father, their friend, their defense against all comers. I was certain that they reassured themselves silently that I would *know what to do.*

"*Captan Keng Keng*" (Very-Clever-Big-Strong-Number-One) was, by then, their name for me when something I had done pleased them, or when I had been overgenerous. Those boys could flatter a frog.

Under the sheet, now dripping rain, I slid along my wet mattress and delved under it. I felt for our rusted but trusted samurai sword, to reassure myself that it had not slid down into the bilge. I sighted, too, our hunting bow, all wrapped up in its plastic bag to keep its drawstring bone-dry and taut.

My toilet over, I grabbed my false leg and hauled it from where it lay under a plastic sheet, to keep it from further rot, where the plastic had frayed around the top. I winced as I heaved it onto my wet, raw stump. I poked my head out into the rain from under the sheet and briefly glanced at them. I watched my two fellow sentinels, one a small boy with one leg half as long as the other, and the other another urchin, but stronger, with half his head a patched-up mess, and I prayed silently that their Allah and my God were good friends.

Then, only three-hundred yards from the main railway line of Southeast Asia, north to south, Singapore to Chiang Mai, we settled down, our minds on our weapons, such as they were, to guard our boat, to keep our eyes open, the boys to seaward, I to landward.

The two boys, gimlet-eyed, watched each and every one of the many boats in the offing, and I, squinting through my binoculars, wiping the rain and salt spray off the lenses every minute, inspected carefully each and every foot of the shadows cast by the late-afternoon sun over the now-deserted beach.

48

A Rainbow

The weather in the northern Gulf of Thailand was like some vast regular machine. Every day, as the sun grew hotter, warm air rose from the coastal plain and, high up, met cooler monsoon air from over the Burmese mountains, and turned to rain. The hot air from sea level was replaced by cooler air from the Gulf; a wind that increased as the afternoon wore on. By dusk a full gale blew until early the next morning.

Henry Wagner was on a dead lee shore. Powerless, if our anchors dragged, there could be no stopping our boat being driven ashore in the breaking seas.

As dusk approached, Nok, Anant, and I kept watch. Our boat heaved and pitched and tossed and jerked like a maddened steer.

Just before dusk deeper shadows appeared in the gloom under the trees. We watched them intently, wondering who it would be, and what they might demand of us.

I knew by their gait, even before they emerged into the light, that it was Thomas and Som. They were empty-handed. They grabbed our long mooring line and made as if to pull us in to the shore, to show us that we should ease off on the anchor lines. There was no sense in hollering; the roar of the wind, the lashing of the rain, would overwhelm any human voice. If they wanted to get on board, they'd have to swim for it. There was no sense in beating our boat on the seabed closer to the beach, or trying to board our dinghy in those heavy beachcombers.

Having to swim on board through breakers was not too bad for Thomas; he could drag himself, hand over hand, along our bowline.

But for Som it was a different kettle of fish; with him having only one arm, we had to pull him on board with a line thrown to him on the wind, by Nok.

"What news?" I asked Thomas as he shook the salt water from his body.

"Everything closed," he gasped. "It's Sunday!"

It showed how preoccupied we were with guarding ourselves from possible predators: We had forgotten the day of the week! That would, perhaps, be cause for a smile among landsmen, but among ocean sailors, necessarily meticulous about knowing the exact time and the date, it showed me how potentially dire our situation was. *If only we had sail!* I found myself thinking time and again. But in a power boat, engineless, we were trapped.

It's a poor sailor who can't find some advantage, though, when everything seems to be against him. I found we had two advantages; and both due to the weather. The first was that the sea in which we were anchored was now so rough that no marauder could approach us from seaward without risking being wrecked on the shore, and the second was that no predator could hope to get on board easily through the breakers.

Thomas added, "There's a couple of good repair shops. They will be open in the morning."

We ate rice and mackerel (caught by Nok) in the rain, then set our night watches. All night long it rained and the swells rolled in, on and on, and our boat jerked on her anchor lines. All night long someone was awake, watching the dark shore and our bouncing dinghy, while the others dozed fitfully, wet through. Then toward dawn the wind and rain eased off, and we were left plunging in middling-sized but smooth swells. Then it was like being in the back of a damp fish truck in which a raucous party had been held the night before, trundling along over rough mountain tracks. Bad enough on two legs, but on one . . .

I decided that one night off Ban Nong Kok had been enough. If those fishermen had woken with any ideas of. . . Before anyone on the shore was awake, even before the first lightening of the eastern horizon, we got the outboard motor that Thomas had managed to get hold of onto the dinghy, lashed it alongside *Henry Wagner*, retrieved our mooring line, heaved our anchors, and, only fifty yards from the shore, set off slowly up the coast. In that way, in a couple of hours, we limped into the little bay at Tha Sakae. But even as we approached the anchorage, our outboard engine gave up the ghost. We dragged out our awning and again sailed *Henry Wagner*, this time using early-morning zephyrs, as light as a gnat's breath, up to the beach.

Thomas and Som headed ashore for the longtail repair shop. The rest of us guarded *Henry Wagner*. In two hours they were back on board with a new shaft. It had not been possible for the old one to be repaired. A Chinese-Thai had shown them a store full of round metal rods. They had chosen one the right size, taken it along the street, to where a lathe sat in a shed, and in short order it had been threaded and milled exactly the same as the old, broken shaft had been. It was amazing to Thomas that so near to a place as primitive and somehow primevally sinister as Ban Nong Kok, a piece of machinery could be made so well and so fast.

The Chinese workshop owner had not tried to cheat us, Som told us. They had bargained, of course, but eventually he had charged us only three-hundred baht ($14) for the whole outfit, shaft and milling.

As we fitted the shaft to our engine, a fight broke out in a small trawler alongside. It was extraordinary. One man, who seemed to be perhaps the first mate, hammered and punched, beating the living daylights out of another, who for some reason I cannot recall seemed to be the cook. This latter did not defend himself, but merely crouched, his hands over his head, let himself be beaten senseless, and ended up spread-eagled facedown over the fishing craft's bulwark. All the while another man, who seemed to be the skipper, sat smoking only a yard away, in their small wheelhouse, and stared vacantly at the garbage-littered foreshore. No one on the crowded decks of a dozen other fishing boats seemed to think the fracas was anything unusual. Everyone smiled and nodded at everyone else, and carried on with forenoon chores, or gazed dreamily at the town. I stared at the collapsed cook, and reflected that in almost fifty years at sea, that was the first time I had ever seen fighting on board a fishing boat.

A sense of impending disaster, should we delay in getting through the Gulf of Thailand, did not allow time for engine trials. Without waiting to eat, as soon as the new longtail shaft was buttoned up to our engine, we pushed *Henry Wagner* off the muck-strewn beach of Tha Sakae, and took off, in calmer seas, north, headed for Prachuap Khiri Khan.

Our new longtail shaft was all right. We made good time—twenty-five miles in three hours. It was still before noon when we roared past the low headland to the south of Khiri Khan.

Over the peaks in Burma black clouds piled up into the sky. Rain deluged the town, so that all we could see was a sheet of dull gray velvet. Suddenly, as we headed for a narrow, rainswept channel between two islets, from the east, where the sky was clear over the Gulf, sunshine poured in and set up a perfect rainbow. It was one of those rare celestial arcs of such firm symmetry, of such density of color, that looking at it in the sea offing, no one could deny the existence of a Supreme Being.

Then the sheets of rain cleared over the shore, and the town was bathed in a silver glow. Below the exact center of the rainbow, shining silver and scarlet and gold, atop a perfectly placed hillock, was revealed a tiny, elegant temple.

The bay at Khiri Khan was big, very shallow for the main part, and well protected to seaward from the afternoon onshore gales by a line of lovely green islands. *Henry Wagner*, with her shallow draught, sought the southern end of the bay, and anchored in about two feet of water. That would be enough; it was low water and the range of tide was only two feet or so.

All work and no play makes Jack a dull boy. I sent the whole crew ashore to walk and exercise, while I guarded our boat. Apart from that, I wanted to tend my sores, and try to dry them off. In a crowded boat it was too awkward, and with a leg stump it was too embarrassing, even among other stumpees. When others were on board, I had to try to do the whole thing under a sheet dragged over me. Then it was a pain in the neck and everywhere else.

This was not so much modesty on my part. It was more a recognition of our Thais' innate modesty, and their essential decency where bodily functions were concerned. I doubt if, on the whole of that voyage in *Henry Wagner*, from Phuket to Bangkok, at sea, in rivers, jungle, or on mudbanks, over two months, I was ever aware that our crew defecated or urinated. Everything in that line was done so secretly, so quietly, that there was never a clue that it had happened. As for me, it meant having to balance over the side at sea, in a pitching boat, or through the Kra, up the rivers, fling myself over the side and crouch in muddy water, or hobble into jungle undergrowth. Even then there'd had to be a Thai standing around not too far away to watch for snakes.

The vast majority of Thais past puberty that we had observed (and girls always—outside of the tourist sextraps) had been most modest and took great care never to expose themselves too much. They had come down, sometimes in droves, to the riverbanks and shores, and covered themselves with sarongs pulled about them, and had bathed their whole bodies with not one hint of immodesty, or shame, only feet away from where we had sat in our boat. When they had wanted to be, they could be the most asexual people I'd ever clapped eyes on.

Nok and Anant, although they were lively and obviously pleased about something, said nothing to me when they came back on board. It was only later, from Som, that I learned they had been recognized ashore. Street urchins who were poking fun had been chased away from our boys by passersby. Schoolboys who had stared and laughed at them as they passed had been scolded by their teachers. Girls had smiled at them as Anant limped along. A chug-chug driver had given them a free ride! They had been spoiled and even cuddled by chubby-armed, elderly ladies in a coffee shop, and feted with free sticky rice and ginger beer. They Had Been On TV!

I didn't know then if Nok and Anant appreciated fully what had happened to them; that they had become famous in their own land. I didn't think so. It seemed to me that, if they thought about it at all, they conceived of the marked change in attitude of strangers, the little marks of admiration and respect they found in strange places when they were recognized, as being the will of Allah.

Perhaps it was?

49

A Head of Rocks

If you worry about not getting back into port safely, sail with a skipper who can't swim. If you worry about getting into bad seas, sail with a skipper who's seasick-prone. But if you worry about not getting enough sea time, sail with one who can't get ashore.

There's nothing worse than being in a beautiful-looking place, and unable to get ashore. In Prachuap Khiri Khan, as I sat on board *Henry Wagner* nursing my sores, it was like gazing at the town through the bars of Cambridge police cells. I knew that because I'd done it in my youth, forty years before, during a wild shore spree. For Thomas's better understanding, when I told him that, I likened Cambridge to Heidelberg, and then he laughed.

We ate a supper of fresh *pla thoo* (a mackerel) fish presented to our boys by the ladies of Khiri Khan. We slept or kept watch through a lovely moonlit night. The chain of islands between the bay and the Gulf were great dark humps that rose steeply out of a black sea. The town was a wide necklace of twinkling lights, and behind it massive black mountains reared into the night sky. A few fishing boats, their wakes aglow with phosphorescence, churned the waters of the bay at odd hours, but none approached us.

We never, on the western shores of the Gulf of Thailand, set an anchor light. We always had a light ready, in case a boat passed us too close, but as much as we could, we let the darkness hide us.

Seamen are minions of the moon and tide, not the clock. In the hour before dawn Nok hove our anchor rode. Our big mud-hook was soon awash, our cat-fall hooked on by Anant, and with my help the muddy, dripping anchor was hoisted and lashed down.

Under power, departure was never the same as it was under sail. I missed the throwing off of gaskets and tiers, and the heaving home of halyards and sheets, the intent sensings of every breeze. Compared to sailing out of a harbor, motoring out was a bit like climbing onto a bus. I still found myself absentmindedly gazing aloft for a mast and sails that weren't there, and then dropping my eyes and somehow feeling a mite ashamed, as if I were naked in a crowded room.

Into the night, with no lights showing, we made for the northern end of the bay, dodged a big fisherman, and took off into the open sea. There was no sense in calling attention to ourselves. There were no TV cameras in the Gulf of Thailand at dawn.

Our run—and a run it surely was—from Prachuap Khiri Khan to Hua Hin, our next port, was about ninety miles. We made it all by noon. We started off before dawn and, laboring thirty minutes on, one hour off at the shuddering, willful helm, Som, Thomas, and Nok made a good thirteen knots all the way.

That sunrise! Beautiful as sunsets in the tropics are, sunrises are even more so. They were often, to me, the most glorious sight on God's earth. But they had a fault—they were too common. They happened every day, whereas if they had only occurred once in a lifetime, travelers would have come from all over the world to marvel at the sight. To see in a few moments the velvety blackness of night tremble through veils of pale purple, hueless gray, all shades of azure, delicate rose, and flashing gold to the imperial blaze of the risen sun was a thing unforgettable.

As we witnessed that holy sunrise, I told the boys that the people who believed in a Christian God thought that he was light. Nok and Anant wondered if Allah was light, too, and I replied that I thought he might be, but I wasn't sure, because the people who believed in him lived mostly where the sun was not a friend. Som said that he thought Buddha might be in the sun, even though he might no longer exist. As Anant handed me a cup of hot Lipton's tea, I stared carefully all around the horizon for any suspicious-looking craft, but their gods and mine were awake, and we were safe.

For us it was a hot forenoon; the slight morning breeze was almost dead astern of us the whole way, and we were outrunning it. It was as though we were rushing forward in the slight swells in still, muggy air. The unforgiving sun rose ever higher, and *Henry Wagner* plunged into the rising seas, one after the other, with our engine roaring at full tilt.

A little to the north of Khiri Khan was as far as our land-survey maps extended. Now we were left with the rough map on the front of the hotel's tourist brochure. It was like nothing in the map room of the Royal Geographical Society; it was of the whole of Thailand and three inches square. It was little to go on; it gave only a general (and very inaccurate) idea of the shape of the Gulf Coast, but then our draught was only a foot, and it was better than nothing.

Hua Hin ("Head of Rock") was, we knew, Thailand's oldest seaside resort. The kings of Siam and their families had spent their summers there for about sixty years. There was, Som had told us back in Surat Thani, a royal palace at Hua Hin. Hua Hin had sounded like the Promised Land of Ease and Quality.

For days, ever since we had started out through the Gulf, Thomas and I had looked forward with mounting anticipation to our visit to this tropical Brighton. I wondered aloud what edifice the Thai equivalent of our prince regent might have erected at the pier's end. Instead of, as on Brighton's pier, a model of an Indian palace, perhaps one of a Venetian house, or a Schwabian castle?

Our discussions, our hopes, our dreams, about the pier at Hua Hin turned out to have been futile. There was no pier, or at any rate nothing like Brighton's. Instead there was a great clump of black rock jutting out to sea, against which massive seas rolled and broke in splendors of rainbow spray two score feet in the air.

The peaks in Burma, dull blue, had distanced themselves from the coastline, and lay almost forty miles back, across a low, steamy plain. Beyond the rock we found an indentation—it was too modest to be called a bay—on the shores of which stood a vast, old-fashioned, tastefully built hotel. There was no sign of a port, none of a haven of any kind except this little curve in the coast.

Old posh hotels had telephones that often worked better than the ones in new hotels. It was urgent that we telephone, as we had arranged to do, our friends at the British Embassy in Bangkok. One more day without word from *Henry Wagner* and our contact would raise the alarm and have, perhaps, the Royal Thai Navy or Air Force searching for us.

North of Hua Hin rock, the seas rolling into the indentation were too heavy and violent to allow *Henry Wagner* to enter any closer than four-hundred yards off the beach. If our engine failed for any reason, we would be wrecked on the rock-strewn foreshore. We prepared our dinghy, and Thomas and Nok, greathearted, set off in it, bouncing on top of the swells and disappearing in the troughs.

"*A good skipper never worries; he concerns himself.*" Nail-biting concern was the order of the day, until we finally breathed again and sighted little patches of color moving up the beach, and knew that our two brave stalwarts had made it safely through the steep, heavy breakers, onto the sunny shore.

This was one of the most distressing consequences of my disability: I had to ask others to take risks I could not take myself except in utter extremis, perhaps to save other lives. This to me was far worse than any jeering looks or sniggers. As we say in Wales: "The limping wolf in winter knows bitterness indeed."

When Thomas and Nok returned, wet through and glowing with their small victory, their news was good. The telephone had worked. Our friends were relieved, they said, and there was a fishing port a mile north of where we lay rolling in the offshore swells.

But this latter tidbit I had already reckoned; the fishingboat traffic in and out, from behind the next headland, had told me.

As we rounded the headland, full speed, Nok at the helm, nimble-eyed and weaving for risk of collision with the many boats rushing to and fro, I wondered at the lack of smiles, a seeming trepidation, of our Thai lads. I asked Som about it.

"Hua Hin is near Petchaburi," he said, mysteriously.

I stared down at our tourist brochure. The city of Petchaburi was marked, a little dot. "But it's miles away!" I exclaimed. The distance wasn't clear, perhaps it was forty miles.

"*Mae pen rai.* . . . It doesn't matter. Petchaburi has many very bad people! They're all gangsters. Everybody knows that!"

For the rest of that day, all the long windy afternoon, as we wallowed away in a steep swell in the middle of the harbor, close to the beach, out of the way of rushing fish trawlers, and watched for our anchors to drag, our boys tried to hide themselves, scrunched low below our gunwales.

Hua Hin stands in my memory, as I write, as one of the most uncomfortable small-craft havens I ever encountered. There had been a few that had topped it, like Bratislava in Czechoslovakia,

Assab in Ethiopia, or an oil-refinery port on the lower Thames that had been so smelly and mucky that I never even bothered to record its name. At Hua Hin the hard afternoon wind blew straight in to the anchorage. The heavy seas it pushed before it, rising ever higher, heaved and rolled at full co⁻quering strength, straight into the bay. Hua Hin had been recommended to us as a pleasant, visit-worthy small-craft haven so often that we were expecting something like (well . . .) Brighton Marina.

The only calmish shelter at Hua Hin was alongside the fishing wharves, which poked out straight into the open sea. They were crowded with working craft lying six or seven deep. Heavy fish trucks and cranes rumbled along the wharves. The harbor water was an oily, filthy mess. The noise was so loud that we, pitching and tossing a hundred yards away, had to shout to be heard. The hard wind rushing by us took our voices and sent them flying toward Burma. But even at the wharves, two-foot waves bounced back from the shore, and the whole time we watched, the jumbled fleet of fishing boats banged and bashed heavily against each other until their work was done. Then there were violent scrambles and loud groans of protesting iron and timber as boats next to the wharf were somehow edged out of the teeming mess, and once escaped, roared at full speed to anchor in the wallow of the open harbor. Their decks were crowded with refugees from the impoverished northeastern province of Esan, laboring for pittances. It seemed that these men and boys were the fathers and brothers of the often lovely "bar girls." No wonder some of them, it was reported, sometimes turned to piracy.

By the first signs of dusk we'd all had more than enough of Hua Hin. Any voyagers worth their salt could take any amount of banging about and discomfort at sea, on the move, but in harbor it was a different matter. Especially with, between us, an arm and two legs missing.

I aimed for a course for us straight across the open Gulf of Thailand, east for eighty miles, to Pattaya. There was no sense in risking a crossing in daylight, when we might be sighted by possible predators from miles away, when we might better make it under cover of darkness and, showing no lights, hide as we moved.

To us, on passage through the Gulf of Thailand, all the things that the seaman normally abhors—black night, no lights, mist, fog, rough seas, and rainstorms—they were all sturdy, true friends.

50

Wetting the Elephant

Henry Wagner departed Hua Hin as soon as daylight faded. We had to get across as much of the eighty miles of open Gulf as we could before daylight exposed us to curious eyes. We didn't leave the bay and head straight out to sea. Unlit as we were, to avoid collision with fishing craft rushing in and out of port, and to deceive prying eyes, we followed the coast north for a mile or so before we changed our course east and headed out into the dark offing. Then, even as we threaded our way through hundreds of bright fishing-boat lamps bobbing offshore, we were but darker shadows in the night. We were by no means the only unlit vessel out in the Gulf. They were all over the place, hove to or roaring around, far and near.

We must have had a dozen of them come tearing past us out of the black night, at anything up to twenty knots, and we must have disturbed more than a few of them, too. For the first ten miles east, I came to realize, we were not only hidden by the dark; we were actually disguised, by our lack of lights, as a local fishing boat. No strangers shone their floodlights on us, and played their beams around us, as they would have assuredly done had we been properly lit. (A tropical fisherman's bad habit, worldwide.)

When we departed Hua Hin, there had been a strong wind

with gusts well up to gale force, and mountainous swells from the southeast. The wind eased down slowly from an hour or so after dusk, but it left heavy showers that wet us through and through, and a steep, jumbled sea that slowed us down to nine knots. We smashed and crashed and bashed at full tilt into ten thousand waves an hour. Streaming water, salt, and rain, wet through to our skins, we ignored the pelting rain and the jerking, pounding, hammering, and sudden sliding of our hull, and the buckets and buckets of spray slashed over our bows by the resisting, resentful seas. Elation was aboard. "Wetting the elephant," we called it.

All that black evening, and most of the black night, in the spray and the rain, we showered the elephant. No one slept. Not even a rat, not even a bat, could have dozed on board that night.

Past midnight, then past the dead hour of landsmen, we crashed, bashed, wallowed, sluiced, and soaked our way east.

Dawn was upon us again, magic and holy. We were all far too weary to enjoy the scenery much as we pushed our way, in dry weather now, past the off-lying islands west of Pattaya. As the sea eased off, and the violent movements of our boat with it, we managed to cook some fish and rice and make a hot drink. As soon as we sighted our first tourist longtail, to the south of Ko Phai Island, we knew we were safe, more or less, from any potential molestation. The tourist police would be watching, perhaps. We eased our speed down to six knots. Our Thai lads fell into deep slumber in the early sun.

With Thomas on the helm, half-falling from exhaustion, me conning our course for him and struggling to keep my eyes open, *Henry Wagner* rambled into Pattaya Bay. I tried to square up our topsides. Tired as we were, we thought she must look as much like any respectable tourist-toting local longboat as we could manage.

We needn't have bothered to try to disguise ourselves. Before we reached the first of a hundred longboats at anchor in the bay off the beach, loud shouting and waving told us that everyone in them already knew very well who we were. We Had Been On TV!

The shouting from the other longboats woke our lads, and in a minute Nok was strolling our deck like the captain of the *Nina*, Som was up forward coiling down a line (try that with one arm!) and, Anant had crawled back down in our bilge and was busy pumping out water as fast as he could. There never was anything like payday and a looming shore to wake a sleepy young sailor.

We wended our way through the longboats at anchor, and inspected the shoreline at Pattaya town. Without a map or chart, it was all very confusing. Finally I decided to head right for the middle of town, and we steered for a broken down–looking pier. There we anchored our bows off, ran a sternline ashore, and slept for the rest of morning. Or tried to.

The Pattayan Thais wouldn't let us rest. They crowded around our stern and chatted with our lads, who all basked in the glory and the glamour that were the customary deserts of the elect, worldwide, who Had Been On TV.

Thomas and I understood quite a bit of what was exchanged in Thai. Our boys (the two that could) talked about the Kra and the rivers, the jungle and the sea. Nok was not shy and gesticulated and made loud noises, while Anant (his Dr. Watson) interpreted for him. But the people inquired about the TV cameras and the interviewer, because, evidently, those were the things that they thought were far more novel and important. To the people ashore, our crew seemed to be no longer mere boys. Now they were the configuration in human flesh of magic images. Behind the crowd around our stern, on the edge of the beach, a large spirit house was ablaze with flowers and candles. If ever there was an example of the Great Clash of Cultures, of the East and the West, of the ancient and the modern, of the nurtured and the imposed, it was there, on that stretch of beach in Pattaya.

Still I could not walk very far; it was too painful. Most of what I observed in Pattaya was along its foreshore. From my vantage point by the old spirit house, under the shade of an old gnarled boa tree, I thought that for a crowded, noisy town with a capacity of ten thousand beds for visitors and all the frenetic activity going on along its beach, Pattaya's foreshore was surprisingly well kept. But there was an air of transience about it.

In the late afternoon, after we had rested, I paid our lads some bahts and preached them a good old Welsh nonconformist hellfire view of the hazards to young sailors ashore in a lively town, and sent them off.

Thomas and Som, as always, went off across the busy seafront road together. Nok and Anant, all spruced up and hair combed, shoved off up the beach. I watched our two smaller crewboys. Nok strolled along confidently, as though he were about to inquire about some luxury condominium in which to invest his treasure; Anant limped alongside him on his crutch, and laughed at Nok's comments (or at his own embarrassment) as they passed girls sitting at the roadside stalls. Only Anant could understand with any clarity his friend's attempts at speech.

Soon Nok and Anant were part of a shuffling crowd of people, mostly visitors, it seemed, along the opposite pavement. I recognized Thais, *farangs*, Indians, Japanese, Malaysians, Arabs, Singapore-Chinese, all intent on enjoying themselves in their own ways, and happy, when necessary, to suffer to do it. As our two *enfants terribles* were lost in the crowd, it struck home to me just how insignificant, just how utterly unimportant and defenseless they really were, and my mind boggled at what they, and we, had done. Then they were gone, and I thanked God that, all the same, whatever they had done, they had done it like sailors, good and true. I prayed that they would not do the same in Pattaya.

I had no need of concern. They were all back, all four of them, within the hour, with still some baht in their pockets. I said nothing, and they said little, but I knew that—subconsciously maybe—they had sensed what I already knew: Compared to what they had witnessed and experienced in *Henry Wagner* at sea, across the Kra, they had realized the spiritual poverty of practically everything that Pattaya was about.

All the triteness and futility of what they were seeing; all the showy drinking, the forced mirth and loud music, all the games and pretense, the bright, gleaming bars crowded with young women from the poor, parched Esan, ready and waiting to pick the *farangs* clean; all this they had seen although they could not have put it into words, as the dross it was.

All the pasty, potbellied, long-nosed, middle-aged *farang* men, all the pushy Arabs and shoving Chinese, free at last, they thought, in a place where only the cash in the pocket mattered. All the hairy-legged nut-turners and bottle-washers from Munich, Melbourne, Miami, or Manchester, who played out their Rambo-Bond fantasies as they basked in never-ending smiles of approval, so they thought, the fools, and toted around, behind their flabby shoulders, their refugee girls (or boys) on hired motorbikes. Now our crew knew the real reason for that name Thai peasants (no fools they) had bestowed so neatly on these pale bodies that dropped from out of the sky: *kee-nok*. Birdshit! A bigger heap of perambulating birdshit than Pattaya's had never been seen since Sodom and Gomorrah.

As our lads, safe and returned on board *Henry Wagner*, turned on Anant's cheap little tape player, I was pleased beyond measure to think that they were, perhaps, learning to distinguish the false and true, the futile and worthy. That night, as they kept watch, I slept for more than an hour for the first time in four days.

We stayed in Pattaya for three days. We contacted a local Catholic-run home for disabled kids and took fifty or sixty of them around the bay for boat rides, ten or twelve at a time. Those kids were so excited and happy that some of them almost forgot their crutches when they scrambled on board, or tried to leave their wheelchairs. It had been, they told me, the first time anyone had ever offered them a boat trip.

"I hope," I told them, "it won't be the last."

There were almost as many longtail boats based in Pattaya Bay as there were "service" girls and boys based on its beach.

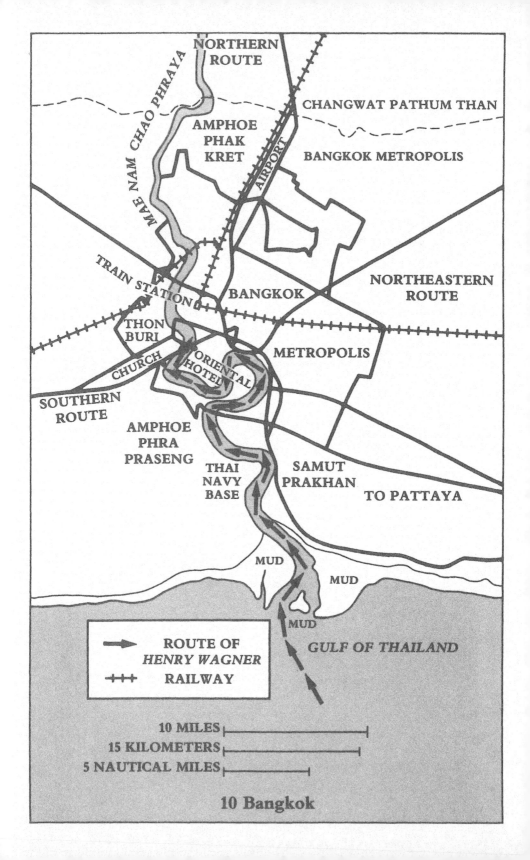

10 Bangkok

51

The Tumult
and the Shouting

On our second day in Pattaya we moved our berth. I was fed up with being importuned with explicit gestures day and night by small, ragged urchins as young as six of both sexes. We shifted a mile away to the south end of the bay. Besides, traffic was quieter, and there was a bit less swell there when the tide rose.

No sooner had we anchored off and dragged our stern to the new beach than four policemen on two motorcycles arrived. Their faces, as they jumped off the bikes, were serious and suspicious, as befitted their role. The most bemedaled one, whom I took for the senior of the squad, patted his pistol as he marched down to the water's edge. They all peered over our stern and screwed up their noses at our shabby state. I can't say I blamed them.

It took us a good half hour to convince the cops that we were not committing any heinous crime by not staying in a hotel, and that we would be moving on as soon as we had dried our boat and ourselves a mite and obtained supplies. They had not seemed convinced, and had all waited, silently, and stared at my pockets for some time for some reason, until a beach-umbrella attendant rushed down and told them that We Had Been On TV. Then they had all smiled the smile that said, "You might have connections?"

and had roared off, and that had been the last, and only, evidence
of any law enforcement I saw in Pattaya.

During the time we were at Pattaya, many Thais who knew
who we were smiled a friendly greeting and sometimes stopped
to chat with our lads. Although plenty of *farang* visitors (and
residents, too, probably) strolled along the beach, not one of them
took any notice of us. The only sign of any curiosity that I remember was from a group of four Arab-looking men. They had
chattered and pointed with their beer bottles at our Saudi flag. But
they were escorted by eight prepubescent Thai females, and soon
moved on to evidently more interesting activities than staring at
longboats.

I commented to Thomas that they probably thought that the
Koran's strictures about alcohol stopped as soon as they boarded
a plane for Bangkok.

"They might be Maronite Christians from Lebanon,"
Thomas pointed out.

"Yes, and the lasses they're with might be from the local
nunnery," I rejoined.

It rained only once in our three days in Pattaya, and that was
a mere light shower. Our stay there, when I ignored most of what
was going on ashore, did us good. We could buy food at the stalls
on the waterfront, and that gave us relief from cooking on board.
In between taking groups of disabled kids out for spins around
the bay, we cleaned our whole boat, and ourselves, thoroughly.
That was so that Bangkok would find our appearance more acceptable, perhaps, than had the Pattaya police. As I told our lads,
"It's a poor boat that doesn't arrive at her destination better than
she left her home port."

I sent Thomas ashore to telephone Nat Page, first secretary
at the British Embassy, and tell him that we would arrive in
Bangkok on the evening of the following day, July 31. We intended to leave for Bangkok at midnight on the thirtieth. But there
was no sign of Thomas until the small hours of the morning of
the thirty first. Then, "not feeling too well" (in fact three sheets
in the wind, as we sailors say), he turned up, fell over our stern,
and collapsed in the bottom of *Henry Wagner*. I told our Thai lads
to move him forward and wedge him between our treasure chest
and the boat's side, and make him comfortable. Silently and carefully they did this, while I watched.

Most Thais had an almost reverent way of handling people

who might have had a few too many. They believed that because
the man was off-guard, a spirit, good or bad, had entered the
person, and that spirit must not be offended. The problem was
not the man who was drunk, but the spirit that was displaying
itself. It had nothing to do with approving of the man or encouraging drunkenness or being "friendly," as so many boozy
farangs imagined. In most cases of drunkenness that I witnessed,
I got the impression that, deep down, most, if not all, sober Thais
felt quite the reverse.

As for me, my first rule in getting along with shipmates was
"Moderation on board, toleration ashore." It's a poor young sailor
who can't be allowed to work off steam. God knows, Thomas
had plenty to work off. He had been, for six weeks and more,
hardly able to see clearly more than six feet, worked to a frazzle,
mostly confined with three Thai lads, whose behavior and expres-
sions had been, to say the least, often puzzling or exasperating.
Not to mention (he must, surely, have thought to himself time
and again) his captain, an elderly man in continual pain, who
seemed at times to be driven almost to the point of megalomania
trying to prove a point that might (who could know?) never be
taken.

But drunk or sober, sick or glowing, rich or poor, a shipmate's a shipmate, and he has to be looked after. So Thomas was
made comfortable, and I checked that his head was down, so that
if he were sick at sea, he would not drown in his own vomit while
we were unable to hear his gurgles and death rattle over the roar
of our engine. It had happened more than once, as I told our silent
lads.

Now we had, on the surface of things, an awkward situation.
Nat Page at the British Embassy in Bangkok was expecting us,
and would have, as he had offered, arranged a berth for our boat
and perhaps accommodation for us ashore. We were all ready for
the fifty-mile sea passage to the mouth of the River Chao Phraya,
and then to head upstream to Bangkok. The weather looked fine
for a forenoon passage across the open sea, and the sea would be
at its least rough. But one of our two 4 limbed people was out of
action.

It's a poor skipper who can't find something good in an awkward situation. I quietly told our lads that now was their chance
to prove that Thai fisherboys didn't need any *farang* help to steer
an open boat across an open sea. They could relieve each other

every fifteen minutes and drive at full speed for their country, their capital, their own honor, and for me. And if they couldn't, or wouldn't I, somehow, would do it myself. Now, would they please set up all six flags and wet our elephant?

It might have sounded corny, perhaps, but my Thai boys listened to me patiently, but excited. Eyes gleaming, they smiled and nodded. And then that's what they did.

By God did those lads work! Our dinghy was on board almost before I could turn and look at it. Nok hopped onto the steering poop, and in a second or two our engine was clattering away. Som took in our stern anchor from the beach, Anant hove up our main anchor, and we were off into the false dawn and a gently rolling sea. Once we had safely passed the anchored longboats in the bay, I peered at my compass and set our course for the Chao Phraya River, northeast by north, and from that moment on, for three hours, until the seas rose with the wind, our brave boys laid a wakeline astern of us as straight as a billiard champion's cue. Their straight steering, and the way they fitted our stern neatly onto each rolling sea, time after time, the whole way to the river, would have made any America's Cup skipper, any Admiral's Cup captain, roll with envy. And all the time our mate, bless his memory, caught up with his sleep in the bottom of *Henry Wagner*.

Our last dawn in the Gulf of Thailand was dry and glorious. To the east the sky was clear, and as daylight crept upon us, sunbeams shot into the sky from behind mountain peaks one hundred miles away in Cambodia. It would not have surprised me to have seen angels in the sky.

Broad daylight showed us a sky clouding over. The high coast to starboard threw a heavy belt of gloom along the shoals between the islands, which, in the calm of expiring light, were unmarked by the slightest ripple. The air was heavy with moisture, and the wind had the faint acrid smell that told of chimneys.

As we came level with Ko Si Chang, a big island behind which we could see big merchant ships hiding, all over the sky little clouds were scattered evenly, but over the island there was a mound of cumulus. It looked like a sheep in a field of lambs.

As we neared the northern shore of the Gulf of Thailand, the sea was almost flat calm. I noticed a line in the sea ahead of us. At first I thought it might be a breeze rippling the water, but as we drew near it, we saw that it was only a skim of dust. Soon it had closed around us, and on all sides, as far as my eyes could see, stretched a level gray plain. It was dust from the industries and cities of Central Thailand. It had been caught up in the night breeze as it had swept down from the mountains of Burma, and then dropped from the heavens like rain. The sea was so still that the dust had not sunk, but had settled down on the surface in a thick film.

In the early forenoon we reached the entrance to the Chao Phraya River, and pushed upstream against the current between low, almost invisible banks. A short while after, we came to what was obviously a naval base. There were several warships, all clean and gleaming, ensigns hoisted, lined up before a shipshape wharf.

It was getting on for noon. I decided to wake Thomas and shook him gently. As always, he woke with a start.

"Thomas! Wake up! *Bandidos!*" It was our alarm word for pirates giving chase.

Thomas jumped up and stared, red-eyed, over the side at half the Thai Navy. There was not one soul in sight on any of the warships' decks. Then, half-grinning, half-apologetic, he glanced at me, then he slumped down again while I got him a cup of coffee.

"We're safe now. Have a good time last night, mate?" I asked him lightly.

"*Ja.* I met some people from Munich, and they knew a place where they have Munich beer. . . ."

"Did the phone work?"

"Yes, the English know we're coming!" He meant our contact at the British Embassy, of course.

"They might have some good old English ale . . ." I sardonically suggested.

It goes to show how colloquial Thomas's English had become. It goes to show the standard of the English he learned from me. "Bloody gnats' piss," he muttered. Then he made his way to our stern to relieve Som on the engine and to steer our boat for the rest of the day, all the way to Bangkok.

We had been able to obtain no chart or accurate map of the river. People we had asked in Pattaya thought there were about fifteen miles of river between the sea and the city. It turned out to be closer to thirty. With the tide and the river current pushing down against us at around five knots, it took us six hours. We reached Bangkok just before dusk.

The scenery that we moved through, as we pushed our way upstream, reminded me of Joseph Conrad's description of it, written a hundred years before, except that now there were hundreds of power tugs to shift rice barges, instead of sweating, straining rowers.

All the way along the river, from eighteen miles and more south of Bangkok city, were thousands upon thousands of great fat Chinese-looking rice barges from upcountry. They all had high sides and rounded tin roofs over their holds to keep their cargoes dry. Aft there was an open-sided wooden cabin where the family who worked them slept, ate, and made love. The rice barges lined the banks or sat patiently to anchor in long lines, sometimes of a half-mile or more, midstream. Dozens moved in any stretch of the river, towed along by immaculate little diesel tugs. All the loaded barges were full to their absolute gunwales, so that the river lapped over their midships decks. The whole passage upstream was a kaleidoscope of heaving tugs, dirty big factories, filthy, crowded docks alive with half-naked laborers toiling in the sun and shade, dark, shadowy godowns, and, interspersed between these gloomy sites of toil, perfect, clean little temples, all red and gold, their frontages ablaze with flowers.

For the first few miles, as we neared the city, big ocean-going merchant ships from half the world rode at anchor in midstream or were being unloaded at the wharves. But it was the people on the smaller craft who welcomed us: They all knew us. We had Been On TV!

There was hardly one yard of river's edge that was not crowded with people, either in boats or on the wooden balconies of houses that teetered, some at alarming angles, on piles right out over the water. There were whole families living in sampan boats no longer than fifteen feet. There were dozens of huge houseboats with what appeared to be schools of youngsters on them. There were men, mothers and babies, children, youths, girls, women, young, middle-aged, ancient, thousands and thousands of them. It was as though the whole of the Orient was afloat.

And practically every single one of those people, when they sighted Henry Wagner pushing up the mighty stream, stopped whatever they were doing, and waved shirts and sheets and shouted and cheered. I listened to the voices of those people of the Chao Phraya as they cheered and cheered our three brave Thai lads, and I heard a welcome for them at last, into the comity of humanity.

* * *

As we passed mile after mile of cheering throngs, I hid low down in our boat. I was exhausted, weary, old, and tired. Only the noise of human voices, even above the roar of machinery everywhere, like ocean waves beating on a shore, told me that, so far, Atlantis was winning.

But my inner voice told me that there was much, much further to go. That murmuring beat of recognition—to me not for ourselves but for all disabled kids—must come not only from the banks of one river, but from everywhere in the world, and others besides me must make it so.

I dragged myself upright, and peered ahead. I squinted against the sun, low down to our east. Our boat's bow swung as Thomas rounded a wide bend. Out of the sun's glare appeared the form of a cross. It was all in a blinding flash. I could see nothing but a black cross in the sky, as though it were hovering unsupported over the riverbank. It was like a photograph snapped against direct sunlight. Below the cross, and all around it, was only the brilliant, blinding glare of the sun.

Half-blinded, I turned my eyes away from that blaze of light but pointed my stick in the direction of the hovering cross. Our elephant, its head down, as if in contrite homage, as if in worship, turned toward it.

52

City of Angels

As *Henry Wagner* closed toward the riverbank, and the sun dropped behind the city, whose Thai name, *Krung Thep*, means "City of Angels," we found that below the cross—surprisingly somehow—was a church. On the bank before the church was a small landing stage. On the stage was a notice: FIRST EPISCOPALIAN CHURCH OF BANGKOK, and immediately beyond that was a wire-mesh fence and an open gate.

After our traipse through the Gulf of Thailand any fence, any gate, between our boat's resting place and the shore was more than welcome. In sultry heat now that the breeze had dropped, we made fast to the landing stage—and were mobbed by young men in soccer gear.

They were all, it seemed to me, of purely Chinese descent. Some of them spoke some English, some French, a couple some German, and one even some Italian. Very quickly, as I laid myself down to rest a while, a bedlam of Babel was in full swing, and it stayed so until about an hour after darkness descended on the city around us, and the footballers went home to their evening meal.

All the while, graceful sleek longtails with stilettolike bow-stems and long roofs, had roared past, and set up a continual chop on the river, so that we had rocked—and were to rock—all night.

It goes to show the exhausted state of my mind that I didn't get around to asking Thomas details of his previous day's phone call back in Pattaya until well after he returned from buying food for supper from somewhere behind the church.

"Nat Page is going to look out for us at nine o'clock in the morning," Thomas replied.

The roar of traffic on the Bangkok bridges nearby was almost deafening. "Where? It's a big city, mate!"

"Nat said on the landing stage at the Oriental Hotel. . . ."

That, weary as I was, meant little to me. "Good, then we'll take off about eight and go and look for him."

Then I set our watches and fell asleep until my own watch at three in the morning. For the first time in weeks I felt, somehow, we were all much safer.

Very soon after we started off the next morning into the crowded river, we were accosted by a cross-river ferry and, in a flurry of shouts and arm waves, shown where to go. Nat Page and a half-dozen reporters and the hotel management and hearty handshakes were all waiting for us on the steps above the Oriental landing pontoon, which with all the river chop was moving like a whale in heat. All the Thai boatmen on it were staring at the name of *Henry Wagner*'s port of origin, painted in Thai on our stern: Phuket. They stared at our crew. I knew their thoughts: Surely they should be in the dust of the temple yard, holding out their hands for alms! They stared at us all again: we had come one thousand miles in six weeks, and we had *crossed the Kra!* And we had run the gauntlet of the Gulf!

It was all overwhelming. I fended off a hundred hands stretched out to help me off *Henry Wagner* and so ashore. My stump and good foot howled silently. I stood on the shifting pontoon, balanced with my stick, and watched as our lads secured our boat shipshape and Bristol-fashion. That done, and them all ashore, I turned and mounted the steps. I felt as if I could easily lie down and gratefully die on them. Instead I had to order Nok to accompany us. He wanted to stay on the pontoon and fish in the river. Sulkily Nok obeyed me.

We all passed into the cool, immense lobby of the Oriental Hotel. No one here asked us for our passports as security. No one here told our boys not to walk in the hotel grounds. No one here looked down their noses at our boat, or at Anant's short-cut trouser leg and crutch, Som's short-cut shirtsleeve, Nok's clamped jaw, Thomas's plastered sores, and my stick. Here was not a hall of distorting mirrors, a place of empty smiles. No one here made us *farangs* feel we were perambulating, gift-loaded Christmas trees. This, no one needed to tell us, was the *world's best hotel*.

Nat had booked me a single room, he said. In the coolness I could rest.

"Please, can my crew have a shower?" No sooner had I asked it than we were all whisked to the very top floor of the Oriental Hotel and shown two huge suites—one for Thomas and me, and one for our crew. "Both yours for a week, sir, courtesy of the management."

My smaller Thai lads were so obviously overwhelmed with all the wonders so suddenly all around them, so out of their depths, that I sent them out with a few baht into the city streets to a nearby Muslim restaurant. Thomas took off with Som to find an optician's shop to buy himself some spectacles, and a place where his photographs might be developed. I knew his pictures might not tell the tale too well, except to people who might, one day, know the whole story. It wasn't because he could only see a mere six feet: Whenever anything significant had happened, Thomas had always been too busy to even think of his camera and film and lens adjustments.

My suite was two huge rooms with big picture windows. The furniture was grand, the bathroom sumptuous, the service superb. I soaked in a great warm bath (with handholds and a telephone within reach!), then I dressed my sores and myself and slumped down on a small couch and stared at the gleaming river and the temple roofs of the city below. I draped a sarong over my stump. I was in the depths of utter gloom. *Has it all been worth it?* I was able to think nothing else. I had no answer. Mountaineers will know the feeling.

It must have been midafternoon when I came out of my half-trance. There was someone standing near. I stirred to look around, and put my hand right on top of something freezing cold.

I saw Nok and Anant grinning, and then looked down at my chaise longue. It was all white silk and little embroidered flowers and lovely mahogany. And on the silk, alongside me, sat a Thai coffee-shop ice cream: a great dollop of the stuff slapped between two pieces of dry bread, sandwich-style. It was starting to melt and ooze out onto the silk. I grabbed it and held it, and stared at it. It must have cost them all of five baht (25 cents). It dripped onto a fine carpet.

I was so surprised I broke out in English: "What the hell is this? . . ." Then I remembered some bits of Thai. "Who put this here?"

Both of them grinned shyly. Anant, as almost always, spoke for the pair of them. "It's for *Captan!*"

"Who bought it? Who wasted money?" I demanded.

"Nok bought it for *Captan!*"

I gazed at Nok. His split upper lip quivered with pleasure and pride in his gift to me.

I tried to look stern. "Why did Nok bring this? What does Nok want?"

"Nok wants *Captan* to have ice cream!"

"What for?" I tried being sarcastic. "Is it because Nok likes *Captan* now even though *Captan* didn't let Nok stay down at the river and fish? Is that it? Now Nok likes *Captan* again?" I glared at Nok. He was staring at the carpet.

In one hand, held out at arm's length, I held out their ice-cream sandwich. It was dripping onto my other, cupped hand. "Nok doesn't do what *Captan* says this morning, and now Nok thinks Nok can buy back *Captan's* respect with one ice cream? Now Nok thinks *Captan* believes Nok likes *Captan?*" (*God, can you believe it?*)

They were both outstaring the carpet now. Then Anant looked up and smiled. He spoke, as always, very quietly. I strained to hear him. "No. *Captan* is not speaking true. Nok didn't say he likes *Captan*. Nok said he bought *Captan* ice cream because *Nok likes Nok now, and Anant likes Anant now, too!*"

For a moment there was a still silence. I laid the dripping ice-cream sandwich on my stump. It didn't matter if it melted on my old sarong. I could hardly look at their eyes. "Go now, thank you," I croaked, and I tried to crease my lips into a smile, and they were gone, and the river below me dissolved.

Alone again, I turned and faced down toward the City of Angels, and I cried. I didn't cry as a baby cries, for what it wants. I cried as a man should cry: for all that he should give and cannot. To get just three of the innumerable specks of human mud to raise themselves from the sunken continent of despair, and to show my more fortunate fellow men what their gods and their universes demanded of them, I'd half-killed myself: *but I was winning*.

Thomas, at last, got his goggles. Now, thank God, he could see again. I stayed at the Oriental for a week. Thomas and the boys took *Henry Wagner* to the Italthai shipbuilding yard at Samut Prakhan, to take up its owners' offer of free storage of our boat, in a locked shed, ashore. Then Thomas and I and the crew returned to Phuket. Thomas checked out *Outward Leg*. I bought a second, thirty-foot longboat for the boys, and we made her ready for them to earn a living, fishing and tourist-toting. I named this second boat *Joe Gribbins*, after the editor of *Nautical Quarterly*, from whence, for a short version of our Kra story, came the money to buy her. All that took just ten days.

Sick, tired, and almost dead with bronchitis, I set off by air with Thomas for England. I needed a refuge. I needed a home, even if for only long enough to get well.

By the time *Joe Gribbins* and all her gear had been paid for and we arrived in London, we had little cash in our kitty. I could afford no fancy hotels. My former London friends were mostly either dead, or departed. In the very early morning we made into London-town on the tube and headed for the Union Jack Club in Waterloo Road. This was a hostel for British ex-servicemen, and compared to a London hotel, the room rates were cheap: $20 each for a single.

In pouring rain we crossed the road from Waterloo Station to the club. I was hardly able to breathe, but somehow I managed to climb the stone steps and enter the small lobby. Behind the desk was a personable, efficient-looking young lady. She was of East Indian aspect and spoke with a broad Trinidadian accent. I'd been to Trinidad many times, so I recognized it. I bade her good morning and asked her for two rooms. She asked me for proof that I was an ex-serviceman. I had none on me. I had a pension certificate somewhere back in Thailand. . . .

"Sorry, sir, you can't stay here with no proof!"

I tapped my prosthesis, "Well, I've got this leg . . . and I did write about this club once in a book . . ."

"Why don't you get someone on the phone, to vouch for

you?" she asked, helpfully. My jet lag was drumming me down into the floor.

A burly porter was beside us. He took my arm. I had just enough strength left to shake him off, but none to argue.

"Sorry, mate, you'll have to leave," he told me. "We get so many blokes trying to get a cheap doss here . . . and . . ." He glanced knowingly at Thomas. *A young man, a foreigner, with a much older man; what was going on?* "What's your mate, he's not English, eh?"

"German," I replied.

"Well, there you are. Him being German, like . . . and you with no papers . . . not on, is it?" He guided me through the door and out into the rain. It was 6:30 A.M.

We hauled our gear to Paddington Station and took a train to Devon. There we found my good friends Wally Herbert and his wife, Marie, both of them polar explorers, who understood. For ten days, they nursed me and fed us, and talked of ice and cold —anything but the Kra or the Gulf of Thailand. During the days I dragged myself to a nearby hill, and, rain or shine, sat silently there and let the Atlantic winds and soft cold rain roll over me, and they made me well, and I could breathe again.

"What's next, Tristan?" asked Thomas. We were off to America, the next day, to earn more money for our Atlantis cause.

I had been silently ruminating on my hill. "I'm not . . . Look, when Wally gets home, ask him if he has a good atlas . . . but of course he does. Ask him if we can borrow it this evening, eh?"

Thomas's eyes brightened. "South China Sea?" he asked.

I knew he was hoping we'd continue our voyage in *Outward Leg,* on to Japan and across the Pacific Ocean, back to sunny California. I might as well tell him the truth. . . .

"No," I replied, "the River Mekong and Laos . . . maybe Vietnam. . . ."

But that's another story.

Envoi

I have made for you a song,
And it may be right or wrong,
But only you can tell me if it's true.
I have tried for to explain
Both your pleasure and your pain,
And, Thomas, here's my best respects to you!
Rudyard Kipling, "Prelude to
Barrack-Room Ballads"

Thomas Andreas Nicholas Ettenhuber died of a heart attack on the north bank of the River Mae Nam Ping, in Chiang Mai, on December 26, 1988. Until then, only his family knew of his heart problem. His death at the age of twenty-four, however, was completely unexpected and a shattering blow to our enterprise. Within two weeks I had retreated (advanced backward) with *Henry Wagner* to Phuket and rebuilt a thirty-foot longtail training boat, which I named *Thomas*. That boat, our achievement, this book, and a carved hardwood statue of a charging bull in my garden in Phuket (Thomas, as am I, was a Taurean) are his memorials. We shall meet again, he and I, and laugh together again, even as we laughed together on vast oceans and dangerous rivers, at death's feebleness.